Return to the City of Joseph

# RETURN TO THE CITY OF JOSEPH

## Modern Mormonism's Contest for the Soul of Nauvoo

SCOTT C. ESPLIN

UNIVERSITY OF ILLINOIS PRESS
Urbana, Chicago, and Springfield

Publication of this book was supported by Brigham Young
University Religious Education.

Library of Congress Cataloging-in-Publication Data
Names: Esplin, Scott C. (Scott Clair), 1974– author.
Title: Return to the city of Joseph: modern Mormonism's
    contest for the soul of Nauvoo / Scott C. Esplin.
Description: Urbana: University of Illinois Press, [2018] |
    Includes bibliographical references and index.
Identifiers: LCCN 2018019672 | ISBN 9780252042102
    (hardcover : alk. paper) | ISBN 9780252083815 (pbk. : alk.
    paper)
Subjects: LCSH: Nauvoo (Ill.)—History. | Mormons—
    Illinois—Nauvoo—History. | Nauvoo (Ill.)—Church
    history.
Classification: LCC F549.N37 E87 2019 | DDC 977.3/43—dc23
LC record available at https://lccn.loc.gov/2018019672

Ebook ISBN 978-0-252-05085-5

*For Janice,*
*and for McKenna, Spencer, Adelyn, and Thomas*

# Contents

# Acknowledgments

"I felt something in that room. What was it?" my five-year-old son inquired as we walked out of the historic Carthage Jail one sweltering June afternoon. I knew what he was asking, for I had felt it too when I was young. I reflected on the journey that had brought both of us there that hot summer day. His question elicited a flood of memories of crisscrossing the country with my own parents, crammed in the back of a station wagon with my siblings in equally hot midwestern summers. Admittedly, the hotel swimming pools, baseball stadiums, and sports halls of fame we visited kept the attention of five boys more than the religious sites. However, while indulging our parents with stops at Mormon sacred spaces like Sharon, Vermont; Palmyra, New York; Kirtland, Ohio; Independence, Missouri; and Nauvoo, Illinois, I too felt something. I continue to feel that something each time I return.

Mormonism stands, in the words of sociologist of religion Rodney Stark, "on the threshold of becoming the first major faith to appear on earth since the Prophet Mohammed rode out of the desert."[1] Like the world religions that preceded it, with their Galilees, Calvarys, Meccas, and Jerusalems, Mormonism is also rooted in the physical space from which it emerged. Similar to other sacred spaces around the world, the sites sacred to Mormonism's founding attract thousands of visitors who blend pilgrimage with tourism. Most prominent among these locations is Nauvoo, Illinois, the former home for the Mormon faith in the 1840s, final resting place of its founder, and arguably its most contested site among the branches of Mormonism.

Like the city it examines, this book blends an academic interest in contested sacred space with personal religious feelings for the events that occurred there. Though rurally isolated, Nauvoo is the most visited of any of the early Mormon locations. But this distinction is not without controversy. As my parents' efforts to take me to religious sites sometimes elicited vocalized opposition, Nauvoo's restoration generated verbalized declarations that Mormon vacations should occur in someone else's hometown. Yet the development of restored Mormon Nauvoo also unites the two largest branches of Mormonism, The Church of Jesus Christ of Latter-day Saints and Community of Christ, with local, unaffiliated residents of Nauvoo, Illinois, in influential, positive ways. More recently, after decades of conflict, these parties now cooperate, navigating and sharing sacred space with hundreds of thousands of visitors.

Personally, I am grateful for these same people and parties in Nauvoo and elsewhere who willingly shared with me their experience with Mormonism's restoration of the City of Joseph. The project began with the unfortunate passing of R. J. Snow, a colleague and mentor who envisioned capturing the history of Nauvoo Restoration Incorporated following his own experience in Nauvoo at the time of the temple dedication. With the encouragement and support of the Religious Studies Center at Brigham Young University, I stepped into a project that defined my work for more than a decade. I am grateful for the Religious Studies Center directors, as well as for my administrators, colleagues, and research assistants within Religious Education at Brigham Young University, whose research skill, personal support, and financial subvention made this book possible.

Countless individuals facilitated this book's production. Directors of Nauvoo Restoration Incorporated, and later officials including Reid Neilson in the Church History Department of The Church of Jesus Christ of Latter-day Saints, provided remarkable access to hundreds of thousands of pages of documents narrating the story of western Mormonism's return to Nauvoo. From the same department, knowledgeable employees of the Historic Sites Division and the Church History Library shared their expertise. Additionally, generous contacts and friends within Community of Christ, including Lachlan Mackay, Rachel Killebrew, Mark Scherer, and Barbara Bernauer, did the same with the story of their properties in Nauvoo, rounding out the narrative and balancing my perspective. People who have made Nauvoo their home—namely, multigenerational families, faith leaders, site directors, tour guides, missionaries, and the Sisters of St. Mary's—shared their stories of Nauvoo's transformation. Regional and national repositories, including the Hancock County Historical Society, Western Illinois University, Colonial Williamsburg, and the National Archives in Washington, D.C., provided additional context, insight, and assistance. The Huntington Library in San Marino, California, supported me as a Mormon History Fellow with the time and resources necessary to complete my writing in their remarkable facility. David Howlett, a kind friend and gifted scholar of sacred space, coached me through the submission process, and Dawn Durante and the staff at the University of Illinois Press polished the finished product. While I am responsible for its flaws, these many friends are responsible for its strengths. Without their help, this project would have remained merely an unorganized collection of notes.

Finally, I am grateful for parents who fostered a love for sacred space and my wife Janice and our four children who indulge my desire to stand in and study it. Over the course of this project, I have been to Nauvoo enough times to build our children a small playhouse from the souvenir brick collected on each visit. While this construction project remains incomplete, the research for this book has built a passion for a sacred past in me and a desire to instill those feelings in those I love. As mentioned, one son experienced those stirrings in the June heat of Joseph Smith's martyrdom site. Another daughter bravely stepped out on the frozen Mississippi River in early February, the snow and wind whipping around her as she experienced the commemoration of an exodus from Nauvoo nearly two centuries earlier. Our two other children playfully wore the pioneer bonnet and coonskin cap that aided in their dressing up like their Bird and Browning ancestors who once exchanged a home in nineteenth-century Nauvoo. Our family was even blessed to live on the other side of the world for a year to immerse ourselves in sacred religious sites of other faiths, lamenting their contestation and appreciating cooperation. While the book bears my name, it is truly a collaborative product. Ultimately, it reflects a combination of research on religious tourism and the positive transformation sacred space can create. I know I am better for it.

Return to the City of Joseph

# Introduction

## *"Come After Us"*

•

"THE LORD HAS BEHELD OUR SACRIFICE: COME AFTER US," someone inscribed in gilded capital letters on the wall of the assembly room of the Mormon temple in Nauvoo, Illinois, in 1846.[1] Though intended as an invitation to join in the exodus of members of The Church of Jesus Christ of Latter-day Saints (Latter-day Saints, LDS, or Mormons) as they sought a new home in the West, the message powerfully summarizes what has occurred in this sleepy Mississippi River town during the twentieth century as well. Beholding the sacrifice of those who built and then abandoned Nauvoo in the nineteenth century, the Church and its members have come back to the place they call the City of Joseph, after its founder, Joseph Smith. By the hundreds of thousands, they have "come after" the earlier Mormon residents of Nauvoo, returning as pilgrimage tourists to a city restored to a glimpse of the splendor it enjoyed in the 1840s.

However, this return to and rebuilding of Mormon Nauvoo has not been without controversy. Indeed, for some descendants of early Nauvoo residents there was no need to return because they did not leave. Most prominently, for Emma Smith, widow of Mormonism's founder, their oldest surviving son, Joseph Smith III, and the Reorganized Church of Jesus Christ of Latter Day Saints (RLDS or Community of Christ) that their family led, Nauvoo remained home. While the "mountain saints" built up Utah as their stronghold, these "prairie saints" maintained a foothold in Nauvoo. For this reason, during the last half of the nineteenth century and the first half of the twentieth, Nauvoo's

FIGURE 1. C. C. A. Christensen (1831–1912), *Crossing the Mississippi on the Ice*, ca. 1878, tempera on muslin, 77⅞ x 114 inches. Brigham Young University Museum of Art, gift of the grandchildren of C. C. A. Christensen, 1970.

Mormon presence was almost entirely Reorganized Mormonism. The return of a rival faith in the mid-twentieth century was met with resistance, as a bidding war and then a building war emerged across the city. A contest of "anything you can build, we can build better" dominated Nauvoo relations between the strands of Mormonism for more than two decades, with each Church seeking to convey their versions of the history of Nauvoo. More recently, as both faiths have matured and, in some significant ways, diverged, cooperation has replaced competition, a welcome development in a long-divided city.

But Nauvoo is more than the 1840s Church headquarters that the branches of Mormonism revere and restore. For the most part, the homes and businesses they have renovated did not merely pass peacefully from builder to present occupant, patiently awaiting restoration. Rather, while some homes lay abandoned, persisting romantically in the memory of the people who deserted them, others became residences to those unaffiliated with Mormonism who made the vacant city their home. Indeed, a French Utopian movement, followed by hardworking German immigrants, also dominate Nauvoo's nineteenth-century past. Appropriately, the descendants of these French communalists, German vintners, and midwestern farmers view their history as integral to the story of Nauvoo. However, too often their story has been deemed less important as some restoration efforts in Nauvoo brushed aside any history that was not 1840s Mormon history.

As a result, while the restoration of Mormon Nauvoo has been beneficial to some elements of the local economy, Nauvoo's dependence on Mormon tourism has created divides within the city. Understandably, not all segments of society have benefited from the changes, nor have they been as welcoming. "Change is best kept in a vending machine," one longtime resident wittingly revealed when asked about the town's feelings for the Mormon return.[2] Unfortunately, the religious tension that was a hallmark of the city during its 1840s Mormon heyday remains a strong undercurrent of the community a century and a half later. For these reasons, modern Nauvoo and the restoration boom it has experienced stands as a testament to the truth expressed by historian Hal Rothman, "The embrace of tourism triggers a contest for the soul of a place."[3]

## Context for Memorials across America

The contest for the soul of Nauvoo is more than merely a Mormon or even a midwestern story. In the midst of the local conflicts within the city, the construction of Nauvoo's memorial to Mormonism mirrored larger national trends for commemoration. Responding to "anxieties about national unity . . . unleashed by the rapid advance of modernism, immigration, and mass culture," the early twentieth century witnessed the proliferation of public and private monuments across the United States. First statues, and later commemorations and pageants, led to what Professor Erika Doss termed "memorial mania."[4] Following World War II, increased leisure time, coupled with robust consumerism and the proliferation of the automobile, connected the monument boom with tourism.[5] Coinciding with this growth in tourism, spiritually motivated travel in a "search for truth, enlightenment, or an authentic experience with the divine or holy" likewise increased.[6] Obsessions with the past and the desire to connect with it created an environment where "commemoration has become utterly commonplace," something that is "deeply rooted in the cultural practices of the nation."[7] Indeed, in the words of anthropologist Paul Shackel, "We live in a society that has an unquenchable thirst for nostalgia."[8]

Both for Mormons in Nauvoo and Americans across the nation as a whole, this thirst, satiated in small measure by the act of erecting memorials to the past, involved more than mere brick and mortar. The "heritage phenomenon," as historian Michael Kammen called it, served several critical social functions,

including the construction of unity, continuity, and loyalty among diverse popu-
lations.[9] Because "heritage connotes integrity, authenticity, venerability, and
stability," the preservation and presentation of history creates what Shackel
argued is a "usable past . . . [one] that serves our present needs." In this way,
a nation like the United States "uses heritage to create collective memory, to
look for more innocent and carefree days."[10] By carefully crafting "a unitary
and coherent version of the past" through the preservation of sacred space,
a society in commotion authors "collective scripts capable of replacing a lost
sense of community."[11]

But it was not merely an American majority that used memorials and heritage to its advantage. The fabric of the national narrative, and with it the country's historic sites, is a patchwork of diverse groups and their stories. Describing
the tapestry, Shackel wrote, "Memories can be public as well as private, and they
serve to legitimize the past and the present. Public history exhibits, monuments,
statues, artifacts, national historical parks, commemorations, and celebrations
can foster the myths that create a common history that allows for divergent
groups to find a common bond."[12] Indeed, "American history," historian John
Bodnar asserted, "is replete with examples of minority groups mounting spir-
ited defenses of their own versions of the past and resisting pressures to acqui-
esce to nationally dominant traditions."[13] The restoration of Mormon Nauvoo
was a project uniting the past of a minority religious body with the national
dominance of western expansion.

For their part, memorials represent the desire to visibly display what matters
to a society. "Today's growing numbers of memorials," argued Doss, "represent
heightened anxieties about who and what should be remembered in America."[14]
However, communities look to the past for more than merely the past's sake.
Monuments and the act of visiting them are "a way of claiming that the past
has something to offer the present, be it a warning or a model."[15] Geographer
Katharyne Mitchell asserted, "There is a deep politics to memory, and each
age attempts to refashion and remake memory to serve its own contemporary purposes. Memory is sustained through the interplay between collective
recollection and repetition."[16] For this reason, the way a society preserves and
presents its heritage may reveal as much, if not more, about how it views its
future as it does its past.

The creation of an idealized historical image, like the one fashioned in
Mormonism's restoration of Nauvoo, requires conscious decisions regarding
what and whose past will be celebrated in a process Rothman called "script-
ing space."[17] In the words of Bruce VanSledright, it includes "a celebration of
selected memories of the past leavened with a considerable degree of historical

amnesia."[18] The people, places, and events that were either chosen or ignored for commemoration shape the historical narrative. "Societies," Kammen asserted, "in fact reconstruct their pasts rather than faithfully record them, and . . . they do so with the needs of contemporary culture in mind—manipulating the past in order to mold the present."[19] Indeed, "we remember what we perceive as good and forget the rest," Shackel noted. "Heritage can create a national mythology based on even the smallest kernel of truth."[20]

In the choices made regarding what will be commemorated, and thus remembered, governments often take an active part. Nations control the past by shaping public memory, Shackel argued, in the interest of "promoting and preserving the ideals of cultural leaders and authorities, developing social unity, and maintaining the status quo" and "to reduce competing interests."[21] During the 1930s, the same era in which Latter-day Saint interest in acquiring property and restoring Nauvoo began to rise, the federal government "intervened in the discussion over public memory in a very substantial way. . . . As it came to regulate areas like the workplace and the family," historian John Bodnar wrote, "the government also attempted to influence and, therefore, distort the discussion over how the past related to the present."[22] Eventually, these desires impacted Nauvoo's restoration as well.

As the century progressed, the National Park Service become one of the most prominent governmental shapers of the remembered past in America. In an advisory role, this included the historical preservation and interpretation of Mormon Nauvoo. Increasingly, the agency found itself considering important interpretive questions like, "What exactly would they tell the American public about history and what function should that information serve in the first place?"[23] These questions were especially important for a site like Nauvoo, where reconstruction was being funded by a religious society. Accordingly, the federal government chose to celebrate Mormonism's influence on the settling of the West, highlighting Nauvoo as a launching point for westward expansion as a way to coincide with Cold War–era efforts to honor the nation's greatness.[24] The object of their attention "was not people in the past but the minds of citizens in the present" through a "selective or symbolic presentation of the past."[25]

Across the nation, private individuals and groups often augmented governmental efforts to shape memory through commemoration. One early chief benefactor of national commemoration efforts was John D. Rockefeller, whose expansive funding of the restoration at Colonial Williamsburg was aimed at reinforcing the notion "that the past was indeed glorious and a source of inspiration." Through these and other projects, "the United States appeared to feverishly turn to its past for entertainment, consolation, patriotic renewal, education, and inspiration from the deeds of ancestors."[26] On a smaller scale, Mormonism's Nauvoo project sought similar results, openly patterning itself after Rockefeller's work and proclaiming itself as the Williamsburg of the Midwest.

The selection of Nauvoo as a nationally significant historic site and Mormons as an important subject demonstrated America's multifaceted approach to its heritage. In addition to commemorating prominent sites like Philadelphia's Independence Hall, New York City's Statue of Liberty, and Washington, D.C.'s Lincoln Memorial, Mormons helped Americans remember an isolated rural farming town in western Illinois. Doss described the phenomenon that allowed a place like Nauvoo to occupy the nation's collective memory: "Memorial mania's affective conditions may call attention to those facets of American national identity gone awry, or bordering on ruin, or in need of revision. . . . Many American memorials are sites of reformation and transformation: spaces and places where history and identity are frequently reconsidered in order to cultivate, or revive, citizen identification with an inconstant nation."[27]

These twentieth-century trends toward memorial building, historical and religious tourism, and enshrining the past emphasize core questions of social memory posed by historian Kirk Savage. "Who guides the process of remembering and towards what ends? Why do specific commemorative projects take particular forms? How do commemorative practices actually shape social relations and cultural beliefs (rather than simply reflecting them)?"[28] The story of the restoration and reconstruction of Mormon Nauvoo confronts these queries by revealing religious tensions within the branches of Mormonism and social conflicts between residents of a rural midwestern farming town and outside tourists. The decisions made regarding what to restore and how to present the story also reflect the values and vision of the participants involved as the faiths and the city move toward their third centuries of existence.

## Mormonism's Makeovers

Mormonism's insertion into the national phenomenon of commemoration and heritage or religious tourism coincided with its own public transformation during the twentieth century. As the century dawned, The Church of Jesus Christ of Latter-day Saints was in the midst of a makeover of its image. Throughout most of the second half of the nineteenth century, the Church and, by association, its members, were vilified nationally. Driven from state to state, they eventually settled in the American Intermountain West, where they hoped to find refuge and relief through isolation. However, as an ever-expanding nation closed in around them, political organizations, private associations, and religious bodies lined up to attack the faith for its controversial beliefs and associated practices. By December 31, 1889, Church president Wilford Woodruff privately remarked in his journal, "Thus Ends the year 1889 And the word of the Prophet Joseph Smith is beginning to be fulfilled that the whole Nation would turn against Zion & make war upon the Saints. The Nation has never been filled so full of lies against the Saints as to Day. 1890 will be an important year with the Latter Day Saints & American Nation."[29]

Woodruff's prediction proved prophetic, as decisions made in 1890 changed the trajectory for the faith and its relationship within the United States. That fall, Woodruff announced the cessation of the faith's long-defended practice of plural marriage, marking, in the words of Thomas Alexander, a historian of the era, "the end of one phase of Mormon history and usher[ing] in the transition to a second." The change, however, was much greater than merely to the faith's familial practices. It involved its paradigmatic core. Alexander explained that Mormonism's model of integrating "religion, politics, society, and the economy into a single non-pluralistic community . . . was simply unacceptable to Victorian America." Reacting to this social reality, "Mormons began groping for a new paradigm that would save essential characteristics of their religious tradition, provide sufficient political stability to preserve the interests of the church, and allow them to live in peace with other Americans."[30]

Ironically, for a faith that had spent decades defending its right to be different through periods of isolationism and civil disobedience, an important aspect of its new paradigm was the positioning of Latter-day Saints as model American citizens. Throughout the nineteenth century, Mormonism's dominant story was that of "an international church in the process of consolidating its resources and establishing a homeland from which to become solidly international again."[31] The faith's commemoration of Nauvoo in the second half of the twentieth century marked the reversal of its consolidated gathering in the West, a return to its historical roots in the Midwest, and a projection for its future within a grand American narrative. The development of a Mormon religious site beyond the faith's traditional western footprint served the purpose of connecting the faith with this accepted national discourse. It was a tangible example of what professor Kathleen Flake called "creating a new future out of the Mormon past."[32]

Mormonism's new future sought to replace conflict with an American society that sought to exterminate it with supreme loyalty to that same society and its ideals. Latter-day Saints shifted from being one of the country's most despised religious groups to becoming, in the assessment of historian Martin Marty, "super-American."[33] The transformation was slow but persistent. Initially, "the public shifted its distrust of Mormons as a people to Mormonism as a belief system," Flake observed. "The change in public opinion from a distrust of the Latter-day Saints to a suspicion of their beliefs fit the permissible limits of American religious difference." Eventually, Mormons and Mormonism were "no longer perceived as a political threat, merely an ethnic peculiarity." In Flake's assessment, "the Latter-day Saints had succeeded in becoming merely odd. Like the Amish pietists of the Midwest and Orthodox Jews of the East, the Mormons in the West became part of America's cultural diversity, a reassuring reminder of its capacity for religious liberty."[34] Though still less than ideal, the change in perception from Mormons as destructive to Mormons as distasteful was profound.

Through active, and at times prominent participation in the nation's wars, its educational institutions, its politics, and its economics, the faith and its members further turned public opinion in their favor as the twentieth century progressed. "Americans had been convinced of the Latter-day Saints' tolerance, obedience, and loyalty," Flake noted, "and had bestowed upon them denominational citizenship with its constitutional privileges and protections."[35] Latter-day Saints historians Leonard Arrington and Davis Bitton similarly concluded, "A half-century and more of heated confrontation with the U.S. government had taught Latter-day Saints the practical limits of religious life in America. By the end of World War I, if not before, the Mormons were more American than most Americans. Patriotism, respect for the law, love of the Constitution, and obedience to political authority reigned as principles of the faith."[36]

Monuments like reconstructed Nauvoo allowed the faith to demonstrate these positive aspects of their character to visitors on its own terms. Mormonism's memorials to its past, as Flake described them, "signaled the church's intent to come out from behind its mountain barrier and claim a place in America at large."[37] In this way, the faith accomplished what Doss wrote of historic sites in general: "Memorials embody the feelings of particular publics at particular historical moments, and frame cultural narratives about self identity and national purpose.... [They] embody the histories and feelings that respective Americans choose to remember at particular moments."[38]

By the middle of the twentieth century, when the restoration project in Nauvoo was in full swing, the transformation of the faith was complete. National legislative and bureaucratic bodies once opposed to Mormonism sought ways to assist in enshrining its past. Prominent Latter-day Saints, including George W. Romney, the former governor of Michigan and once a candidate for the presidency of the United States; David M. Kennedy, Treasury Department secretary and later U.S. ambassador to NATO; and J. Willard

Marriott, businessman and entrepreneur, were involved in the project, with Kennedy and Marriott serving on the restoration group's national board. They were joined by non–Latter-day Saints members, including A. Edwin Kendrew, senior vice-president of Colonial Williamsburg; J. C. "Pinky" Harrington, famed historical archaeologist; and Harold P. Fabian, chairman of the National Park Service advisory board. Though not without conflict among those with differing views for how Nauvoo's past should be remembered, Mormonism had moved onto the national historic stage.

However, it was not merely the larger branch of Mormonism that was transformed during the restoration of Nauvoo. Its sister faith, the Reorganized Church of Jesus Christ of Latter Day Saints, underwent its own dramatic restructuring. Following its founding in 1860, this smaller Midwestern Mormon offshoot repeatedly struggled to define itself in contrast to its more well-known, though not well-liked, western relative. Seeking to secure its own space within the parameters of modern Mormonism, "the Reorganization was defined mostly by what it was not," asserted Richard Moore, an expert on relations between the faiths. "Adversarial from the start, each group determined to prove the other wrong," leading to "hard feelings . . . and misunderstandings."[39] Indeed, "the most important issue facing the Reorganized Church," noted former Reorganized Church historian Mark A. Scherer, "was denominational identity," with the interpretation of events from the earlier Nauvoo era as "ground zero in the historical and theological boundary separating the two major denominational segments of Latter Day Saintism."[40]

Among the prominent early points of debate between the faiths, the most significant included interpretations of leadership succession, temple rituals, and marital practices, all of which were rooted in the historical presentation of Nauvoo. From its founding, the Reorganized prairie Church adhered to the practice of lineal prophetic leadership, believing that the posterity of Joseph Smith should lead the faith rather than the seniority successorship model practiced by Brigham Young and his fellow mountain Mormon followers. Additionally, in the earliest years of the Reorganized Church, its leaders repeatedly challenged their western relatives over the continued practice of performing baptisms for the dead in their sacred buildings called temples. Though they acknowledged the practice had occurred in the unfinished Nauvoo Temple, the faith viewed both the practice and its Mormon practitioners as having been rejected by God for failure to complete the building. Similarly, Reorganized Church leaders and scholars sought to exonerate Joseph Smith for any involvement in the controversial practice of plural marriage, originated in Nauvoo but expanded significantly by Brigham Young and the leadership of the Utah-based Church.

As rival buildings and competing presentations between the strands of Mormonism were developed in Nauvoo in the twentieth century, these theological differences were slowly resolved between the faiths. In the second half of the twentieth century, scriptural passages that addressed temple practices like baptism for the dead were removed from Reorganized scripture, careful historians acknowledged the active role Joseph Smith played in Nauvoo's controversial polygamous marriage practices, and Church leadership pivoted away from lineal successorship. In the place of these and other fundamental positions, the faith focused instead on community building. "Our history is not our theology," summarized Reorganized Church historian Mark Scherer, reflecting the changes. "No longer did church leaders aspire to replicate the Nauvoo, Kirtland, Independence, or even Palmyra churches" of early Mormonism. "Instead they shifted their primary emphasis to the church in the world."[41] The current mission statement of Community of Christ reflects this focus: "We proclaim Jesus Christ and promote communities of joy, hope, love, and peace."

The resolution of the differences between the faiths centered on what appears to be a subtle shift away from Joseph Smith and Nauvoo theology. Community of Christ theologian Tony Chvala-Smith summarized, "The Community of Christ no longer treats the Joseph Smith story as the normative lens through which it interprets the Christian message." Former Community of Christ Apostle Andrew Bolton added, "We used to see Jesus through the eyes of Joseph; now we see Joseph through the eyes of Jesus."[42]

Pivoting from an emphasis on Joseph Smith makes Nauvoo, a location affectionately termed the City of Joseph, an interesting base of operation for Community of Christ. Because it controls the most significant Smith family properties in the city, Nauvoo remains important to the faith, even if its past is far from central to its present theology. With approximately one hundred thousand visitors to their sites in the City of Joseph each year, only 5 percent of whom are members of Community of Christ, leaders acknowledge that their historic-sites program in Nauvoo is "the single most popular method to introduce the Community of Christ to North America."[43] But by the end of the century, the theological Nauvoo of Joseph Smith was not the model for the faith, a dramatic change for the longtime owners of his properties in the city.

## An 1840s Religious River Town

Modern visitors to Nauvoo are rarely introduced to these stories associated with the city's restoration project, the conflicts it created, or what the project reveals about the parties involved. Rather, traveling along Illinois's scenic Highway 96, the tourist steps back in time. Horse-drawn carriages pass a bustling blacksmith shop and brick furnace. Visitors stroll through manicured gardens, venturing into open doorways where guides recreate life in a religious city on a bend in the Mississippi River during the mid-1840s. The picture is one of prosperity, presided over by a stately temple monument on a bluff overlooking the community. Within minutes, if they did not know it already, visitors to the area quickly learn about the Latter-day Saints' founding of the City of Joseph. They hear the story of the city's creation in 1839, learn of its meteoric rise, and trace the exodus to the river's edge and the West in 1846.

Little mention is made of how the town was preserved and rebuilt, why the Mormons returned, and how the homes were transformed from ruin to repair. Few examine the tension this return created between the strands of Mormonism as well as within the local community. Rarely does the visitor learn about the faith interactions, positive and negative, within Nauvoo, or the attempts by those without ties to Mormonism to shape and preserve their own community heritage. More broadly, few pause to consider what the restoration project reveals about the branches of Mormonism and their development as modern expressions of Nauvoo's past. Nevertheless, the inquisitive visitor wonders: How was this city on the banks of the Mississippi River transform from abandonment to become a Mormon Mecca, the most frequented historic site of the faith? What is the twentieth-century history of Mormonism's restoration of Nauvoo?

As a social history of the City of Joseph, this work examines Nauvoo's recent past in an effort to reveal the values of its major stakeholders. The work begins with the decline of Mormon Nauvoo following the death of Joseph Smith in 1844 and the exodus of the main branch of the faith two years later. It continues with the occupation of the vacant properties by French communalists and German immigrants who joined a small but significant segment of reorganized Mormonism that remained in the city. Controlling the most important surviving properties of the faith, the Reorganized Church of Jesus Christ of Latter Day Saints led the earliest efforts to develop religious tourism in Nauvoo. The story continues with the return of The Church of Jesus Christ of Latter-day Saints, seeking to place itself within the national narrative by acquiring, restoring, and developing Nauvoo as a memorial to Mormonism. The contest, cooperation, and compromise that ensued make the story of the restoration of Nauvoo a case study for the faiths involved and an example of the development of religious tourism in America.

# CHAPTER 1

# The Mormon City in Decline

"A few years ago, ascending the Upper Mississippi in the Autumn, when its waters were low, I was compelled to travel by land past the region of the Rapids," wrote Philadelphia lawyer and friend of the Mormons Thomas Kane in 1850. "I was descending the last hillside upon my journey, when a landscape in delightful contrast broke upon my view. Half encircled by a bend of the river, a beautiful city lay glittering in the fresh morning sun; its bright new dwellings, set in cool green gardens, ranging up around a stately dome-shaped hill, which was crowned by a noble marble edifice, whose high tapering spire was radiant with white and gold."

Kane continued in his narrative, capturing his tour of an abandoned Illinois river town. "I procured a skiff, and rowing across the river, landed at the chief wharf of the city. No one met me there. I looked, and saw no one. I could hear no one move; though the quiet everywhere was such that I heard the flies buzz, and the water-ripples break against the shallow of the beach." Moving into town, Kane continued, "I walked through the solitary streets. The town lay as in a dream, under some deadening spell of loneliness, from which I almost feared to wake it. For plainly it had not slept long. There was no grass growing up in the paved ways. Rains had not entirely washed away the prints of dusty footsteps. Yet I went about unchecked."

Turning to the marks of mid-nineteenth century industry, Kane recalled, "I went into empty workshops, ropewalks and smithies. The spinner's wheel was

FIGURE 2. View of Nauvoo, Ill., from across the Mississippi River, ca. 1855. Steel engraving published by Herrmann J. Meyer. Retrieved from the Library of Congress, https://www.loc.gov/item/2002705511/.

idle; the carpenter had gone from his work-bench and shavings, his unfinished sash and casing. Fresh bark was in the tanners's vat, and the fresh-chopped lightwood stood piled against the baker's oven. The blacksmith's shop was cold; but his coal heap and ladling pool and crooked water horn were all there, as if he had just gone off for a holiday. No work people anywhere looked to know my errand." Exploring abandoned gardens and vacant homes, Kane found, "No one called out to me from any opened window, or dog sprang forward to bark an alarm. I could have supposed the people hidden in the houses, but the doors were unfastened; and when at last I timidly entered them, I found dead ashes white upon the hearths, and had to tread a tiptoe, as if walking down the aisle of a country church, to avoid rousing irreverent echoes from the naked floors."

Wondering if he were witness to a recent catastrophe, Kane turned his attention to the outskirts of town, where he found the city's graveyard. "But there was no record of Plague there, nor did it in anywise differ much from other Protestant American cemeteries. Some of the mounds were not long sodded; some of the stones were newly set, their dates recent, and their black inscriptions glossy in the mason's hardly dried lettering ink." Beyond the graveyard, however, he did find "a young orchard had been roughly torn down" and "the still smoldering embers of a barbecue fire, that had been constructed of rails from the fencing round it. It was the latest sign of life there," Kane surmised. Across the surrounding countryside, "fields upon fields of heavy-headed yellow grain lay rotting ungathered upon the ground. No one was at hand to take in their rich harvest. As far as the eye could reach, they stretched away—they, sleeping too in the hazy air of Autumn."[1] The scene, as Kane captured it, was the city of Nauvoo, Illinois, just days after the expulsion of the last of its Mormon residents in September 1846.

It was this generally vacant city about which Kane and others wrote in the late 1840s. However, it was not merely Mormons and their friends, like Kane, who wrote about the deserted city. Those unaffiliated with the faith also described their visits to the region. For example, J. H. Buckingham, the son of a prominent Boston newspaperman, published his 1847 visit to "the Holy City of the Mormons." Like Kane, Buckingham was initially impressed by the waterfront scene that confronted him. "The city is situated on the left bank of the Mississippi, in the state of Illinois, on a lot of land gently and gradually sloping down to the water, but extending back over a prairie some two or three or more miles." Also like Kane, he was struck by the orderliness and accomplishment he found.

> It appears to have been laid out by somebody, originally, into streets running in squares, and each house is built with regard to the original plan. The families have erected each one their house on their own lot, and of course the dwellings are not compact, but are scattered over a large extent of ground. There is but one block of dwellings, or stores, in the whole city, and that appears to have been left unfinished. Most of them are of brick, two stories and a half high, and square, with a gable roof. There are, however, a number of buildings of wood, and some of them three stories high.

However, Buckingham was also moved by the sense of abandonment.

> It has had eighteen thousand inhabitants; it now has eighteen hundred, or at most, two thousand. . . . Time was, and that not two years and a half ago, when every house was full, and every farm under good cultivation. Now, every thing looks forlorn and desolate. Not half the buildings are occupied, and of these not half are half full. The stores are closed. The farms are running to waste. The streets are overgrown with grass. The inhabitants look like any thing but an industrious people, and every thing tells of ruin instead of prosperity.[2]

This scene of abandonment, ruin, and loss captured by Kane and Bucking-ham stands in stark contrast to the period immediately previous to their visits to Nauvoo. The Church of Jesus Christ of Latter-day Saints flourished for seven eventful years in this town on the bend of the Mississippi River. Settled by their Prophet Joseph Smith in 1839, the community began as a refuge for thousands fleeing persecution in nearby Missouri. Bolstered by the constant influx of immigrants moving to the region due to the faith's proselyting efforts across the United States, Canada, and Europe, population boomed across the city and the surrounding region.[3] Hundreds of log, frame, and brick structures dotted the landscape as homes, schools, shops, and social halls were quickly erected. Overlooking it all, a stately temple slowly rose in prominence on a bluff.

However, in spite of the apparent peacefulness in town, disaffection slowly simmered, both in Nauvoo and in the surrounding communities. "Many resi-dents of Hancock County were as unprepared for Nauvoo's meteoric rise as were the newcomers themselves," historian Richard Bennett observed.[4] Some within and outside of the Church were troubled by doctrinal expansion pushed by Smith and his associates. Teachings on man's potential in the afterlife, deity, salvation for the dead, and plural marriage resonated with many but troubled others. The growing political power of the community and its leaders was also worrisome. Additionally, rival towns along the river suffered economic losses as commerce shifted to the bustling ports of Nauvoo. "The economic and political jealousies of surrounding Illinois communities, the ongoing bitterness between the Missourians and the Mormons, the Mormon habit of block voting, their clannishness, and their religious fervor, contributed to an atmosphere of mount-ing tension and instability," summarized Bennett. "Eventually it was determined that the Mormons must be dislodged whatever the cost."[5] The powder keg of violence erupted when Joseph Smith and his brother Hyrum were arrested and then killed by a mob in nearby Carthage, Illinois, on June 27, 1844.

The death of Mormonism's founder shattered the faith's hopes for an extended peace in the city of Nauvoo. Following a protracted struggle over leadership, the Church's Quorum of the Twelve Apostles and especially its president, Brigham Young, emerged as Smith's successor. Initially, the Twelve encouraged the continued development of Nauvoo, including the completion of its chief building project, the temple. "The murder of Joseph will not stop the work; it will not stop the Temple," the Apostles wrote to members of the Church in Great Britain.[6] The charge to complete work on the temple domi-nated their discourses over the subsequent months following Smith's death.[7] In January 1845, leaders issued a call for help to finish the structure. "We wish all the young, middle aged, and able bodied men who have it in their hearts to stretch forth this work with power, to come to Nauvoo, prepared to stay during the summer; and to bring with them means to sustain themselves with, and to enable us to forward this work; to bring with them teams, cattle, sheep, gold, silver, brass, iron, oil, paints, and tools." Those unable to come in person were invited to "send all the money, cloth, and clothing, together with the raw material for manufacturing purposes; such as cotton, cotton yarn, wool, steel, iron, brass, etc., etc., as we are preparing to go into extensive manufacturing operations, and all these things can be applied to the furtherance of the temple."[8] Young and his associates even halted the faith's well-known proselytizing efforts in order to put all the community's endeavors into completing the structure. "I do not want any man to go to preach till he is sent," Young declared in March 1845. "If the world want to hear preaching let them come here, and if they really want the gospel, let them clean Carthage jail," a reference to the site where their leader, Smith, was killed.[9] Appealing to biblical precedence for emphasis, Young boldly decreed, "We want to build the Temple in this place, if we have to build it, as the Jews built the walls of the Temple in Jerusalem, with a sword in one hand and the trowel in the other."[10]

As Young expected, while work progressed on the temple, opposition to the Saints' continued presence in Illinois increased. Attacks began in Mormon settlements outside Nauvoo in the fall of 1845. Cordelia Morley recalled being driven from her home in the community of Yelrome, approximately thirty miles from Nauvoo, that September. "In 1845, the mob was doing all they could to drive the Mormons out again. They drove off the stock in the fall when the grain was in the stack, they burned it to the ground, the houses were also burned and all was desolate."[11] Perrigrine Sessions wrote in his journal, "The months of September and October [were] a continual scene of work and turmoil and the labour on the Temple was almost oblige[d] to stop and the workmen many of them carried small arms with them all the time and all kept their muskets where they could put their hands on them at moments warning."[12]

While external threats of physical violence plagued the Church's continued presence in Nauvoo, internal leadership conflicts sought to divide it as well. Though Brigham Young and his supporters had repulsed Sidney Rigdon, a former counselor to Joseph Smith, in his efforts to lead the faith in August 1844, Rigdon retreated to Pittsburgh, Pennsylvania, where he regrouped and eventually reorganized. In April 1845 he established his own Church of Christ, patterned after the earlier Church and sustained by several adherents formerly loyal to Smith. At the same time, James J. Strang, a charismatic elder of the Church in Wisconsin, attracted thousands to his message that Smith had appointed him as his prophetic successor. Among his followers, Strang counted Smith's lone surviving brother and former Apostle, William Smith, as well as other prominent Church leaders. Many Nauvoo residents flocked north to hear his message, further weakening Mormonism's presence in the city.

By late September 1845, Church leadership decided it was best to leave Nauvoo. On September 24, 1845, William Clayton, who acted as scribe for the Twelve Apostles in their deliberations, wrote in his journal, "It is very evident that the time is come for this people to separate themselves from all gentile movements and go to a place where they can erect the standard and live according to the law of God."[13] A committee of residents from neighboring Adams County negotiated a tenuous promise from those opposing the Church "to agree to restrain and withhold all further violence, and that [the Latter-day Saints] be permitted to depart in peace next spring."[14] At the Church's general conference in early October, "a vote was taken that this people move to the West en masse and [the vote] carried."[15]

During the fall and winter of 1845–46, Latter-day Saint residents of Nauvoo continued their work on the interior of the Temple, received personal sacred ordinances within its walls, and prepared to leave their beloved city. "Nearly every man was some kind of a mechanic to build wagons," remarked twenty-year-old Irene Hascall, "and the whole mind of the people was engaged in the great work of emigrating west in the Spring."[16] By late winter, with the temple nearly finished, the Saints quietly began closing their doors, bidding goodbye to a once bustling city. In early February 1846, Brigham Young recorded his farewell, summarizing the feelings of many: "I met with the Council of the Twelve in the southeast corner room of the attic of the Temple. We knelt around the altar, and dedicated the building to the Most High. We asked his blessing upon our intended move to the west; also asked him to enable us some day to finish the Temple, and dedicate it to him, and we would leave it in his hands to do as he pleased; and to preserve the building as a monument to Joseph Smith. We asked the Lord to accept the labors of his servants in this land."[17] On May 22, 1846, fellow Apostle Wilford Woodruff reflected in his journal his feelings as he looked back at the city he loved: "I left Nauvoo for the last time perhaps in this life. I looked upon the Temple & City of Nauvoo as I retired from it & felt to ask the Lord to preserve it as a monument of the sacrifice of his Saints."[18]

It initially appeared that these prayers would be answered and the temple preserved. Before even leaving Nauvoo, Church leadership considered renting, leasing, or selling the building, together with other Church property. When negotiations developed between Church agent Almon Babbitt and officials from the Catholic Church in the communities of Quincy, Illinois, Cincinnati, Ohio, Detroit, Michigan, and Chicago, Illinois, Babbitt reported to the Church's

Twelve Apostles in December 1845 that prospects were "good and Cheering."[19] In his journal on December 1, 1845, Heber C. Kimball wrote, "Some of them would be here in a few days, to rent some of our Publick buildings."[20] However, negotiations failed when Catholic officials countered with a plan to purchase only part of the Church property, raising concerns that they could not secure funding in the brief time prior to the Saints' departure.[21]

Recognizing that completion of a sale would be impossible before leaving for the West, officials appointed Almon W. Babbitt, Joseph L. Heywood, John S. Fullmer, Henry W. Miller, and John M. Bernhisel as agents, authorizing them to remain behind in Nauvoo and represent Church interests.[22] Church leaders' intention to sell the temple along with the rest of the public and private properties in the city sparked great interest across the region. On May 13, 1846, the *Hancock Eagle* reported, "THE TEMPLE IN THE MARKET.— the deliberations of the great Mormon Council, which was held Sunday last (on the occasion of the dedication) resulted in the passage of a resolution to sell the Temple, for the purpose of obtaining funds to effect a removal of the poor from the State."[23] Two days later, the same newspaper began advertising, "TEMPLE FOR SALE. The undersigned Trustees of the Latter Day Saints propose to sell the Temple on very low terms, if an early application is made. The Temple is admirably designed for Literary and Religious purposes. Address the Undersigned Trustees."[24] Though several options presented themselves, nothing immediately materialized.

Prospects for the sale of properties worsened when the social climate in Nauvoo deteriorated in September 1846. Determined to force the expulsion of the poor who had been unable to flee the city during the general exodus earlier in the year, conflict erupted in Nauvoo on September 12, 1846. The Battle of Nauvoo, a five-day standoff of approximately one hundred Mormons and new citizens against more than fifteen hundred armed men aimed at driving them from the region ended on September 17 with the death of participants from both sides and the surrender of the defenders of the city. A "poor camp" quickly formed on the Iowa side of the Mississippi River as the city was hurriedly vacated.

From his camp in western Iowa, Brigham Young learned of the dire situation in Nauvoo. He counseled the trustees, "If you conclude to sell the temple, sell it as soon as possible, and all other property—settle your affairs and come up and winter with us."[25] Nevertheless, the agents pressed on. In September 1847 John Fullmer lamented, "The Temple is still unsold, and I do not know but the God of Heaven intends to have it so remain as a standing monument of our sacrifice, and as witness against the nation. Sold or unsold, I should think it such as we shall not be able at best to get one dollar in twenty of what it cost."[26] Their efforts were repeatedly thwarted both by reluctant buyers and by legal challenges that clouded any potential transaction. In particular, James J. Strang, a rival successor to Brigham Young and the Twelve Apostles, claimed control over the temple's fate. At the same time, land speculator Isaac Galland placed a $20,000 lien against the property. "All these impediments clearly affected the trustees' attempts to dispose of the Nauvoo Temple," summarized historian Lisle G. Brown.[27]

Psychologically, some of the former residents of Nauvoo moved on. Soon after departing, Brigham Young offered his reflections on the city in a letter to his brother, "[Nauvoo] is not the place for me any more till this nation is scourged by the hand of the Almighty, who rules in the heavens. This Nation shall feel the heavy hand of judgment. They have shed the blood of Prophets and Saints, and have been the means of the death of many. Do not think . . . I hate to leave my house and home. No! far from that. I am so free from bondage at this time that Nauvoo looks like a prison to me. It looks pleasant ahead, but dark to look back."[28] Returning to Nebraska to gather additional followers after leading an initial company to the valley of the Great Salt Lake, Brigham Young further counseled the trustees in November 1847 to "leave the keys of the Temple in care of Judge Owens and the building itself in the hands of the Lord."[29]

Abandoning hopes for a ready sale of their properties, other Latter-day Saints nevertheless maintained a keen interest in Nauvoo. Traveling through the area on the way to a two-year mission in the East, Wilford Woodruff called upon the trustees in Nauvoo in July 1848, visiting the city in spite of earlier premonitions that he was leaving it for good. "I visited the Temple & went over it from the bottom to the top whare I once more had A full view of the once beautiful but now desolate city of Nauvoo," Woodruff recorded in his journal. "The temple was in a much better state of preservation than I expected to find it," he continued.

Though two years removed from the conflicts that drove the Saints from the area, Woodruff reported that tensions were still high in the region. "The people in the City of Nauvoo were much excited from A report that Elder Hyde would preach in the Temple that day. They had made many threats upon the subject & some Came in waggons from the Country to hear & see but the excitement was all among themselves for Elder Hyde gave out no such appointment." However, Woodruff did record his own preaching to a man from Michigan who had come to Nauvoo "to enquire after the gospel & to see the saints." Following an hour-long discussion, Woodruff baptized the man, confirmed him in the

Church, ordained him an Elder, gave him a license to preach, and sent him on his way rejoicing.[30]

As Woodruff's experience indicates, the temple and the city of Nauvoo continued to attract interested non-Mormons who passed through the area. One visitor to Nauvoo recorded in his journal the beautiful but sad state of both the temple and the city as he found them in June 1848.

> The site of Nauvoo is one of the most beautiful in all the western country as well as in the country immediately surrounding. . . . The temple of which so much has been said and written stands at the highest point of land in the city about 150 or 200 [feet] above the river . . . [and] at a distance it has the appearance of an immense church. . . . On ascending to the top one of the most grand and charming prospects meets the eye. The country on the east is an immense prairie and has once been peopled by the Mormons. But everything about the place is dull and stagnant. There are less than 2000 people now in the place.[31]

In spite of continued efforts to lease or sell the temple, the peaceful transfer of the building was eventually blocked by catastrophe. On October 9, 1848, an arsonist set fire to the structure. Joseph Smith III, the sixteen-year-old son of Joseph and Emma Smith, described the alarm of fire that sounded across the town. Smith was intimately acquainted with the temple, having been "over every foot of [the] building while it was being formed, and after it was enclosed . . . often visit[ing] it in company with many who came to view it, both before and after the exodus of the Saints." From a small bedroom above his father's Red Brick Store, he was "aroused by someone shouting, 'Fire!'" Smith later recalled, "That night the whole interior of the Temple burned out."[32]

The *Nauvoo Patriot* reported the event. "Our citizens were awakened by the alarm of fire. . . . The fire was seen first about three o'clock in the morning, and not until it had taken such hold of the timbers and roof as to make useless any effort to extinguish it. The materials of the inside were so dry, and the fire spread so rapidly, that a few minutes were sufficient to wrap this famed edifice in a sheet of flame." Though its builders had created conflict in the region, the local newspaper lamented the building's loss. "It was a sight too full of mournful sublimity. . . . Although the morning was tolerably dark, still, when the flames shot upwards, the spire, the streets, and the houses for nearly a mile distant were lighted up, so as to render even the smallest objects discernible. The glare of the vast torch, pointing skyward, indescribably contrasted with the universal gloom and darkness around it: and men looked on with faces sad as if the crumbling ruins below were consuming all their hopes."[33]

From across the river, the *Keokuk Register* similarly captured the scene:

> The fire presented a most sublime spectacle. It commenced in the cupola, and as the flames shot up to the sky, they threw a lurid glare into the surrounding darkness. Great volumes of smoke and flame burst from the windows, and the crash of falling timbers was distinctly heard on the opposite side of the river. The interior of the building was like a furnace; the walls of solid masonry were heated throughout and cracked by the intense heat. The melted zinc and lead was dropping from its huge block during the day. On Tuesday morning the walls were too hot to be touched. The naked walls still stand, and if not demolished by the hand of man, for centuries may stand.[34]

Far away in Utah, Latter-day Saint response to the news was mixed. Possibly reflecting his frustration with the various efforts to sell the structure or a desire that others not desecrate the sacred building they had sacrificed so much to build, Brigham Young remarked, "I hoped to see it burned before I left, but I did not. I was glad when I heard of its being destroyed by fire, and of the walls having fallen in, and said, 'Hell, you cannot now occupy it.'"[35] Not all Latter-day Saints, however, shared Young's view regarding the fate of the temple or Nauvoo. Recalling his visit to the city while en route to Europe during the winter of 1849–1850, Lorenzo Snow wrote to his sister Eliza,

> I proceeded to Nauvoo—I gazed upon its ruins—the direful work of mobocracy. My heart sickened as I contemplated that once beautiful city. . . . But now, O how sad the change! The moss was growing upon the buildings, which were fast crumbling down; the windows were broken in, the doors were shaking to and fro by the wind, as they played upon their rusty, creaking hinges. The lovely Temple of our God, once the admiration and astonishment of the world and the hope of the Saints, was burned, and its blackened walls were falling upon each other.[36]

Abandoned, the homes and temple shell fell into other hands or into complete disrepair and remained in this state for decades to come.

## French Takeover of Nauvoo

Though years after the Latter-day Saints had hoped—and too late to save the building from arson—Church agents did eventually succeed in selling the Nauvoo Temple, thus paving the way for the post-Mormon era of Nauvoo's history. On April 2, 1849, officials sold the fire-damaged structure, together with property west of the building, to Étienne Cabet, leader of a French utopian society known as the Icarians, for $2,000.[37] The founder of a communalistic movement in France that numbered more than four hundred thousand by the mid-1840s, Cabet had sent sixty-nine of his most devout followers to establish a model society along the Red River in western Texas in 1848. Failing to establish a community in the rugged region, the survivors returned to New Orleans, where they were bolstered by additional emigrants as well as by news that Cabet himself would soon join them. While awaiting his arrival, the Icarians learned of the abandoned city of Nauvoo upriver in Illinois. In early 1849, an exploratory party surveyed the region, returning to New Orleans with a report of vacant houses and land in cultivation. On March 1, 1849, Cabet, whom the community elected as their president for a ten-year term, started upriver from New Orleans for Nauvoo with 280 followers.[38]

FIGURE 3. Etienne Cabet (1788–1856), French philosopher and founder of the Icarian movement. Courtesy of Archives and Special Collections, Western Illinois University Libraries.

Cabet sought and received a charter for his community from the state of Illinois in February 1851. The Icarian Constitution summarized the group's beliefs: "In a word, old society is based on selfishness, inequality and individualism: let the new be based on FRATERNITY, EQUALITY, and LIBERTY, Communism or COMMUNITY."[39] Emile Vallet, one of Cabet's Nauvoo followers, expanded in practical terms the application of the group's beliefs, "The new society was based on marriage and the family. . . . To the exception of the family, everything was in common among them. No private property, no monies, no poor, no rich, no competition, no antagonism; complete solidarity. The strong working for the feeble, the sick; the one working for all and all working for one; everyone producing according to his strength, his talent, his skill and consuming according to his wants. . . . Women rehabilitated, cherished and respected. Love, confidence, security, happiness."[40]

Vallet also captured the group's settling of Nauvoo. "They were offered land, farms at very low figures," Vallet continued, "but Cabet had examined the ruins of the Mormon Temple. . . . They had not money enough to buy both, land and the ruins, but those ruins worked on Cabet's brains. They were renowned already and when connected with his name, they both would add to each other's glory." Against the counsel of some of his advisors, Cabet and the community purchased the temple while merely renting other land.[41] Cabet hoped to transform the damaged temple into a school, while his followers occupied the many abandoned homes in the region.

Throughout the early months of 1850, workers assembled lumber and began rebuilding the interior of the temple. The society's secretary reported, "Many preparations were already made—An agent has been sent to the pine forests in the North to buy timbers of dimensions necessary for re-establishing the roof and floors. Some other pieces of wood were ready; a steam mill was purchased to fit up a saw-mill; the saw-mill was nearly finished; a vast shed was raising near the Temple, to shelter the carpenters; the masons were laying in the interior the bases of the pillars."[42]

However, their hopes for repurposing the temple were dashed when a tornado toppled the north wall and damaged the others in May 1850. Working inside the building at the time of the storm, Vallet recounted his escape.

Suddenly a furious wind began to blow; four of the masons fearing the nonsolidity of the walls, left to seek shelter elsewhere. Seven of us remained, taking refuge in the tool room on the south side [of the temple's basement]. If there is a Providence it was on our side, for hardly had we taken our position than the tornado began to tear small rocks from the top of the walls and flew in every direction. We became frightened. Some proposed to run away, others opposed it on the ground that it was dangerous, as those loose rocks could fall on our heads and kill us. Before we had decided whether we should stay or run, one of us that was watching exclaimed: "Friends, we are lost, the north wall is caving in!" And so it was.

Conveying the fear the men had for their own lives, Vallet continued:

> A wall sixty feet high was coming on us, having only forty feet to expand. We fled to the southwest corner, deafened with terror. I for one heard nothing. The fall of that wall was heard three miles away in the country. We looked at one another. All alive, but white as sheets. The wind was terrific, the rain was blinding us. The cloud was touching the ground. The most severe storm I ever witnessed in Nauvoo. We were mostly paralyzed. We expected every minute the other walls to come down. Some of the top rocks had fallen within three feet of us. The east wall was three feet out of plumb. "Forward march!" shouted one and on we ran over the heaped up rocks more dead than alive.[43]

When the storm was over, the community gathered to assess the damage. Fearing an accident should the weakened walls tumble, the southern and eastern walls were immediately removed, leaving only the main western wall.[44] Residents carted off the rubble for use in their own structures.

With plans to use the temple ruined, Cabet and his followers turned their attention to building the rest of their community. Numerous frame, box-like apartment houses were erected on the north, east, and south of the temple block, with a large community dining hall, kitchen, and workshop nearby. Limestone rubble from the temple was used to build a school. Near the river, the community constructed large flourmills, a distillery, a slaughterhouse, and a washhouse. To disseminate their communal message, an Icarian printing office was opened. The 1850 census listed 276 Icarians living in Nauvoo. Five years later, the Illinois census reported the community had grown to 464 members.[45] "The majority of the members composing the Icarian Society was a selection from the best laboring class of France," Vallet recalled. "The most laborious, honest, economical, intelligent and philanthropic. They had the profound conviction that they were able to carry out the communist principles. They had the determination, the will (they thought) that would overcome all obstacles, all difficulties and enable them to stand and support all privations."[46]

In spite of their intentions, the fall of the temple served to portend the Icarian experience in Nauvoo. Ultimately, the community survived for a similar seven-year period as the earlier Mormon era. Cabet and his followers "were in earnest," Vallet noted.

> But they were human. The ego was too strong to be subdued by the will. They were under the influence of their sensations and without being conscious of it were constantly blaming others and hurting the feelings of those they called brothers. . . . As they had the same rights, the same duties, the same privileges, they naturally thought themselves authorized, entitled to watch, to detect, to mention the negligence, the errors, the lack of skill, the want of economy, the wasting and squandering, the abuse of authority of some of the officers; in one word all that could injure the interest and endanger the existence of the society.[47]

Mormon Frederick Piercy, visiting Nauvoo in 1853, captured the tenuous state of Icarian affairs at the time. "At present the Icarians form the most important part of the population of Nauvoo. I was told while there that they were by no means in a prosperous condition, and that M. Cabet had publicly said, that unless they received assistance from France it would be impossible for the organization to continue. They have used the stones of the Temple to build workshops and a school-house. They live in a long ugly row of buildings, the architect of which, and the school-house, was a cobbler. . . . I very much question whether the Icarians will ever accomplish much."[48]

Discouraged by the challenges they faced in Nauvoo, members of the Icarian community began looking for another location to continue the communal experiment. In 1853 some moved to Iowa, where they homesteaded nearly four thousand acres of land. Meanwhile, in Nauvoo, jealousy and discontentment grew. Followers lost confidence in the society. "They were and had been leaving as fast as they would come," Vallet reported, "so that in six years 1,800 persons came to it and we were never more than 500 members at the same time."[49] For his part, Cabet appears to have grown dictatorial. According to Vallet, "Cabet claimed supremacy and always refused to listen to any motion of reform to his perfect system." When he tried to claim the presidency of the community for life in 1856, his followers rebelled.[50] Fearing civil war, the inhabitants of Nauvoo prepared "to chase the boisterous communists as they had chased the Mormons before."[51] Before violence erupted, Cabet and his minority of 180 followers abandoned Nauvoo for St. Louis, Missouri, in October 1856, where he died of a stroke a month later.[52] The remaining Icarian community in Nauvoo liquidated their property and relocated to Iowa.[53] Others abandoned the society and were absorbed into the Nauvoo fabric of Mormons who did not move West, along with new citizens and a growing German immigrant population.

## The Most German-Speaking Town in Illinois

German settlers wrote the next chapter in the story of Nauvoo's post-Mormon nineteenth-century history. Immigrants from central Europe began moving to the region at the same time as those in the Icarian movement. Seeking opportunity while also fleeing militarization in their native lands, they settled across the Midwest, bringing with them elements of their German culture and heritage.[54] Learning of "a town laid out with streets and stores and homes that could be bought for back taxes," many settled in Nauvoo.[55] Joseph Smith III later recalled, "Chief among these were some Germans who had come in, bought property, and were engaged in gardening, fruit-raising, and wine-making."[56] Irish, Belgian, and French immigrants similarly seeking a new start joined them in Nauvoo. As a result, Catholic, Lutheran, Presbyterian, and Methodist churches emerged, with the German language used in worship services and the parochial schools they established.[57] Capitalizing on the buildings vacated by the Mormon community, Reverend Jacob Haas organized a Methodist congregation that briefly met in the Latter-day Saint Seventies Hall.[58]

Throughout the second half of the nineteenth century, the German language was reportedly more common in town than was English, with some referring to it as "the most German speaking town in Illinois," a reputation that persisted into the twentieth century.[59] Florence Ourth, a girl who, as a teenager, moved with her family to Nauvoo in 1923, later recalled, "When we came it was a German community—the store keepers all talked German, as there were many people who couldn't talk English. They would have German services in the Lutheran church once a month so they always had a pastor who could speak German. . . . So when we came here it really was a German community."[60] This German influence can be seen in the names of many of the Nauvoo businesses of the era, including Ochsner's Emporium, the Leonard J. Schrader School of Aeronautics, Reimbold's General Store, Ritter's Meat Packing Plant, John Laubersheimer's General Store, and the Kraus Café and Confectionary.[61] It is most prominently featured in the inscription at the top of the John George Kaufmann home, which fittingly reads, in German, "This house is mine, but not really. Whoever comes after me, it will be his. I've been here. Whoever reads this must also have been here."[62]

These European settlers shaped Nauvoo both religiously and economically. In the early 1850s, Catholic priest Father J. C. Alleman purchased the former home of Latter-day Saint Apostle Parley P. Pratt, converting it into St. Patrick's Church. As German immigrants outnumbered the Irish population, the church was renamed after Saints Peter and Paul. Alleman also brought grapevines to

Nauvoo, dramatically altering the local economy. Emil Baxter, a director in the Icarian community, remained in Nauvoo following the Icarian departure and opened the first winery in the community in 1857, a family business that persists today, five generations later.[63] Other trades emerged in town as residents filled the void created by the Mormon and Icarian departures. By 1860 the town boasted seven blacksmiths, two cigar makers, three or four harness shops, three wagon makers, six cooper shops, two tin shops, six shoemakers, four or five tailors, six grocery stores, cabinet makers, carpenters, and mills.[64]

## Dismantling the Mormon Remains

While Nauvoo, as a town, survived after the Mormon and Icarian eras, its size paled in comparison. There simply were not enough residents in town or demand across the region for the number of vacant structures, and many fell into disrepair. Frederick Piercy's description of his 1853 visit to Nauvoo captures the state of the city:

> The first objects I saw in approaching the city were the remains of what was once the Temple, situated on the highest eminence of the city.... On the banks of the river lie broken blocks of stone and shattered bricks, and the visitor's first steps are over evidences of ruin and desolation. Foundations of what must once have been substantial buildings are broken up and exposed to the light, and houses, once noted for neatness, cleanliness and order, and surrounded by flower gardens, evincing taste, care, and a love of the beautiful, after being pillaged of all that was valuable and portable, have been abandoned by their ruthless destroyers, and are now monuments of their selfish, jealous and contemptible hate.[65]

The temple ruins, which Piercy described so dramatically in 1853, were finally removed a decade later. Describing their demolition, the *Carthage Republican* reported in 1864, "One day last week a mine was placed beneath the remaining portion yet standing; and with the blast that followed the last of the famous Mormon temple lay prone and broken in the dust. We understand that the stone, much of which is uninjured, has been sold to parties who contemplate building residences and wine cellars." The newspaper lamented the loss:

> The last remaining vestige of what the famous Mormon temple was in its former glory has disappeared, and nothing now remains to mark its site but heaps of broken stone and rubbish. The southwest corner, which has braved the blasts of ten or fifteen winters,—towering in sad grandeur above the sad buildings,—a marked object for many miles, the shrine of the pilgrimage

FIGURE 4. Nauvoo Temple ruins, ca. 1853. Steel engraving by Frederick Piercy. Historic Sites photograph collection: Nauvoo, Nauvoo Temple—Oblique view, 1853. Church History Library, The Church of Jesus Christ of Latter-day Saints, Salt Lake City.

of thousands who have annually flocked to gaze in wonder and awe upon the beautiful ruin,—is no more. The eye of the stranger and traveler who approach the classic city of Nauvoo will no more rest upon the towering ruin that first gives notice of their proximity to the sacred soil, where once tread the hurrying feet of thousands of the "Lord's anointed."[66]

Though the temple itself was gone, Mormon visitors to Nauvoo continued to be fascinated with the city's fate. J. C. Rich, a Latter-day Saint born in Nauvoo in 1841, returned to the town of his birth in 1869. Writing to his father-in-law and former Nauvoo resident, Edward Hunter, Rich characterized many of the city's prominent structures in the late 1860s: "The outside of the Mansion House looks even more dilapidated & forsaken than the inside. It does not seem that one improvement has been made since the prophet left it. . . . The Nauvoo House . . . still stands as it did when the work on it ceased. It has the appearance of recent work in its masonry. The bricks are as good as the day they were made and the finishing touch of the trowel indicates that it was done but yesterday. . . . The old Masonic Hall still stands, but looks old." Rich also reported on the condition of several prominent homes, "Prest. Young's house remains in good repair and Bro. Kimball's as good as the day he left it." He also described the final resting place of many early Latter-day Saints. "I visited the Old Mormon graveyard—now a complete forest of oak and hickory. There is probably fifty tomb-stones standing, among the number I found one to the memory of my sister. The fence around the graveyard is down and exposed. . . . At present it belongs to no one and having a fine forest of timber thereon the probability is that ere long some one will enclose it and forever obliterate its existence as a graveyard."

Summarizing his experience in Nauvoo, Rich reflected his feelings for its demise:

> The settlers in this Co. are generally of the opinion that land once occupied by the Mormons, no matter as to the richness of the soil, has never seemed profitable to the owners since the Saints were driven away. They say the curse of God is visibly manifested in the earth's production. I have told some of them that I wished to God it would refuse to produce even white beans, but I realize it would not do for me to judge these matters. The old mob spirit has about died out and a general feeling of regret at the manner of treating the Mormons is very prevalent.[67]

Local feelings regarding the Mormons, together with the state of the structures they had left behind, were captured in the accounts of others who visited the city. Richard W. Young, a Latter-day Saint personally unacquainted with the earlier experience in Nauvoo, reported a stopover in an 1883 Church periodical. "The greater part of the town at the present time—it seems to have been otherwise in the days of '38–'46—is located on the ridge," Young noted, "with a few houses nearby on the meadow land, and an unoccupied strip a quarter of a mile wide between the houses and the river on the west." Unable to orient himself initially, Young continued, "The Temple we at once concluded must have been erected on one of the highest points on the ridge, and so we walked up to what we considered a likely location; our first conjecture was further strengthened as to the site by the presence in that neighborhood of a drug store and several other buildings constructed of finely wrought white stone, which we assumed to have come from the walls of the Temple." Finding a neighbor to take him on a tour, Young reported little remaining visible evidence of the once-imposing structure. "Here was a house and yard, not even on the corner of a block; with all the usual surroundings of a semi-rural home, distinguished from its neighbors in no special manner, perfectly level, with fruit trees and flowers—and this, we were thrice assured, was where the Nauvoo Temple used to stand."

Young next inquired after the homes of Joseph Smith as well as of his grandfather, Brigham Young. Visiting the latter, he found it occupied by a Dr. Parker, and to be "in astonishingly good repair," a "solid and cheerful, and historically interesting" house. At the Smith property, he found both the Mansion House and the Nauvoo House, together with their caretaker, Lewis Bidamon, the second husband of Emma Smith. Young described Bidamon as "a massive man, cordial in his treatment of us, and apparently neither a very strong advocate of Reorganism nor a bitter enemy of the Church." Inquiring about what might remain from the earlier era, Bidamon told Young that "all relics of the Prophet Joseph . . . had been removed by the 'boys' at the time of Emma's death." Concluding his visit, Young captured the state of Nauvoo at the time. "An old German . . . having learned our names, said he would like to have our people all back there again—but since he was the proprietor of a corner grocery, we suspected him of sinister motives."[68]

As the generation of Latter-day Saints who personally experienced Nauvoo dwindled in the late nineteenth century, a new reality for the town emerged. The conflicts that doomed the earlier Mormon and Icarian periods of the city's history had dissipated. In their place, European immigrants committed to an agrarian rather than a religious or communal future rebuilt the abandoned city to the best of their abilities and resources. Their quiet takeover of the city, with little public recognition for the Mormon past, reflected how the majority controls social memory. Far away in Utah, however, some hoped for a revival of the Latter-day Saint presence in the Midwest. Writing in 1887, Latter-day Saint editor B. H. Roberts predicted, "While the people who once made it the abode of peace are thriving in other lands, made rich and fruitful by their industry, this languishing city awaits their return to recover the lost glory that won for her the proud name, 'Nauvoo the Beautiful.'"[69]

Recovery of Nauvoo's Mormon past was not on the minds of all who experienced it. For these, a return to Nauvoo was unnecessary because they never left the city. In fact, before the Utah branch could ever return, some, including the Smith family and the faith they founded following their father's death, led out in using Nauvoo for interpretive purposes. Quietly but actively participating in community affairs, this first family of the Restoration lived among the residents of Nauvoo for decades, mourning with them when the temple was burned, witnessing the rise and fall of the Icarian experiment, and even worshipping for a time alongside them in the local Methodist congregation. As their Utah cousins sought to survive in the deserts of the Intermountain West, the midwestern Mormons thrived in the city along the Mississippi, eventually leading out in the preservation and celebration of Mormon memory in the early twentieth century.

# CHAPTER 2

# Nauvoo as a Reorganized Church Foothold

While much of the city of Nauvoo lay abandoned by Latter-day Saints and only partially occupied by their successors, an important connection to the Mormon past lingered during the second half of the nineteenth century. Emma Smith, widow of the slain Prophet, together with their five children, remained in Nauvoo after the exodus, preserving the memory of Joseph Smith in the region as well as buildings important to the Mormon legacy. As much of the city fell into disrepair, Smith family occupancy of their waterfront properties preserved a toehold for Latter-day Saint presence in the city through the combination of religious and familial memory. However, their presence and these properties also set the stage for controversy because of the varying interpretations of the memory of Joseph Smith, especially as those competing interpretations became entrenched within American society.

## The Smith Family in Post-Mormon Nauvoo

Following Joseph Smith's death in 1844, property held in his name quickly became a point of contention between Emma Smith and Brigham Young. However, the conflict between these two imposing figures within early Mormon history ran deeper than property lines and personal possessions. In the wake of the martyrdom of Joseph Smith, differing views on succession, coupled with sometimes opposing views on the memory of the Prophet, including the faith

FIGURE 5. Emma Smith, widow of Joseph Smith,
the founder of Mormonism, with son David Hyrum,
1845. Unknown photographer, reproduction by
George Edward Anderson. Used by permission,
L. Tom Perry Special Collections, Harold B. Lee
Library, Brigham Young University, Provo, Utah.

he founded and the theology he practiced, drove a wedge between Smith and
Young, creating a wound that outlived each of them.

Concerned initially for her temporal welfare as well as for the welfare of her
fatherless children, Smith maintained control of the Mansion House, Homestead, Nauvoo House, and Red Brick Store, as well as several other lots in town
and in the surrounding countryside. Young, on the other hand, concerned himself with the debts of the Church, many of which were complicated by the overlapping nature of Joseph Smith's roles as husband, citizen, and Church leader.
Upon reviewing the Prophet's financial affairs a week after the martyrdom,

Joseph Smith's clerk William Clayton summarized the problem: "The situation looks gloomy. The property is chiefly in the name of the Trustee in Trust while the obligations are considered personal."[1] Because of the intersection between Church and personal property, the question of ownership plagued Smith's widow for nearly a decade. "Most of the assets were in Joseph's name as trustee-in-trust for the church," Emma Smith's biographers noted. "The liabilities were in Joseph's name as private citizen and Emma was now accountable. . . . [She] had inherited a debt that would plague her for years."[2]

Creditors turned to Emma for satisfaction of her late husband's debts. Smith's mother-in-law and fellow widow, Lucy Mack Smith, warned her about the difficulties she faced: "Creditors will come forward and use up all the property there is."[3] The prediction proved prophetic even before the Saints' exodus from Nauvoo. As early as two months following the martyrdom of Joseph Smith, Emma Smith received a financial notice from the interim mayor of Nauvoo, Daniel Spencer, a Young follower. "Where as Joseph Smith, Mayor, John P. Greene, C[ity] M[arshall], and Wm. Clay[ton] Treasurer did borrow of Mr. John Robinson the sum of fifteen hundred dollars for the use of the City of Nauvoo & Joseph Smith did retain one thousand dollars of the same in his hands you are requested to pay to Mr. Robinson the above $1,000."[4] Understandably, debts like these complicated an already difficult circumstance for the grieving widow.

Legal action eventually determined the fate of the Smith properties. In 1850 the Mansion House, Homestead, Nauvoo House, and farm were considered exempt from creditors' attempts to acquire them. In a subsequent lawsuit in 1852, their exempt status was reversed, forcing Emma to purchase them for herself in order to save them for the family.[5] While she worked to get the properties securely in her possession, Smith also sought ways to supplement the family income. As early as August 1844, she arranged for Nauvoo Stake president William Marks to rent the Mansion House, retaining several rooms for her personal use. A year later, she tried to rent out Joseph's Red Brick Store to a friend, Joseph Heywood.[6] During the Battle of Nauvoo in September 1846, she leased the Mansion House to Abram Van Tuyl and fled with the children, who ranged in age from fifteen to not yet two, 150 miles upstream to Fulton, Illinois.[7] There, she waited out the conflict.

Learning that Van Tuyl was planning to defraud her and depart with her possessions, Emma made a hasty return to Nauvoo in the winter of 1847.[8] She succeed in protecting her interests from Van Tuyl but lamented, "I have no friend but God, and no place to go but home."[9] Later that fall, Major Lewis Bidamon, a non-Mormon new citizen of Nauvoo and widower himself, courted Smith.[10]

"You are alone and I am alone. Let us live our lives out together," he reportedly proposed. The two were married on December 23, 1847, bringing a measure of financial stability to Smith while helping her raise her five children.[11] Her oldest son, Joseph, fifteen at the time of his mother's remarriage, later summarized the "new conditions and environments" introduced into their family by Bidamon. "He was a man of strong likes and dislikes, passionate, easily moved to anger, but withal ordinarily affable in manner, decidedly hospitable, and generous in disposition," Smith recalled. "He made friends easily, but unfortunately for him, lost them quite as easily. His love for intoxicating liquors and his lack of religious convictions were the two most serious drawbacks to the happiness of our home, and tended to affect and color materially the after-events of our lives." In spite of these failings, Smith nevertheless expressed gratitude for Bidamon's influence. "While his moral character might not be considered to be of the highest quality he did possess a certain pride of manhood, a deeply-rooted dislike of being in debt or under obligation to anyone, and, so far as the ordinary transactions of life are concerned, a desire to deal honorably with his fellow man. I can but give Major Bidamon credit for considerable foresight in providing comfortably for the family from the resources at hand."[12]

In the years that followed, the Bidamon family eventually found acceptance within a Nauvoo community that was detached from its Mormon founding. "I mingled freely in the society of the place," Joseph Smith III later recalled. "The Mansion House attracted those of the highest order and it was recognized as one of the centers of Nauvoo's social life. There was a good spirit of comradeship among all the young people there, and the group included Catholics, Presbyterians, Methodists, and Lutherans, as well as those of no religious affiliations. All of these mingled freely in the social activities of the place without friction arising from denominational proclivities." Describing his own religious affiliations after the Mormon exodus, Smith continued, "I was a constant attendant at church services, usually the Methodist and Presbyterians, though occasionally attending Catholic services which were conducted in both the English and German languages."[13]

While Emma Smith's marriage to Lewis Bidamon brought a dramatic social change for the entire family, decisions regarding religion by her oldest son ultimately added another. In the years following Joseph Smith's death, the many factions of Mormonism had repeatedly sought out Emma and her children. "I have always avoided talking to my children about having anything to do in the church, for I have suffered so much I have dreaded to have them take any part in it," Emma reportedly told one courter for the family's faith. "But I have always believed that if God wanted them to do anything in the church, the One who called their father would make it known to them."[14] In 1856 Joseph Smith III rebuffed attempts from some that he reorganize the Church and lead it as a lineal successor to his father. However, by 1860, Smith reconsidered his position. Attending an organizational conference of believers in Amboy, Illinois, on April 6, 1860, the twenty-seven-year-old Smith, accompanied by his mother, presented himself for leadership in the Reorganized Church of Jesus Christ of Latter Day Saints. "I came not here of myself," Smith announced to the congregation, "but by the influence of the spirit. For some time past I have received manifestations pointing to the position which I am about to assume. I wish to say that I have come here not to be dictated by any men or set of men. I have come in obedience to a power not my own, and shall be dictated by the power that sent me. God works by means best known to himself, and I feel that for some time past He has been pointing out a work for me to do."[15] Deciding to headquarter the newly formed Church in Nauvoo where he lived with his wife and three-year-old son, Smith experienced opposition from locals who feared a return of Mormonism that, by that time, was openly advocating its practice of polygamy. Smith calmed the concerns, strongly denouncing the Utah Church's controversial marital practices while promising that he and the followers of his faith were more moderate.[16]

Over time, the Smiths and, by association, the Reorganized Church of Jesus Christ achieved a measure of respectability in Nauvoo. Joseph Smith III, who had married Emmeline Griswold in 1856 and moved into the old family homestead, was elected as justice of the peace in 1858. In spite of opposition from some because of his religious views, he won reelection by nearly a four to one margin in 1862. He later recalled, "So far as the purposes of the election were concerned, I had many friends among the Germans, French, and Austrians of the community. When they found that leading church people with their respective followers and adherents banded together to defeat me for the office, they rallied to my support."[17] Of the larger extended family and their acceptance within the community, one neighbor added, "Mrs. Smith Bidamon was awfully nice. There wasn't a better woman in Nauvoo. She was a good soul, a good christian woman. She was good to everyone. Everyone thought well of her. She was always busy, a great woman to work. She did a good job raising her children. Her boys, Joseph, Alexander, and David were good boys. She was good to Mr. Bidamon's son, Charles."[18]

Many confirm the assessment of both the Smith/Bidamon family and their faith. Orville F. Berry, a prominent nineteenth-century Hancock County attorney, reported from interviews of longtime area residents and his own lifelong observations, "There are in this county quite a large number of members of the reorganized church, and as citizens of the community they stand high; while it is possible that some feel, even yet, peculiarly about them on account of the history of the church here, as individuals they could not so feel in regard to them."[19] William R. Hamilton, the son of the hotel keeper in Carthage who assisted with the bodies of Joseph and Hyrum Smith following their martyrdom and, by the end of the nineteenth century, was "perhaps the oldest settler in Hancock county," similarly noted, "Immediately after the killing of Joseph, all kinds of trouble began at Nauvoo. This ended in the final driving away of the entire crowd, except a small number who believed that Joseph's son should be the successor to his father. They remained here. At least they did not go with Brigham Young, and they are now known in this county as the 'Reorganized Church of Jesus Christ of Latter Day Saints.' No just criticism can be made of the acts of this branch of the church here."[20]

Interestingly, while the Prophet's widow and her family gained respectability locally, they drew increased criticism from Mormons living more than a thousand miles away. Visitors from the West to Nauvoo frequently sought them out, unflatteringly reporting their condition back to associates in Utah. In May 1853 Hannah Tapfield King visited Nauvoo and produced an oft-repeated characterization of Emma, "Power is the principle that seems to be stamped on her, but it is like the lion when couchant," King wrote. "Her mind seemed to me to be absorbed in the *past* and lost almost to the present . . . neither does she seem to desire to form any intimacy or renew it. . . . She did not even seem to respond to kindness, but she looked as if she had suffered and as if a deep vein of bitterness ran through her system. I felt sorry for her."[21]

The statement may say more about the tensions between the Latter-day Saints in the West and Emma Smith Bidamon than it does about the Prophet's widow herself. Critically, King continued, "She seems to have shut her eyes to the light and knowledge she once possessed, and how great is the darkness that envelopes her! She seems to be absorbed in the past, and to take no cognizance of passing events or people.—I feel she is not worthy of the Prophet Joseph Smith, but I leave her. I am not her judge."[22] Similarly, J. C. Rich wrote his observations of a visit with the family at the Mansion House in 1869: "Emma looks very old and broken; she never spoke while I was in the room only to give direction to the hired girl who waited on the table. While in conversation with Bidamon at the table, I stated in answer to his questions that I was from Salt Lake City at the same time telling who I was. I looked over to where Emma was sitting, knowing that she was well acquainted with my parents, but she never raised her eyes or said a word while I remained there. I could not help thinking what a change has come over that woman; [now] she is the wife of a man whose character, even among his friends, is reproached as a drunkard and an adulterer."[23] While his comments likely reflect his perception of the visit, they also reflect the nineteenth-century tensions between Brighamites and Josephites.

By 1866, Joseph Smith III relocated the headquarters of the Reorganized Church away from Nauvoo to Plano, Illinois, where he could oversee production of the Church's periodical, the *True Latter Day Saints' Herald*. His brother Alexander, who had affiliated with the movement in 1862 after some initial opposition, joined him shortly thereafter. Their other surviving brother, David Hyrum, likewise joined the faith in the early 1860s.[24] Alexander and David made repeated proselyting trips to Utah, taking them both away from Illinois. Emma and Lewis Bidamon, together with Lewis's son Charles E., remained in Nauvoo. Lewis finished his work transforming the unfinished Nauvoo House into the three-story Riverside Mansion, which the Bidamons occupied in late 1871.[25] The Major used foundation stone from the Nauvoo House to erect a stable on adjoining property to the north.[26] An official branch of the Reorganized Church, commonly called "the Olive Branch," was also formed in the city. Meeting in the upper room of Joseph Smith's Red Brick Store, it boasted as many as seventy-five members by 1864, including Emma and the Smith sons.[27] When the boys moved away, however, the branch struggled. "Our meetings are rather poorly attended," Emma lamented to her son Joseph in 1866. "The outsiders have left off attending. I think some of them are a little like myself, They miss my boys."[28] The branch was eventually disbanded in 1875.

Though away from Nauvoo, the sons kept in frequent contact with their mother. However, on a visit in the spring of 1879, Alexander Hale Smith found her sick in bed. "I had the testimony from God that my mother was dying," he later recalled. He sent word to Joseph, "If you expect to see mother alive, come quick." He did, and they bid farewell as she passed away a few weeks later.

## Securing and Preserving Smith Properties

With Emma Smith Bidamon's death on April 30, 1879, Smith presence and property in Nauvoo shifted to her posterity. The Homestead, Mansion House, and Red Brick Store properties were deeded to her surviving sons, while the Riverside Mansion (Nauvoo House) was given to her second husband, Lewis Bidamon, who passed it on to his son, Charles, at his death in 1891.[29] In the absence of the Smith sons due to their having moved away from Nauvoo, the properties slowly declined. In 1893 the Nauvoo city council condemned the long-dilapidated eastern wing of the Mansion House, forcing Alexander Hale

Smith, Joseph Smith III's brother and Reorganized Church Apostle, to have it removed.[30]

However, while the Smith leadership no longer headquartered the Reorganized Church in Nauvoo, it did recognize the importance of its properties to their movement. Significantly, Alexander Smith expressed the need to maintain Nauvoo as a historic site. Hearing a rumor that the Riverside Mansion was up for auction in 1893, Smith wrote to Reorganized Church Bishop E. L. Kelley, "I haven't for years felt a particle of interest in the old place until late. I feel we ought to take advantage of every opportunity to get a foot hold there again."[31] Over the next two decades, the Smiths and the Church they led sought to solidify their presence in the City of Joseph.

Reorganized Church interest in historic properties was heightened in 1905 when Latter-day Saints from Utah constructed a monument at the Prophet's birthplace in Sharon, Vermont, and, the same year, held a mission conference in Nauvoo. Following the conference, Reorganized Church historian and Apostle Heman C. Smith wrote to Church Presiding Bishop E. L. Kelley, "The Brighamites have recently been here over fifty strong and held a conference. We are following them with a series of meetings in City Hall. They have made quite an impression on those who want to sell property by giving out the impression that they are coming back to build up the place within two years. The story is out that they have bought the Nauvoo House, but Mr. C[harles] E. Bidamon, in whom the title is, answers me that it is not so."[32]

Because of these rumors, Heman Smith repeatedly reached out to Charles Bidamon, seeking either to secure title to the Nauvoo House for his faith or at least to block the Utah branch from doing so. In December 1905, Bidamon wrote Smith, "I have not offered the Nauvoo House for sale. I have however received a very good offer for the place from the Utah people who seem very anxious to get the property and as they say fulfill the revelation which they say they will do."[33] Strapped for cash, Bidamon requested a loan of up to $500 against the property. Later the next May, Heman Smith agreed to a loan, provided he receive "a guarantee that you will give me first chance of purchase should you con[sider to sell] and providing the title is all right." At the same time, Smith pressed for a sale, "I note also that you say that you might sell if you could get your price. Will you please . . . let me know what the price is[?] I am not in a hurry about purchasing however as long as you hold it yourself it is all right but when it goes out of your hands I would like to have a chance." Explaining his motivation, Smith continued, "I do not know that there is so very much importance attached to the place from a church stand point, but you know that there are a great many pleasant memories connected with the place—my wife and we [*sic*] do not wish to see it go into the hands of strangers unless the price gets unreasonably high."[34] While it is unclear why the sale did not occur at the time, Smith did secure a promise in the loan contract. Among other conditions, the documents stipulated, "It is also further expressly agreed that the property will not be sold by the makers of this note during the period of this loan without first giving the payee herein a chance to buy it at the time."[35]

Interestingly, in spite of this clause, Bidamon contacted Latter-day Saint Church president Joseph F. Smith three years later, offering to sell the Nauvoo House to the Utah Church. Possibly pitting the two faiths against each other in hopes of instigating a bidding war, Bidamon wrote, "Heman C. Smith Historian of the Reorganized Church has been negotiating with me for the purchase of the Nauvoo House property (of which I am owner) they desiring it on account of church association and revelation regarding its building." Offering it for sale to the Utah Church leader, Bidamon continued, "Sometime ago I had a conversation with one of the elders of your church about the property and the revelation. In the conversation he requested me that if at any time I desired to sell to communicate with you and secure your offer. The property is now for sale, and if your church wishes to secure it, please let me hear from you at once, or the property will soon pass into the hands of the Reorganized church."[36]

When a sale to the Latter-day Saints failed to materialize, Bidamon reentered into negotiations with Heman Smith and the Reorganized Church. This time, Smith was more cautious in his deliberations. "I have been in consultation with Bishop Kelley regarding your property, the Nauvoo House, and he has advised with Joseph, and Fred Smith, and also with the Bishop's Counsellor [*sic*] G. H. Hilliard," Smith coyly wrote in September 1909. "It seems to be the general opinion that the possession of the property is not of so much importance to the Church as might be thought as the house designated by revelation was never completed, and this house built by your father has no special value attached to it on account of revelation." Informing Bidamon that "it would therefore be impossible to dispose of [the property] to the church at . . . any special price," Smith countered, "I can not therefore take the property at the price you offer, but I am prepared to offer you the sum of Three Thousand Dollars, and make you the payment down you designated as soon as negotiations are complete. This is the best I can do at present, and can make no promise of . . . anything better in the future."[37] Accordingly, the transaction was consummated.

This would not be the last time Bidamon ruffled feathers by seeking financial gain from his possession of Mormon memorabilia. Years later, Mary Dean Haycock, a cousin to Joseph Smith III, recalled the feelings of the family as Charles Bidamon parted with some precious family possessions. In particular, she recalled Joseph Smith III's final visit to Nauvoo and the sad scene that ensued. "I never heard the [Smith] cousins ask for any piece of furniture or any keepsakes for *years* later when no one was left in the old home except 'young Charlie B.' as they called him with his shiftless family," Haycock recounted. Capturing the poignant experience, she continued, "Joseph said, 'I would like once more to go thru the old home.' . . . He was almost totally blind & very heavy but my sister and I armed him to the door & Charlie let us in & followed us from room to room but Coz. Joseph payed no attention to him as Chas. was bleary eyed and staggering—Joseph noticed he'd been selling off many pieces of the house furnishings and said, 'Where is the great roast pig platter & its ladle?' Chas said the platter has the corner knocked out that held the gravy—But here it is—A great willowware platter & ladle to match."

Moving together to another portion of the home, Haycock recalled,

> Then he asked to see his mother's room & was led to the top of the stairs & to the S.E. a large corner room still furnished with a great 4 poster bed with steps—a curious old chest of drawers & a small walnut rocker. Joseph run his fingers over the rocker & said "How oft has my dear Mother sat here rocking & overlooking the great father of waters, & dreaming of those other days." After a moment of silent thot [*sic*] he moved on to a small square table and murmured as tho to himself—"Ah, this is my father's favorite old checkerboard table. See! The top is inlaid with two different sorts of wood for the checkers." I noticed one square was light the next square of dark wood then his hand moved to the edge of the drawer & reaching under he pressed a spring when out popped the drawer which I believe still contained the checkers. We were all surprised and had to exclaim which made him smile. Then he asked—"Charlie what will you take to let me have this old table of father's?" Charlie mumbled, "I've been offered $35 for it" to which Coz Joseph answered as he turned away "Oh well anytime you feel like giving it to me send it along."

Haycock summarized the pathetic encounter:

> I walked off. Joseph was pretty feeble that day & I don't think he ever visited us or Nauvoo again. My sister & I scolded at him for allowing Bidamon to sell all the old family furniture & even they claimed the old home too but Joseph sighed & said it's not worth fighting for and the church is in need of what we can gather in & more. Later I knew a Carthage collector bragging of going after night with a team & wagon & driver & a nice bottle of whiskey for Charlie & when he was just about down & out he gave them the key to the Old Homestead & went with them and they got all they could haul in the wagon that night.[38]

While priceless possessions slipped away from within the buildings' interiors, over time the Reorganized Church did slowly consolidate its land holdings in Nauvoo. Church leadership obtained the deed to the family cemetery in 1908 from members of the Smith family. In 1916 the Church officially received the Mansion House from the estate of Alexander Hale Smith. Finally, three years later, Frederick M. Smith, son of Joseph Smith III and head of the faith following his father's death in 1914, deeded the remaining Smith properties, the Joseph Smith Homestead and the lot for the Red Brick Store, to the Reorganized Church.[39] Subsequent land purchases continued in the surrounding area until, by 1963, the Church had acquired all of the sixteen blocks that comprise the Joseph Smith Historic Site.[40]

## Nauvoo as a Reorganized Church Proselytizing Site

Understandably, Reorganized Church officials were not merely interested in property ownership in Nauvoo. As early as 1906, a Sunday School was organized in the town under the direction of Mark Siegfried, a local schoolteacher. Recognizing interest in the properties and "looking toward the permanent protection of the grounds at Nauvoo and to the preservation of the house still standing known as the homestead of Joseph, the Martyr," the 1917 General

FIGURE 6. Joseph Smith Homestead, Nauvoo, Ill.
Used by permission, Utah State Historical Society.

Conference of the Church called for immediate action to save the buildings.[41] Later the same year, Church officials reported that the Nauvoo House and the Homestead "were in need of extensive repairs and protection from the river." They authorized the expenditure of up to $5,000 of General Church funds "to put the property in condition and protect it."[42]

Acting on these encouragements, John and Ida Layton were assigned as the first caretakers and guides at the Smith family properties in 1918. Tours were conducted and limited restoration efforts of both the Mansion House and the Homestead were begun.[43] The Laytons found that visitors were interested in the Smith properties and, by association, the Reorganization. In 1919 Ida Layton reported in the faith's *Zion's Ensign,* "Sundays in Nauvoo are usually quiet, restful days, but occasionally they differ. June 15 was one of the days that was different." She reported the visit of a member family with their three young sons, a baptism with about twenty-five people present, as well as a number of excursionists. "We were very busy for over an hour, showing them around," Layton noted. "There were thirty who registered, making fifty for the week, including those of the Sunday before. Counting to-day's visitors we have 1,094 to date."[44] Later that July, the Burtons, a Reorganized missionary couple in Nauvoo, summarized, "We feel that a good work is being done at this place and many a sermonette is preached to those who visit the buildings. In the country around this place we can see a new interest being taken in the gospel. Six have been baptized in the past four weeks, and several are near the kingdom. We are glad to welcome visitors at any time."[45]

A year later, the Saints in Nauvoo celebrated the opening of a new meetinghouse, the first ward schoolhouse that they had acquired and renovated for Church use. Located in an area of the city known as the flats, "the building is a pleasing structure of red brick, pleasing both inside and out," Emma B. Burton reported. "It is well seated. The Saints bought it, together with two acres of land adjoining it. They have made many improvements, making it really pretty inside. It is lighted with electricity, provided with furnace heaters, and a brother in Burlington donated an organ."[46]

Of course, the homes themselves continued to be the main attraction for visitors. In June 1920, Burton continued, "Since my last writing I have visited all the places of note. I have been in the room where the 'elect lady,' Mrs. Emma Smith, closed her eyes to the scenes of earth. This was in the chamber of the Nauvoo House; and in the upstairs room in the Mansion House where the spirit of Brother Alexander Smith left the fleshly house and took its flight to another stage of action. I have stood on the stone slab that covers the old well of Hyrum Smith, and have seen where the house stood, the ruins of which have recently been torn down." In a nod to a popular song of the day, Burton continued, "Many come to drink of the icy cold water from the 'old oaken bucket that hangs in the well' of the Old Homestead. . . . How pleasant it is to sit on the green, sloping bank, in front of the Homestead, in the friendly shade of one of those trees, and watch the steamer coming to the landing, and the gasoline boats darting about, causing the little wavelets to lap the shore almost at our feet."[47] Florence Ourth, the niece of the caretakers, recalled her visit to the town. "You just kind of felt like you were stepping back in history. . . . So many of the old homes were still standing although deserted and we could just wander in and out of them and just imagine."[48]

During the tenure of the Laytons, a Nauvoo branch of the Reorganized Church, absent since the last years of Emma Smith, was formally reestablished. In March 1921, Apostle U. W. Greene and Patriarch F. A. Smith held a conference with the twenty-two members living in the area and appointed Harvey V. Minton as branch president.[49] Both the branch and the historic sites garnered attention. "We have had many visitors here this summer, coming from all parts of the country," P. R. Burton wrote. "They desire to know what we teach and the main difference between us and the Utah Church. We also have many visitors from the Utah people and we treat them kindly, and hope some day they will see the error of their ways and return to the true church."[50]

Reorganized Church proselyting opportunities continued to present themselves through the sites in the city. By 1922, Charles J. Smith announced, "The work is gaining in Nauvoo, but it will take time and faithful service to put it on the high level where we wish to see it. Many tourists and visitors come there every year to see the old historic places and to hear the story of them. Last year one thousand two hundred and fourteen visitors registered in the Mansion House, heard the gospel story, took some literature with them, and expressed pleasure in having come."[51] However, growing a Reorganized Church presence in Nauvoo was not without its challenges. "It may not be the 'easiest' place in the world to prosecute missionary work, but it becomes interesting and inspiring if one will bend to the will of Him who guides us into all truth," Smith continued. "We have not baptized great numbers in this district lately, but those who have been baptized are continually holding up the banner of King Immanuel."[52]

Indeed, while some were attracted to the Reorganized message during the first half of the nineteenth century, others cynically commented on the oddity of the city and its connections to Mormonism. "The Weirdest Place in Chicagoland is Nauvoo, Ill.," read the title to a 1926 *Chicago Daily Tribune* article. "Nauvoo is petrified history," the author declared. "As sheer curio Nauvoo is the most interesting relic in Chicagoland." After summarizing the story of the Mormon exodus from the city, the author continued,

> The departure of Brigham and his hosts did not end the history of Nauvoo as a shrine city. As such it functions to this day. I said the place is petrified history. But there are a hundred thousand members of the "Reorganized Church of Jesus Christ of Latter Day Saints"—that is the present ecclesiastical name of the body of descendants of the Mormons who did not follow Brigham—who devoutly believe that "in the Lord's own time" Nauvoo will be restored to its glory of 80 years ago. . . . So you see Nauvoo is no dead shrine. It functions, and has Mormon pageants and solemn anniversary services near the supposed grave of its murdered "martyr."

Sarcastically, the reporter concluded, "The 'reorganized' Mormons at Nauvoo . . . assured me that the town now drowsing on the Mississippi . . . will be restored by 'revelation.' Pending that, they ought to engage a good, live go-getter and develop a chamber of commerce. Those are genuine aids to the Lord's work nowadays."[53]

## Competing Mormon Views on Nauvoo

Present in all of these narratives was the constant tension between the Reorganized Church, which controlled the properties in Nauvoo, and the larger Utah Church familiar to many of its visitors. In this regard, Nauvoo followed the trend of other religious and historic sites as a contested space.[54] The Chicago newspaperman whose visit to Nauvoo prompted him to call it the "weirdest place" in the area had picked up on the tension.

> Mrs. Layton [the guide] always spoke of Brigham's followers as "those who departed from the original church," but some of her co-religionists, not so gentle spoken as she is, call the Utah hierarchy, "the rejected church." "We," said Mrs. Layton, "have not changed one item of our doctrine as given us by the Martyr and Founder, and twice the United States courts have decided that we are his lawful successors. The Utah Saints—they don't allow our elders to preach in their churches, but we allow them to preach in ours. We treat them courteously, as we would treat you." And so she did treat me, showing me most interesting places, which she will also show you, for the Saints welcome visitors, even from among the gentiles.[55]

Nowhere was the tension greater than in one of the most significant events to occur under the direction of the Reorganized Church during this era, the

1928 discovery and re-interment of the bodies of Joseph, Hyrum, and Emma Smith.[56] The discovery came about following construction of a dam on the Mississippi River near Keokuk, Iowa, approximately thirteen miles downriver from Nauvoo. The dam, begun in 1910 and completed three years later, backed up the river near Nauvoo to form what is now known as Lake Cooper. The resulting higher water levels threatened the Smith riverfront properties. In 1920, Church officials prevailed upon the power company that operated the dam to install riprap along the shore near the Smith properties. However, the rock did little to slow the encroaching erosion of the property. In the Nauvoo House, the increased water levels necessitated filling in the cellar and eventually installing a berm and pumps, as the water reached within twelve feet of the foundation.[57]

By 1928, Church leaders were especially concerned. Not only was the rising water damaging the lot surrounding the Smith homestead, it threatened the unmarked graves of Joseph and Hyrum Smith believed to be located in the area. Following their deaths, the bodies of the brothers had originally been secreted in the unfinished basement of the Nauvoo House. Because of ongoing threats and rumors that the bodies might be taken away, Emma Smith and individuals close to her moved them again several months later with even greater secrecy. The reburial was done under the floor of an outbuilding near the Smith homestead. Those involved kept the closely guarded secret.[58] Decades later, Emma Smith Bidamon was buried in the same general area by her son, Joseph Smith III. Smith was one of the few who knew the location of the graves of his father and uncle. By the time his son and successor, Frederick M. Smith, was ordained as the Church's prophet-president in 1915, knowledge regarding the exact location of the bodies of the Smith brothers was lost. With the rising water level, Smith and others worried that not only would knowledge of the bodies be lost, the remains themselves could be washed away.[59]

In January 1928 the Reorganized Church appointed William O. Hands, a surveyor and civil engineer from Independence, Missouri, to try to locate the remains. Following a week of difficult and discouraging digging, Hands and his companions located the bodies of Joseph and Hyrum Smith on January 16, 1928. "This has been a day that will long be remembered," he wrote in the Nauvoo House Guest Book.[60] To protect the remains, the group dug a new grave for Joseph, Hyrum, and Emma Smith higher on the hill, reinterring their bodies on January 20, 1928. The new grave encased the remains in a concrete slab ten feet square and more than three feet thick. A slab originally marking Emma Smith's grave was divided in thirds and used to mark each of the new graves.

FIGURE 7. Graves of Emma, Joseph, and Hyrum Smith, Nauvoo, Ill.
Used by permission, Utah State Historical Society.

While accounts of the reburial indicate the respect with which it was per-formed, the entire project infuriated officials from the Utah Church. Samuel O. Bennion, Central States Mission president for The Church of Jesus Christ of Latter-day Saints, apparently read of the discovery and impending reburial in an area newspaper. Driving all night from Independence, Missouri, to Nauvoo, he and three other Elders examined the remains and witnessed the reburial. Reporting to the Latter-day Saint First Presidency regarding the occasion, Bennion wrote, "I am convinced myself . . . that the skeletons dug up by Fred M. Smith are the skeletons of Joseph and Hyrum Smith. . . . Great care was taken to lay the bodies just about as near as they naturally were. . . . These men were very careful in their work and had the flag flying during the time." Apparently aware of the controversy the reburial might generate, Bennion continued,

> I said to Fred M. why didn't you let the bodies of these men rest where they were, that it seemed a terrible thing to disturb their graves. He answered me, by saying that he wanted to find out if the graves of these men were down by what was once called the Spring House and rather evasively avoided my questions, but told me that he did not know exactly where they were buried and he wanted to find out. It was my impression . . . that he had heard the reports that Brigham Young took the bodies of Joseph and Hyrum to Utah and that he wanted to prove it untrue.

Reflecting the tension between the faiths, Bennion concluded, "As a matter of history, four men holding the Priesthood in the Church of Jesus Christ of Latter-day Saints stood on the ground from which these bodies [we]re taken and where they were laid in the earth again.... I am sorry they were disturbed and I don't think Fred M. Smith had any business to touch those graves, at least without consulting you."[61]

For his part, Reorganized Church president Frederick M. Smith sent a telegram informing Joseph Fielding Smith, a Latter-day Saint Apostle and grandson of Hyrum Smith, of the discovery of the graves. Frederick Smith wrote,

> Under the direction of engineer W. O. Hands on January 11th search was begun for the bodies of Joseph and Hyrum, and on January 16th in the afternoon they were found in the family cemetery near the Homestead near the grave of Emma.... Disinterment began yesterday and today the remains of the two and Emma will be placed in concrete crypts in what will be part of the foundation of a monument it is planned to erect on the spot.... Would like to have had ... you with me ... Made a hard journey to get here yesterday.... Bennion expected here this afternoon.[62]

In spite of the various communications, Joseph Fielding Smith was greatly troubled by the affair. "These sacred remains should not have been disturbed, and such a despicable act could only be performed by those who are lacking in all the finer feelings and in whom the spirit of reverence for things held sacred and holy by all faithful Latter-day Saints, does not exist," Smith blasted in a Kansas City newspaper and aimed at an audience familiar with the nearby Reorganized Church. "Frederick M. Smith has debased himself in the sight of all honorable men as well as in the sight of God, in this unholy and sacrilegious act. It is almost beyond belief that even he could stoop so low as to photograph the remaining bones of God's prophets, and show them on screens to a morbid following. The Lord will reward him according to his works," the Utah Church official concluded.[63] Latter-day Saint officials even threatened to sue Frederick M. Smith for desecration of the graves.[64] Bothered by the attacks, President Smith responded, "It was unkind, not to say absurd, ... to attribute to me as a motivation an objective so sordid as a 'bid for cheap sensation.' Our purpose was for that of adequately marking by suitable monument in due time.... The location of the grave was a prerequisite."[65]

The discovery of the remains together with the public feud that ensued between the prairie and mountain Mormons generated publicity for sites in Nauvoo. Responding to the interest, Reorganized Church leaders began making plans for improvements in each of their Nauvoo holdings. Though talk of an expanded memorial to the martyrs stalled with the onset of the Great Depression,[66] arrangements were made to furnish the properties with Mormon-era artifacts and inquiries were made concerning surviving temple sun and moon stones.[67] In the 1930s, a document outlining the preservation and development of Church properties in the town listed as the Church's objective "to preserve the cultural, spiritual and religious atmosphere of Nauvoo."[68] Key uses of the properties included missionary efforts, reunions, young peoples' camps, special meetings, and recreation.

Ambitiously, Reorganized officials outlined plans to reconstruct the Mansion House to its former size, develop the Homestead into a museum by transforming the parlor, office, living room and two upstairs rooms into period recreations, utilize the Nauvoo House for group meetings and lodging, erect improved memorials over the graves to the martyrs, and generally clean up the surrounding property, including the waterfront. In terms of staffing, they proposed locating a couple on the temple block, another at the Mansion House, and young people as guides at the Homestead. "Objects for consideration of expansion" included acquiring all of the property along Water Street between the river and Durphy Street, with careful consideration of the buildings located in the area. In addition to the Joseph Smith properties the Church already owned, possible additions included the Hyrum Smith residence, the Hyrum Smith office, the *Times and Seasons* office, the William Marks residence, and the Orson Pratt residence. Finally, planners proposed that "a village street of former Nauvoo could be developed here which would add materially to the interest and effectiveness of the objective for maintaining General Church holdings" in the city.[69]

Outside observers rightly recognized the Reorganized Church's place as leaders in the preservation of a Mormon Nauvoo. "To them goes the credit for preserving the important relics of Joseph Smith's Nauvoo," heralded the Federal Writers' Project of Illinois *Nauvoo Guide* in 1939. "The Joseph Smith Homestead, the Mansion House—second home of the Prophet—the Nauvoo House, which was under construction as a great hotel when Smith was murdered, and numerous other historic dwellings are owned and maintained by the Reorganized Church. The church also has a guide service to the town, and has done considerable research in determining the original owners of the old Mormon homes and in locating the sites of the important buildings that have been destroyed."[70]

The preservation and development of Nauvoo by the Reorganized Church in the early twentieth century placed the faith on a track to control the Mormon message in the city. They owned the most significant remaining structures, controlled the burial site of the founder of Mormonism, and, through their caretaker guides, offered the only interpretation for visitors. In these ways, they could "script the space," picking and choosing what to remember about the Mormon past in Nauvoo.[71]

But while the Reorganized Church and its leaders were solidifying their place and developing ambitious plans, they were not alone in their interest. Individuals associated with their larger sister faith in the West likewise turned their attention toward the city's potential. "In increasing numbers both 'Reorganites' and Utah Mormons make the pilgrimage to Nauvoo and the nearby Carthage jail," the *Nauvoo Guide* continued. "Gradually the conception of Nauvoo as a latter-day Mecca is shaping; this conception, with the martyrdom of Joseph Smith and the hegira to Utah, has given the Mormons three of the fixtures found in many long-established religions. Both the Utah and the Reorganized branches have acquired portions of the Temple lot in Nauvoo; the Utah Mormons expect some day to build there a copy of the Temple. Nauvoo as Mecca is booming."[72] Additionally, private and governmental groups unaffiliated with Mormonism discovered potential in the site. Indeed, a Chicago-area newspaper reporter likewise sensed the prospect of restoring Mormon Nauvoo. "The magnificoes' houses are in such good condition that every one of them would restore beautifully."[73] In the years that followed, this declaration proved predictive as groups beyond the Reorganized Church influenced the way Nauvoo told its story.

# CHAPTER 3

# Latter-day Saint Re-Interest in Nauvoo

While the Reorganized Church was expanding its presence in Nauvoo, Latter-day Saint interest in the site quietly simmered. Like their prairie sisters, mountain Mormons were continually drawn to the City of Joseph as well. Some remembered it as the place where they buried both their prophet and their dreams, while others longed for a return of that which was lost. Encouraging these hopes, former Nauvoo resident and Latter-day Saint Church president John Taylor boldly declared before a general Church audience in Salt Lake City in 1882,

> As a people or community, we can abide our time, but I will say to you Latter-day Saints, that there is nothing of which you have been despoiled by oppressive acts or mobocratic rule, but that you will again possess, or your children after you. Your rights in Ohio, your rights in Jackson, Clay, Caldwell and Davi[ess] counties in Missouri, will yet be restored to you. Your possessions, of which you have been fraudulently despoiled in Missouri and Illinois, you will again possess, and that without force, or fraud or violence. The Lord has a way of His own in regulating such matters.[1]

In the twentieth century, the "way" for Latter-day Saint return emerged because of the combined actions of unique actors and a Church interested in engaging nationally. Church desires coincided with national interests in celebrating westward expansion, creating an environment ripe for restoration, though not without an increase in contested memory over Nauvoo's past.

## Latter-day Saint Visitors to the City of Joseph

The first members of The Church of Jesus Christ of Latter-day Saints to return to Nauvoo from the West in the early twentieth century were more interested in reminiscing than they were in relocating. Frequent visitors included Latter-day Saint missionaries, traveling to or from their assigned fields of labor or even laboring in the Midwest itself. In 1901, while serving a mission in southern Illinois, Elder Thomas H. Burton wrote of visiting Nauvoo with Elders F. S. Parkinson, B. M. Olson, and W. A. Wilcox. The four toured prominent residences and civic structures, all of which, Burton noted, were "very large and durable," evidence that the early Saints had "built to stay." Commenting on the city's thirteen hundred residents, "mostly all Germans" with a "Catholic element," Burton reported the local attitude toward his Church: "We had the pleasure of meeting a number of prominent citizens and aged veterans, and after conversing with them . . . I am pleased to note that the prejudice which used to exist in that city against our people is almost abolished."[2]

By 1905, one local Nauvoo paper reported, "It is only with the last few years that the 'Mormons' from Utah have been visiting Nauvoo in any considerable numbers. . . . It is true, there has been an occasional 'Mormon' visitor, but within the last year it might be said there have been many members of that faith visit us."[3] In Utah, the *Deseret News* shared the observations of two of those visitors, Elders F. M. Mortensen and George H. Smith, who noted, "Many of the buildings erected by the leading brethren are still standing as monuments to their names and the tragic history of those days." Regarding those who preceded them, the missionaries indicated that the local hotel proprietors "have quite a bundle of namecards of Elders who have visited the city in the past."[4]

Later the same year, more than one hundred visiting elders and members descended on the town for a two-day mission conference, where local residents expressed "a strong desire that our people should come back to Nauvoo and build it up again." The plea may have stemmed, in part, from the dilapidated condition of the community and its structures, which one conference attendee described as "literally and completely deserted so far as industry is concerned," standing "empty, sheltering only rats and insects. In many cases," the report continued, "even where the homes are occupied by strangers, not a nail has been driven, a stone or brick replaced, nor a fence repaired in all the years that have elapsed. . . . The foundations and beginning of a great center of activity have been allowed to crumble and decay and to be wrapped in the folds of wild vegetation."[5]

Conference participants visited the former Smith properties, then owned by the children of the Prophet. "The old homestead of the Prophet Joseph, across the street from the unfinished Nauvoo House, has had not improvements save a renewal of shingles," reported conference attendee George A. Startup. In what may have been a subtle dig emphasizing the divide between the faiths over plural marriage, Startup continued, "[It] is occupied by a family which charges 10 cents to each visitor who desires to look upon the final resting place of the first wife of the Prophet Joseph Smith, the grave of Emma Smith Bidamon, and also those of the first wife and children of Jos. Smith, eldest son of the Prophet, in the rear of the old Smith homestead. High weeds surround the graves; in fact, the whole surroundings in this neighborhood have a desolate aspect."[6] While the report of the physical condition of the Homestead and its cemetery were less than positive, participants were welcomed into the Nauvoo House for a meeting by Charles Bidamon, the building's owner.

Lorin Farr, then eighty-six years old, traveled from Chicago to participate in the conference, showing attendees the home he had left vacant and thrilling them with his recollections of abandoning the town as a twenty-six-year-old man. "It was a happy coincidence," one participant noted, "that a great many of the Elders attending the conference were sons of men who were driven out of Nauvoo sixty years ago."[7] The gathering's final session, held in Nauvoo's town hall, generated strong community interest, with as many as four hundred in attendance.[8] The event was highlighted by the baptismal service of Mr. and Mrs. Frank Grimes and their daughter Sylvia, tenants in the old Mansion House.[9] "Three honest souls were baptized in the Mississippi near the Nauvoo House before a large crowd of interested onlookers," one newspaper recorded. "Long will the people of Nauvoo remember the first return of the 'Mormons' to their city, for all are glad to have us return," apparently blind to the fact that Reorganized Mormons were already there.[10] Positive reports from this conference and from others who proselyted in the area filtered back to Utah, where the *Deseret News* later editorialized, "People in Nauvoo are very friendly and anxious to have the 'Mormons' come back and help revive the town to its former condition."[11]

In addition to this early conference, another notable Latter-day Saint visit to Nauvoo during the era was that of Church president Joseph F. Smith in 1906. Returning from a trip to the East, Smith stopped in the town of his youth, visiting his home and recalling "some pathetic reminiscence which brought tears to his eyes."[12] Among these were memories of the murders of his father, Hyrum Smith, and uncle, Joseph Smith. Visits like these spurred speculation in local Nauvoo papers "that the Utah 'Mormon' Church intends purchasing property in Nauvoo, as was done in Carthage, Ill., and Independence, Mo. Looks like the Utah 'Mormons' intend returning to the beautiful land."[13]

## Acquiring the Carthage Jail

The Church had, indeed, purchased the nearby Carthage Jail in 1903, fueling rumors of a return. Decades earlier, the jail had been sold by officials from Hancock County to a Bryant F. Peterson. James and Eliza Browning later acquired it, remaking the structure into their home. The Brownings regularly allowed interested visitors to tour the structure, including the room where the martyrdom occurred.[14] Following the death of Mr. Browning, Church leaders learned of the property's availability through a Carthage attorney who was aware of the faith's interest in the site.[15] After negotiating with Eliza M. Browning, the parties agreed on the $4,000 purchase price.[16] "It was thought advisable to buy it and place someone in charge with Church literature to distribute to callers," officials surmised, "and by this means utilize this property of sad memory in doing missionary work."[17] The Carthage Jail transaction was the first of what would eventually be dozens of acquisitions of historically significant structures for the faith during the twentieth century.

However, though the Church did purchase property in historically significant Latter-day Saint communities in the early twentieth century, including Sharon, Vermont (birthplace of Joseph Smith), Palmyra, New York (location of Smith's First Vision), and Independence, Missouri (city where the faith attempted to establish its "Zion" and headquarters for the Reorganized Church), it failed to acquire any property in Nauvoo itself. Rather, Church leaders contented themselves with assigning missionaries to the area and organizing a short-lived, weekly Sunday School in the vacant *Times and Seasons* building in the city.[18]

Meanwhile, in nearby Carthage, little changed following the Church's acquisition of the jail property. Missionaries touring the site two years later reported, "Old Carthage jail, where Joseph and Hyrum sealed their testimony with their blood, was visited and a photo taken. An admission fee of 15¢ each permits visitors to see the room in which the tragedy took place."[19] A grand restoration of the site may have failed to materialize because of Church president Joseph F. Smith's close connection to and strong feelings regarding it. "I despise this place. It harrows up my feelings to come here," Smith openly declared when he visited the site of his father's death on his 1906 trip.[20]

While the Church did little to formally develop the Carthage Jail site, visitors still came, especially with the increase of tourism generated by the advent of the automobile. A Chicago newspaperman who visited the site in 1926 noted, "The Saints now own that jail, and preserve it as a shrine, and the custodian, turning back the carpet in the main upper chamber, shows you the faint stains made by wounded Joseph's blood when he rushed toward the window to escape the mob leaders upstairs only to meet death before the guns of other leaders who were waiting for him in the yard below."[21] In 1934, Northern States Mission president George S. Romney finally appointed the first missionary couple to conduct tours of the site.[22]

## A Memorial to Relief Society in Nauvoo

While the Latter-day Saint Church dipped its toe into historical site preservation and interpretation in Carthage, the Reorganized Church continued to actively control historic Nauvoo through property ownership and interpretation. The Utah Saints' first foray into a historical presence in Nauvoo began with a cooperative effort with their Reorganized Church partners, initially through an innocuous historical marker that celebrated a common heritage, an organization for women known as the Nauvoo Relief Society. Speaking at a Relief Society conference in Salt Lake City in October 1932, Elder George Albert Smith, Latter-day Saint Apostle and president of the Utah Pioneer Trails and Landmarks Association, sparked the idea for a memorial to the organization in Nauvoo. "We have been marking the pioneer trails," Smith stated. "I may get myself into difficulty by making a recommendation, but I think there is one thing lacking in the City of Nauvoo. There ought to be a monument to the Relief Society in that city. . . . I think this great women's organization ought to be dignified at its birthplace by a fine monument."[23]

Louise Yates Robison, general president of the Relief Society, took up the charge. The *Relief Society Magazine* reported, "It has long been the desire of President Robison and her associates, to give concrete form to the great debt of gratitude felt by the Relief Society for its founders—to perpetuate the site of its organization, and to create, as it were, a shrine where a grateful people could take on new faith and hope from a review of the glorious past." Because the monument would reside near the site of the Relief Society's founding, Joseph Smith's Red Brick Store, permission was required from the property's owner, the Reorganized Church. "This was accomplished through Dr. Frederick M. Smith, president of the Reorganized Church, and grandson of the Prophet Joseph," Church periodicals reported. "Dr. Smith was most gracious and cooperative from the standpoint of his Church and of his family, who were deeply appreciative of the spirit of the memorial and of the honor conferred upon Emma Hale Smith, first president of Relief Society."[24]

In July 1933, Latter-day Saint Relief Society officials erected their marker, an eight-foot-tall piece of Tennessee bur-rose quartzite, on which was placed a bronze plaque summarizing the founding of the Relief Society and a second plaque thanking the Reorganized Church for their generosity while recognizing them as the owner of the property.[25] Additionally, because some considered Nauvoo the beginning point of the Mormon pioneer trail and the idea had been conceived by the Utah Pioneer Trails organization, the memorial also bore the familiar trail symbol of an ox skull.[26] The monument stood next to the foundation of the Red Brick Store, which had been demolished in the 1890s and was subsequently beautified into a sunken garden. George Albert Smith, who had proposed the idea of the memorial, dedicated the marker, accompanied by Relief Society and Young Ladies' Mutual Improvement Association officers from the Utah Church. Representatives of the Joseph Smith family participated in the service, including Reorganized Church president Frederick M. Smith and his three sisters.[27]

While the cooperative endeavor began well, problems emblematic of the relations between the two churches during the first half of the twentieth century soon developed. Over time, disagreement centered on whose memory of

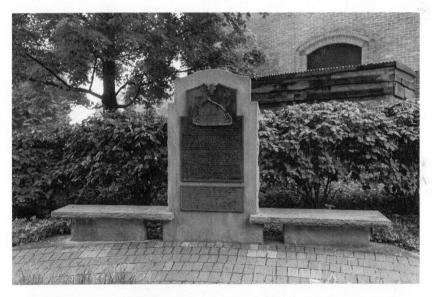

FIGURE 8. Nauvoo Relief Society monument. Originally placed near the site of Joseph Smith's red brick store, the scene of the Relief Society's founding, the monument was relocated to the temple lot in 1952 because of its symbolic connections to The Church of Jesus Christ of Latter-day Saints. It was moved again in 1988 to its present location as part of the Relief Society monument to women gardens adjacent to the Latter-day Saint visitors' center. Photograph by Richard Crookston. Used by permission.

Nauvoo should dominate historical interpretation. An aspect of the controversy between the two faiths played itself out publicly over the location of the
Relief Society monument. Marking the eastern start of the Pioneer trail, the
monument told not only the story of the founding of the Relief Society but, on
property owned by the Reorganized Church, it also highlighted the Latter-day
Saints' exodus, and therefore the mountain Mormon story, especially by its
inclusion of the well-known ox skull symbol on one of the plaques. The pioneer
memorial caused concern for Reorganized Church officials as early as 1939, just
six years after its creation. Developing their own long-term plan for Nauvoo,
one official cautioned, "Please . . . determine the manner in which permission
was given to the Utah people to erect their monument. We should be sure
that nothing even inferentially implies ceding of control over the land itself.
Furthermore, I look forward to an opportunity to have this statue removed.
Our future development of the property will undoubtedly make such removal
necessary."[28]

By the 1950s, the placement of the Latter-day Saint marker on Reorganized
Church property caused increased concern, especially as Utah Church activity
expanded in the region. In May 1952, Lewis Scott complained to Reorganized
Church officials, some of whom were new since Church president Frederick
M. Smith's death in 1946. "Bishop Johnson and I in discussing the Mormon
marker that is located on our property in Nauvoo, came to the conclusion
that it has no place on our property," Scott wrote. "The guide informed us . . .
that it has led to some misunderstandings. It is recommended that the matter
be discussed with the Presidency relative to requesting the Utah Church to
remove this marker."[29] Bringing the matter to the attention of the Reorganized
Church's First Presidency, Presiding Bishopric member G. L. DeLapp wrote,
"[The monument] has proven a constant irritant to our guides at Nauvoo."[30]

In June 1952 Bishop DeLapp wrote to the Latter-day Saint First Presidency
regarding the controversial monument. "At intervals during the last few years
considerable criticism has come to us regarding the location of a marker placed
by your church on property which belongs to the Reorganization at Nauvoo.
This marker identifies the site of the founding of the Ladies' Relief Society.
When this marker was placed it was mutually agreed that you would remove
it upon request. In discussing this matter with our First Presidency it has been
concluded that it is now advisable to have this marker removed. We are sure
that you will be willing to cooperate." Handwritten notes on a copy of the letter
located in the Community of Christ archives reflected the tensions between
the two movements at the time. Bearing initials of members of the Reorganized
Church leadership, one note read, "Hope this is OK. Seemed the thing to do

in view of the complaints continuing to come in." A second comment, more emphatic than the first, declared, "I'll stand with you on this. The Mormons are our enemies at heart and we owe them nothing."[31]

Writing to one of the granddaughters of former Church president Joseph Smith III, DeLapp summarized the problem:

> In regard to the marker which was placed by the Utah Church, with the permission of our church, on a site at Nauvoo . . . [I] would state that this caused so much controversy and discussion over the years, and so many objections were raised by the guides, that by action of the First Presidency and the Presiding Bishopric, the Utah Church was requested to remove the marker. Unless you are in a position to have to meet the individual members of the Utah Church day after day regarding such matters, it is difficult to appreciate the need for such action having been taken. However, it was, in our opinion, the best thing for both organizations.[32]

The Latter-day Saint First Presidency responded, assigning Wilford C. Wood to remove the monument. Wood, a successful Utah businessman with strong interest in the preservation of Church history, had represented the Utah Church in transactions involving historical sites.[33] Complying with the request, Wood tried to smooth over any lingering tensions. He responded to Bishop DeLapp, "In accordance with your request, I will be glad to have your cooperation in moving this marker from your property and I want everything to be done in accordance with your wishes and in a pleasing and acceptable manner. . . . I remember the kindnesses you have shown to me during the past and hope that nothing in the future with my assignments may be displeasing to you and that I shall be able to do the work in such a way that it will be satisfactory to both you and the First Presidency of your Church."[34] In August 1952 Wood negotiated the removal of the six-ton monument from the Red Brick Store property, promising to relocate it and restore the area within four months. Wood moved the monument to the temple lot, a portion of which he had acquired for the Latter-day Saint Church over the previous several years.

The narrative of coming together to commemorate a common story like the founding of the Nauvoo Relief Society, only to de-memorialize the site and request a marker be moved, is an interesting reflection on the growing tensions that enveloped Nauvoo as the twentieth century progressed. As the Utah-based Church expanded beyond its western boundaries back into traditionally Reorganized Church strongholds across the Midwest, the latter group felt threatened. Contests over memory were stronger than the potentially unifying social functions of commemoration.[35]

## Securing the Nauvoo Temple Lot

Relationships between the branches of Mormonism were clearly strained because of their joint interest in the City of Joseph. As Nauvoo's founding had divided people during the days of Joseph Smith, the preservation and development of its properties became divisive a century later, this time within the religious posterity of the faith's founder. The conflict over the location of the memorial originated because it became increasingly clear that the Latter-day Saints wanted a more active interpretive presence in Nauvoo than merely a monument marking the founding of the Relief Society. They had their eyes on a much larger prize, ultimately including the Nauvoo Temple property.

The Latter-day Saint acquisition of Nauvoo's temple square was a process twenty-five years and ten separate transactions in the making. The successful acquisition must be primarily attributed to the efforts of Wilford Wood, who, acting either on his own or as an official representative of the Church, purchased the initial six parcels, the first of which included the actual property for the temple itself. Learning that the prime lot was available, Wood contacted the Church's First Presidency about its purchase in February 1937. Permission was granted to pursue the property, with a maximum bid from the Church set at $1,000. Prospects appeared bleak, however, as the Bank of Nauvoo, which owned the property, had announced that bidding would start at $1,000 and, in earlier sales, had protected its interest by countering any lower bids. In fact, bank officials may have contacted Wood in the first place because they thought he would offer a higher price. Nevertheless, Wood hastily made the twelve-hundred-mile drive from Salt Lake City to Nauvoo to negotiate with the officers. Outlining his constraints, Wood explained that he could not afford to pay "the price of sentiment," nor could he "risk the ill-feelings that might be caused by competitive bidding," and "pleaded for the price to be within reason." Bank officials countered that "the property was worth all they were asking and that they would buy it back at the sale for what they had in it, if necessary, to protect their interests."

In what Wood later called "the most important Council Meeting held in Nauvoo since the Saints were driven from here nearly one hundred years ago," he persisted. He promised that "the Church would put up a Bureau of Information which would be a credit to Nauvoo and that what they might lose in the price of the lot would come back to them many times with the people who would come and pay homage to a desolate city." Bank officials continued to press that "they could not see how they could sell for less than $1,000 to $1,500." Replying with what he called "an impression," Wood questioned, "Are you going to try to make us pay exorbitant price for the blood of a martyred Prophet, when you know this property rightfully belongs to the Mormon people?"[36] Bank officials acquiesced, and the price was set at $900, as long as no one else outbid the Church at the public auction the next day. Providentially, none did, as Wood was the sole bidder. True to their word, bank officers did not influence others or put forward their own counteroffer. On February 20, 1937, The Church of Jesus Christ of Latter-day Saints bought a portion of the temple lot where the Nauvoo Temple had once stood.

The *Carthage Gazette* quietly noted the transaction: "At the master's sale of some of the C. W. Reimbold estate in Nauvoo, held at the court house Saturday, that part of the property known as the old Mormon Temple site was purchased by representatives of the Utah Mormon church for $900."[37] In Utah, a Church periodical more emphatically heralded, "Nauvoo the Beautiful has long been a Mecca for Latter-day Saints. . . . Undoubtedly still more Church members will be eager to revisit the scenes of early Church history now that the Church

FIGURE 9. Nauvoo Temple block, looking west, 1907. George Edward Anderson glass plate negative collection: Illinois sites, Nauvoo, Illinois, Church History Library, The Church of Jesus Christ of Latter-day Saints, Salt Lake City.

once more owns the Nauvoo Temple site."[38] It was this prospect of a Mormon return to Nauvoo that some in town celebrated but others feared.

With public announcement of the Church's acquisition, neighboring properties on the temple square also became available. Prices varied considerably for the parcels, ranging from $1,100 for the next purchase, a large northeast corner lot acquired by Wood only two months later, to $100,000 for lot three, the expansive southwest corner of the property, purchased from the Catholic Church more than twenty years later in 1961. Wood conducted the first six transactions from 1937 to 1951. Church officials themselves negotiated the final four acquisitions from 1952 through 1962.[39] Understandably, the transactions generated great concern among the Reorganized Church that had long dominated Nauvoo.

## Temple Reconstruction Rumors

As the Latter-day Saint Church pieced together again the temple lot property, rumors swirled regarding the building's reconstruction. In fact, plans to rebuild the Nauvoo temple, one of the faith's best-kept secrets of the 1990s, was one of its worst-kept secrets in the 1930s and 1940s. On October 29, 1937, the *Carthage Gazette* reported,

> Although from official circles of the Utah branch of the Mormon church comes the word that at least two other large building projects are anticipated before any new building will be done at Nauvoo, the leaders do not deny that they are planning rebuilding the temple at Nauvoo. Last year the church negotiated for the barren site of the temple and also for some adjoining land. This building site is one of the highest points in Nauvoo and it is no secret that the church is planning a shrine that will compare in beauty and size with the great temple built almost a hundred years ago on the same ground.[40]

A year later, while encouraging commemoration of the centennial of the founding of Nauvoo, Northern States Mission president Bryant S. Hinckley and Chicago-area landscape artist Lane K. Newberry revealed the grand plan they envisioned for Nauvoo. Aspiringly, they proposed:

1. To transfer to the Church that part of the Temple Block that does not already belong to it.
2. To ask the Church to erect a suitable memorial on the block when it is transferred to them.
3. To dedicate as a State Park that part of the lowland where the remaining old Mormon homes stand.

4. To have these homes restored as they were, and maintained as they were.

5. To secure the land lying between the Temple Block and the park land below.

Even more ambitiously, Hinckley and Newberry answered the question, "Who is to do this?" with the response, "Preferably the State of Illinois; if not, her citizens."[41] By proposing such an expansive endeavor for the State of Illinois, the pair hoped to capitalize on growing civic interest in the preservation of historical sites and on an improving image of Mormonism nationally.

Newberry, a descendent of Mormon pioneers but himself not a practicing member of the faith, explained his interest in the project. Among his several reasons, Newberry declared, "I feel that the World should honor men and women who accomplished what the Mormons accomplished in Nauvoo. . . . There is a spirit back of the building of this city that the World needs today, and it can only be attained by honoring those who had it yesterday." From a practical perspective, Newberry also explained that the project would give the State of Illinois the chance to tell "the story of a whole group and not just one man," but that it needed to be done "now while the buildings still remain intact, because, in spite of their fine construction, nature is taking her toll." Additionally, he believed that the restored temple "would give the State of Illinois one of the finest examples of primitive art in America."[42]

As an important official for the faith, Hinckley saw the project from a Church perspective. Concluding the announcement, he outlined his and the Church's ultimate hopes for restoring Mormon Nauvoo. "The Nauvoo visitor of today lingers: he is interested; there is something about the quiet atmosphere of that dream city that charms and fascinates him: it speaks of the past: he feels reverent." Addressing the difficulty in rebuilding the temple, but also its potential impact on the community and for the growth of Mormonism, Hinckley continued,

> The completion of this extraordinary project will be a matter of far-reaching significance. It will bring into relief one of the most heroic, dramatic, and fascinating pioneer achievements ever enacted upon American soil. It will reveal a record of fortitude and self-reliance; of patriotic and courageous endeavor, that should stimulate faith in the hearts of all men, in a day when the strongest hesitate and falter. The dedication of this Memorial will add attractively to the long list of historically important places of which Illinois is justly proud. Annually thousands of Latter-day Saints will visit it. As these developments go forward, Nauvoo is destined to become one of the most

beautiful shrines of America and one of the strong missionary centers of the Church.[43]

In spite of its religious overtones, Hinckley's declaration played into a national narrative interested in celebrating American greatness in the face of the Great Depression. Supporting the plan while at the same time deferring to the role to be occupied by the State of Illinois in its advancement, the Church's First Presidency publicly endorsed the proposal: "We shall be glad to erect in the future such memorial on the Temple Block, if secured by the State of Illinois, as will fittingly carry out your project."[44]

Interested citizens of western Illinois picked up on the news. By March 1939, Carthage's *Hancock County Journal* reported that "the Mormon Church is planning to rebuild the old Mormon temple at Nauvoo at a cost of $1,000,000, work to start within a short time. . . . It is understood the Mormon church has already appropriated $100,000 to finance the beginning of the work of reconstructing the old Temple."[45] The federal government even gave credence to these rumors, publishing in their 1939 *Nauvoo Guide*, "Both the Utah and the Reorganized branches have acquired portions of the Temple lot in Nauvoo; the Utah Mormons expect some day to build there a copy of the Temple. Nauvoo as Mecca is booming."[46]

References to the state's involvement in the project stem from rumors that Illinois government officials were openly planning to convert a portion of historic Nauvoo into a state park. In February 1938, Utah's *Deseret News* printed a letter by Robert Kingery, chairman of the Illinois State Planning Commission, outlining his plans for state acquisition and development of the property. The state would acquire the property "either by persuading the local people at Nauvoo to buy the land and give it to the state, or by some co-operative arrangement whereby the state will buy an equal amount of land to that purchased by local people and presented to the state." Once the land was secured, Kingery proposed that the state "offer the President of the Mormon Church its cooperation in whatever historical restoration may be undertaken by the Church or jointly by the Church and the state."[47]

Later the same year, a delegation of Illinois State Planning Commission officials, the Illinois Chamber of Commerce, the Chicago Association of Commerce, the Quincy Historical Society, and editors from five major Chicago-area newspapers descended on Nauvoo, where plans were further outlined. They included preserving an area covering 230 acres of property extending from the Mississippi River to the foot of the Temple grounds. The site included "about 35 of the original homes . . . many of [which] are still in good condition and would be preserved, while the others would be restored. Buildings of historic import which have been destroyed, such as the shop where the wagons were built for the trek across the plains, would also be restored."[48] Newberry, who led the party in their tour of Nauvoo, even boldly explained, "The Church already owns about one-third of [the temple lot] and the people of Illinois plan to acquire the remainder and present it as a gift to the Church. Church officials have already promised that if this is done they will erect a suitable memorial there."[49]

Talk of an extensive Latter-day Saint presence in Nauvoo, highlighted by a reconstructed Nauvoo Temple, greatly concerned Reorganized leaders during the late 1930s. Lynn Smith, son of Reorganized First Presidency member Elbert A. Smith, was assigned to direct Church efforts in Nauvoo at the time. Reporting on the Latter-day Saint centennial celebration of the founding of Nauvoo in 1939, Smith recorded,

> This is the day that the "Utah" Mormons are in town. . . . Bill Sinnock from Quincy spent some time presenting the idea of the park project and temple rebuilding project. His program is this. The series of radio skits that have been given over the Quincy station will be recorded and sent out to the radio stations of Canada and the United States. This will give a national coverage of the proposed plan. The purpose of this radio advertisement is to request donations which will go for purchasing the temple block and donating it to the "Utah" Church so it can rebuild the Nauvoo temple.

Smith countered the plan, wondering "why the property should not be given to the Reorg[anized] Church." He concluded that project organizers "rather evaded the issue and talked in generalities but left the impression, that the gift would go to 'Utah' because they were in a position to and had said they would rebuild the temple."[50]

Concern centered not merely on reconstructing the building, however. The issues between the two Churches were ones of interpretation and access, largely based on their differing theological views regarding temples and the religious rituals performed therein. Outlining his plan, Latter-day Saint leader Bryant Hinckley hoped that the State of Illinois would purchase the temple block. However, he continued,

> Who will control it when the Temple Block is transferred to the Church? The Church will own and control it and will erect thereon a suitable memorial. When the land below is dedicated as a park and the homes are restored and the project in its entirety is completed, who will tell the visitor who comes to see it the story of those who lived in the homes—laid out the city—built the temple? That is a fair question and deserves a straight and unequivocal answer. Understanding as I do the motive behind this movement and the

character of the men behind it, I do not hesitate to say, in answer to this question, that the wishes of those in whose honor this memorial is established will govern who shall tell the story.[51]

Hinckley knew that control of the message went with control of the building, a reality that mattered greatly to the faith at the time as it sought to move further onto a national stage.

Hinckley's answer clearly bothered Reorganized Church officials. Lynn Smith reported, "I put this question to [those planning the temple project,] 'What assurance do you have that, if the property is deeded over to the 'Utah' church that they will build it?' He replied 'I have statements in writing that they will.' I also asked him if he had any more assurance that they would not use it for private worship? and he replied that that shouldn't matter, whether they used it for that purpose or not it would still bring many people to Nauvoo."[52] Focused on increasing tourism within their state, public officials pushing for the project apparently failed to recognize the long history of tension over temple theology in general, and the Nauvoo Temple specifically, between the western and midwestern branches of Mormonism. Interestingly, some of the same concerns regarding access to the building and its use resurfaced as plans were finally announced in the 1990s to rebuild the temple.[53]

## Rival Commemorations of Nauvoo's Past

While these rumors regarding the reconstruction of the temple swirled around Nauvoo, both faiths sought to celebrate the centennial of the city's founding in 1939. On June 24–25, more than seven hundred Latter-day Saints gathered for historic tours, games, a musical festival, and memorial services in both Nauvoo and Carthage. Metropolitan newspapers across the Midwest covered the event, reporting visitors from thirty-three states and two Canadian provinces. The local *Keokuk Daily Gate City* printed a photograph of hundreds lined up to tour Carthage Jail.[54] Latter-day Saint Apostle George Albert Smith headlined the occasion, accompanied by Bryant S. Hinckley, outgoing president of the faith's Northern States Mission, and Leo J. Muir, new president of the mission. Addressing those assembled, Lane K. Newberry outlined his dream to see the temple rebuilt and the homes restored.[55] According to a Reorganized Church official apparently in attendance, "In the evening service, George Albert [Smith] made the statement that he looked forward to the day when a temple would be built and that Nauvoo would be a state [park] and he said it with fervor."[56]

A week later, the Reorganized Church held its own centennial celebration, headlined by the participation of three of Joseph and Emma Smith's grandsons, Frederick M. Smith, Church president, Israel A. Smith, and Elbert A. Smith. Announcements leading up to the meetings reveal the tensions evident between the two celebrations. "Although we are the inheritors of the unchanged teachings and beliefs of the original church of that day," officials declared in the faith's periodical, *The Saints' Herald,* "we are not alone in our plans of commemoration. . . . As owners of the Mansion House, Nauvoo House, the Old Homestead and a part of the original Temple Site, we occupy the most historically interesting portion of old Nauvoo." Capitalizing on the opportunity, they called on members to donate to preserve the structures and, by implication, Reorganized control of the city. "Please help us protect the interests of the church in that century-old place, Nauvoo the Beautiful."[57] At the commemoration itself, held near the graves of Joseph, Hyrum, and Emma Smith on Sunday, July 2, 1939, several hundred members heard messages from their leaders, including a plea from Church president Frederick M. Smith for an "artistically beautiful" monument, one which "can be seen for many miles up and down the Mississippi river" to be erected as a "suitable marker" for the graves. Smith expressed the hope "that I shall not have to wait many more years to see this accomplished."[58] The memorial rivalry between the faiths in Nauvoo had clearly intensified.

As tensions simmered over the proposed temple project, the outbreak of World War II postponed projects for both faiths as well as the state of Illinois in the city. However, with the war's conclusion in 1945, interest in Nauvoo quickly resumed. Prior to the war, talk had begun among leaders of the Sons of Utah Pioneers of commemorating the exodus from Nauvoo and the subsequent migration westward to Utah by replicating the experience in precise detail, complete with live oxen and covered wagons.[59] In the spring of 1946, leaders of the organization resurrected the idea. They organized a centennial company of 143 men, three women, and two "scouts" to duplicate Brigham Young's 1847 camp in number and to follow the trail to Utah. The caravan timed their journey to arrive in Salt Lake City on July 24, 1947, where they became an entry in the city's Pioneer Day parade.[60] Seeking a spirit of "enthusiasm and good humor, rather than solemn historical accuracy," they traded ox-drawn wagons for modern transportation, traveling in seventy-two automobiles decorated as wagons, with cutout oxen hanging on the sides of the cars and white canvas covering the tops.[61]

The party convened in Nauvoo at the temple lot in July 1947, where they transformed their cars into wagons and prepared for the "pioneer trek"

FIGURE 10. Arrival of the centennial caravan from Nauvoo in Salt Lake City, July 24, 1947. Photograph by Boyart Studios. Used by permission, Utah State Historical Society.

adventure. While in town, members also took in the sites, many of them for the first time. Participant George B. Everton recounted the reception the group received.

> One of the outstanding features of the trek was the kindness with which we were received by all who had any contact with us as we traveled over the trail made by our forebears in their westward movement. An example of this courtesy was the way in which we were received by the Reorganized Church of Jesus Christ of Latter-day Saints [sic] at Nauvoo, of their permitting us to assemble at the home of Joseph Smith, now owned by them, and holding services there on the banks of the mighty Mississippi and afterwards showing us some of the places dear to our hearts as well as to theirs.

Everton described in detail the tour he received from Bishop Siegfried of the Reorganized Church.[62] Caravan accounts likewise made repeated reference to the generosity and assistance provided by the Catholic Church in Nauvoo as well as by its mayor, Lowell S. Horton.[63] Speaking over a Carthage, Illinois, radio station, Apostle and caravan special guest Spencer W. Kimball summarized, "We appreciate beyond our expression the warm welcome we have received in Nauvoo, Carthage, and vicinity. These kind people have literally turned all their facilities over to us. We have the kindest feelings for you."[64] By all accounts, the commencement of the 1947 centennial caravan offered high hopes for relations between the various parties in town.

The positive reception, especially from Reorganized Church officials, was a stark contrast to the tensions evident just a few years earlier. This good will in Nauvoo may have existed because all knew that this group of Mormons was on its way out of town. Indeed, in spite of the cooperation evident at the centennial caravan, tensions flared when the topic of the temple reconstruction surfaced again. Divisions between the two faiths were further aggravated by efforts of the State of Illinois to increase tourism following the war. Resurrecting rumors regarding the reconstruction of the Nauvoo Temple, the Illinois House of Representatives passed a resolution on April 27, 1949, encouraging both the Latter-day Saints and Reorganized faiths to collaborate in the reconstruction of the Nauvoo Temple, a project they claimed "would serve as a fitting memorial to the courageous band of pilgrims who here acquired the heroic determination to found a new state in the West." Additionally, state officials hoped the building "would add immeasurably to the attractiveness of historic Nauvoo and would create on the part of many Illinois citizens a new interest in the great movements which have played so prominent a role in the history of our State."[65] However, the proposal only added fuel to the fire, as it inadvertently gave preferential position to the Latter-day Saint stance on controversial Nauvoo issues by championing both the temple and the westward exodus.[66] Disturbingly for the Reorganized Church, the federal government gave the same preferential treatment to the Latter-day Saint position when in 1959 the National Park Service lauded Nauvoo and the exodus as "one of the most significant mass movements in advance of white settlement to the Pacific" and "one of the most dramatic events in the history of American westward expansion."[67]

## A Bidding War over Nauvoo Properties

Calls for something to be done in Nauvoo turned to action. By the early 1950s, Wood and other Latter-day Saint Church officials were on the move again, attempting to purchase the remainder of the temple block. They were not alone, however. In spite of their insistence that temple ordinances were no longer an essential component of their theology, the Reorganized Church stepped up its efforts to also acquire portions of Nauvoo's temple square. In 1950 the Reimbold property on the square's northwest corner was rumored to be available. Nauvoo resident Charles Kornman wrote to the Reorganized Presiding Bishopric that September: "The lady who owns the building on the northwest corner of the temple site has decided to sell come spring. She intended to sell to the Mormon Church but Bro. Lewis heard about it and went and talked to her so I think that we have first chance at it if we want it. I think it would be a nice gesture for us if we could get a hold of it—if nothing more than to keep the Utah folks from getting a toehold (anymore than they have already)."[68] Reorganized officials acted quickly, directing Harold Smith to investigate the property, its value, and the expected price, as the Church might be "a competitor of the Mormon church in securing this property."[69]

In spite of their efforts, purchase by the Reorganized Church failed. Visiting with Mrs. Reimbold in April 1951, Reorganized officials were informed that "she had made other plans relative to her property" and "was not free to talk further about the matter." Bishop L. W. Kohlman correctly surmised, "While I am not certain what arrangements she has made relative to her property, I do know that the Mormons have contacted her on several different occasions."[70] On behalf of the Latter-day Saints, Wilford Wood acquired the property from Mrs. Clara K. Reimbold on June 8, 1951.[71]

Regarding the availability of another portion of the temple lot, in 1952 Lewis E. Scott negotiated on behalf of the Reorganized Church with a Mr. Schafer for his property, a southern piece of the temple square block along Mulholland Street. Schafer apparently wanted $10,000 for the property. Scott retorted, "I told him that I knew we wouldn't go over $5,000 and that I thought it would probably be more in the neighborhood of $3,500 or $4,000." Scott apparently felt comfortable with these offers because he believed "Mr. Woods [sic] of the Mormon church [had only] offered them $2,000."[72] Within three months, the price quickly escalated. When Wood and the Latter-day Saints purchased the Schafer property in September 1952, Scott sent an internal memo to the Reorganized Church's Presiding Bishopric, "Mr. Woods [sic] gave Shaffer [sic] $9,000 plus the rentals for one year for this property that we had considered purchasing.... That Utah Church now has [nearly] all the land within the block except the corner lot owned by the Catholics and the property we own. The Mormons have been spreading the rumor that they are going to have this land condemned so that they can have the State replace the Temple."[73]

Undeterred, Reorganized Church officials next sought to purchase a small, twenty-five-foot wide lot facing Bluff Street, then occupied by the local telephone company.[74] In spite of their efforts, which began as early as 1954, the Latter-day Saints again succeeded in finalizing the transaction ahead of the

Reorganized Church, purchasing it in 1959 following twenty-two months of negotiation. A historian of the temple lot noted that this transaction was made possible through the influence of city attorney Preston W. Kimball and the town's former mayor, Lowell S. Horton, both of whom energetically supported the return of the Latter-day Saints to the city, seemingly siding with one party over the other.[75] The fact that the Reorganized Church had hopes to buy the Reimbold, Schafer, and telephone-company properties but lost out to the Latter-day Saints highlights the competition over historic properties and the tensions that ensued between the two faiths during the 1950s.

As the Reorganized Church lost out on its acquisition attempts of the temple lot, it also missed on a potential purchase of the Nauvoo Masonic Hall down in the city's flats. In 1950 Clarence A. Skinner wrote to the Reorganized Church Presiding Bishopric, informing them of the death of the building's owner and asking if they were interested in acquiring the property.[76] Bishop G. Leslie DeLapp raised the question with the Reorganized Church First Presidency, "Do you know of any reason why this property should be purchased? I am not sure what the reaction of our church people would be to buying a Masonic building, even though it has historical value."[77] Ultimately, it was decided that the building lacked "any particular value to the church" because it was "pretty well away from [Reorganized Church] property except the local church, and has no historical value so far as the visitors are concerned."[78] Again, the Latter-day Saints from Utah quickly moved in.

In one of the more controversial acquisitions of the era, Wilford Wood acted on the Reorganized Church's decision not to purchase the Masonic Hall, eventually buying the structure in 1954 from Arline Mulch, the daughter of its longtime occupant Charles Mulch. The building had been transformed into a personal residence in the 1860s by removing the third story of the structure and remodeling the building.[79] However, the sale was complicated because of the accusation of improprieties brought against Wood.

Arline Mulch later leveled charges that, prior to her father's death in 1949, Charles Mulch had instructed his daughter to sell his property only if absolutely necessary, providing a guide for the prices she should seek for each parcel. Mulch claimed that Wood knew all of this. She stated that in April 1954, Wood manipulated her into signing a document, selling the former Nauvoo Masonic Hall to Wood for $7,250. Just three days after the transaction, Mulch painfully wrote Wood, "I am very ill and crazed with grief over what I have done. Am unable to work, eat, or sleep. I didn't want to sell the property and why I agreed to your proposition, I will never know. Can't we call the whole thing off for the present time. I will gladly return your money and reimburse you for your trouble but I implore you to please let me keep the property. When I think of the years that my beloved father, whom you knew and respected, deprived himself the necessities of life in order to hold the property which he loved so well. It was his life's work and he gave it all to me. I just can't give it up now." Appealing to Wood's sensitivities, Mulch declared, "You represent a wonderful Church and a great people and I am only a lone woman begging for forgiveness for my great mistake. Only prayer and you can help me."[80]

For his part, Wood felt like the deal should move forward. Seeking to console Mulch, he telegraphed, "Do not worry about the mistake. It will be corrected and be all right. I have business in the East and will be to see you in a few days. Please do not talk to anyone else until I have talked to you."[81] However, according to Mulch, when they met in May 1954, Wood increased the pressure. She claimed that Wood told her "he had talked with her [deceased] father the previous night and her father had told him to advise her." She said that Wood, his wife, and Mulch then joined hands in prayer, "during which . . . Wilford C. Wood represented that he was communicating with [her] deceased father and that she should do as the papers she had signed read." Mulch claimed, "As a result of this weird and unwarranted oppression and persistence [she] became very nervous, upset and unable to eat or sleep and became subject to spells of crying." In this troubled condition, Mulch and Wood went ahead with a modified sale price of $10,750.[82]

With the transaction secured, Wood began examining the property, discovering a copper box secreted in the building's original cornerstone. It contained important artifacts from the Nauvoo era, including minutes of the Nauvoo Masonic lodge, period newspapers, and pamphlets. The items were delivered to Salt Lake City, with replica copies of the materials together with new items returned in their place in the corner of the building.[83] Wood began to make plans to preserve the structure.

The complicated Masonic Hall transaction was not complete, however. In a lawsuit filed in November 1954, Mulch claimed that she was "of a shy, timid and retiring disposition" and that Wood had coerced her into selling the property. As a "result of the misrepresentations, fraudulent acts, false statements, threats and oppression of . . . Wilford C. Wood," the complaint called for the contract to be cancelled.[84] Threateningly, Mulch's attorney reached out to Church officials in Salt Lake City:

> Your organization is willing to accept the benefits of these labors and have not only done that but have indicated that you will permit [Wilford Wood] to continue to prey on other people with his high pressure methods and treat them in the same manner he has treated Miss Mulch. . . . We feel as though your organization, if it continues to use the same methods in this

case, should have its activities called to the attention of the world at large. I do not wish to be indelicate [but] the activities of this kind by the Mormon Church in this area will certainly be news for our local radio station, our Des Moines Register representative and our Chicago Tribune representative.[85]

The two parties eventually found a compromise. The lawsuit was dropped a year later when Wood returned the property to Mulch in exchange for the money paid and an agreement that the Church would be able to buy the property when it became available for sale. More than a decade later, Mulch sold all of her Nauvoo properties, including the Masonic Hall, to Church officials.[86] But the episode foreshadowed community opposition to Latter-day Saint restoration efforts in the city.

Though the Latter-day Saints eventually succeeded in the Masonic Hall purchase as well as in most of their temple-lot acquisitions, they too missed a potential early purchase of property adjacent to the temple lot during this period. In 1952 the Benedictine Sisters in Nauvoo decided to build a new priory, academy, and dormitory for their boarding school, the St. Mary's Academy, across the street from the temple lot. Aware of Church interest in the neighboring property, they offered it to Wood, explaining,

> As you know, our crowded conditions demand that we build as soon as possible.... Your beloved Prophet Joseph Smith must surely have stood on the Temple spot when he named his city Nauvoo, the City Beautiful. We fully understand your love and interest in the spot and your desire to make here a shrine worthy of faith and zeal.... If we could construct any type of building to suit our needs without interfering with the majestic view from the Temple block, we would do so. But there is no way; hence our suggestion to you that you purchase our entire property here, and we will re-establish ourselves in some other section of Nauvoo.[87]

Unable to accommodate the offer, Wood nevertheless responded, "I was advised to thank you for your good feelings and good will towards the Mormon people, and as I told you before, the Mormons and the Catholics will always get along in Nauvoo."[88] The Sisters proceeded with building their new academy adjacent to the temple site, obstructing, as feared, the view of the river and the lower portion of the city.

Tensions remained strained between the two branches of Mormonism as the Latter-day Saints sought to complete the final pieces of the temple-lot puzzle. The purchase of the Saints Peter and Paul school and the Nauvoo Parish Hall property from the Catholic Church on July 22, 1961, for the sum of $100,000 left only a small section on the west of the temple lot unowned by the Latter-day

Saint Church. The Reorganized Church, however, controlled this piece. Eager to conduct an excavation on the temple property, in 1962 Latter-day Saint officials reached out to Reorganized officials regarding the final parcel. Coyly, Reorganized Church officials expressed doubt "if any amount of money would buy that land. . . . But," they countered, "it might be available for trade for some of the Temple property [the Latter-day Saints] have in Independence."[89] Ultimately, Reorganized leaders used this leverage to increase their holdings in Independence, Missouri, their headquarters.

Throughout 1962, negotiations progressed between the two Churches regarding the status of this remaining Nauvoo Temple Lot property. An initial offer was made to trade three Latter-day Saint-owned properties near the Reorganized Church auditorium in Independence for the lot in Nauvoo, with the Reorganized Church paying the difference between appraised values. In March the Reorganized Church's Standing High Council gave its approval for the transaction. However, they also indicated a hope "that a fourth Independence property now owned by the Utah Church will be included in this transaction."[90] Private conversations and documents between Reorganized Church officials repeatedly noted that Latter-day Saints were "in very much of a hurry to get this under way."[91] Using the urgency to their advantage, Reorganized Church officials succeeded in increasing the exchange to four properties in Independence for the lone Nauvoo lot.[92] Furthermore, negotiations stipulated that property be independently appraised "based on the commercial value of the property concerned" rather than any sentimental value.[93]

Additionally, some assurance was offered that the temple in Nauvoo would not immediately be rebuilt. Summarizing the deal, Mark Siegfried wrote Reorganized Presiding Bishop G. Leslie DeLapp, "I had a letter from a friend of mine who recently had word from Joseph Fielding Smith, President of the Council of Twelve in Utah. In this letter J. F. S. states that they have no intention of rebuilding the Temple in Nauvoo. Just to level off the lot and make it look nice."[94] While the deal evidenced cooperation between the faiths, tensions were apparently still high. Bishop DeLapp responded, "I hope that the information you received regarding the intent of the Utah Church at Nauvoo is correct. We will be interested in watching developments."[95]

## Responses to Latter-day Saint Acquisitions

Though they were rebuffed in their attempts to purchase historic properties, Reorganized Church leaders maintained their attention on the important Smith properties they did own in Nauvoo. Preservation efforts included placing a new granite slab measuring 10' × 10' × 1' over the graves of Joseph, Hyrum, and Emma Smith in 1951.[96] Learning that the Homestead was "infested with termites" and "in a very bad state of repair," that structure was elevated in 1953 so that a new foundation could be built.[97] At the same time, the exterior logs were also replaced and electrical wiring improved. Preservation and restoration efforts were likewise conducted on the Mansion House in the mid-1950s, with interior walls rearranged and a new paint color scheme employed. The Bidamon stable, a stone building erected north of the Nauvoo House, was transformed into an office and information center.[98] Concerned about "increased trespass of the Mormons on [their] property," officials investigated installing rustic wooden gates and fencing.[99] In an additional effort to increase safety, they approached the city, seeking permission to close the road between the Homestead and the Nauvoo House.[100] They also reduced fire hazard by installing sprinkler systems in the Homestead and Mansion House in 1955.[101] In total, the Reorganized Church spent more than $50,000 on their properties in Nauvoo during the decade.[102]

In the midst of these endeavors, the Reorganized Church expressed great interest in historical accuracy. In 1952 they sought the advice of experts from Virginia's Colonial Williamsburg restoration. A. E. Kendrew, vice president and resident architect for the Colonial Williamsburg restoration, responded with a willingness "to be of assistance to others," extending an invitation for Reorganized Church officials to visit Williamsburg "to discuss your problems . . . and give you the benefit of our experience in an advisory manner."[103] Ironically, just a few years later, Kendrew was actively involved in restoring structures in Nauvoo, but on behalf of the Utah Church. In the same letter, Kendrew also encouraged the faith to consult with the National Council for Historic Sites and Buildings. Within weeks, officials from the Reorganized Church made application for membership in the National Council. Regionally, they also reached out to the Division of Architecture and Engineering for the State of Illinois for expertise regarding the preservation of the Nauvoo properties.[104]

The improvements to the properties coincided with a steady increase in attendance by visitors to the Reorganized Church sites. In 1950, one guide reported 24,416 more visitors over the previous two-year period, noting, "Of course, this does not show the thousands of visitors that did not register."[105] Two years later, officials reported nearly fifteen hundred visitors reporting in the month of May 1952 alone. These visitors came from nearly every state in the nation and several foreign countries. A July 1955 report listed Illinois with the most visitors per state for that month (300 visitors), followed by Iowa (192 visitors) and Utah (118 visitors). The same report noted that the largest group of visitors reported themselves as Latter-day Saint (13.3 percent in July 1955), with those not indicating a faith second (10 percent), Methodists third (8.5 percent) and Reorganized Latter Day Saints fourth (8.3 percent).

A sampling of comments forwarded to Reorganized Church officials seems to indicate a positive reception by visitors. "The tour is very interesting. You should be highly commended for a wonderful state of preservation of the property and grounds," one Latter-day Saint visitor from Utah wrote in 1955. "Thank you for your liberal and open mind and your courteous hospitality," wrote another Latter-day Saint from Kansas City, Missouri. People not affiliated with either faith were likewise impressed. "Very historic and remarkable. They were most brave," observed a Lutheran from Illinois. "A most interesting presentation on the history and convictions of your church," summarized a Congregationalist minister from Iowa. "It helps tremendously in understanding other religious groups."[106] Of course, not all visits were positive. "I am disappointed with the way the church homes of Joseph Smith are run," one visitor reported in 1953. "When I go to Nauvoo I hear complaints of the service received from both local and visiting people. Yesterday I was there. . . . The guide was a young boy with no enthusiasm at all and talked so low we could hardly hear him. We all waited a long time before any one came around to guide us through."[107]

As visitors to the properties increased, the various parties in Nauvoo looked to the future. Losing out on efforts to control a portion of the Temple lot, Reorganized Church leaders sought to distinguish themselves from their Utah counterparts. For example, the Church worked with the Nauvoo Historical Society on a "Joseph Smith room" for a building at the Nauvoo State Park. However, a guide for the Reorganized Church characterized the mounting tension in an exchange with Church officials. "If we don't take an interest in it then the local people might go to the Mormons and have them do something. There is some indication that the room might be called the Mormon room anyhow and I don't like that particularly."[108]

Meanwhile, local residents unaffiliated with either faith sought to capitalize on the growing interest in Nauvoo. "Say, will you loan 'Historic Nauvoo Vacation Lands, Inc.' a little money?" a local town newsletter entrepreneurially advertised. "We the incorporators Elmer Kraus, Steve Kelley, El Kron, & myself think it's O.K., at least we have our necks out several thousand dollars. We know some are laughing at our sight seeing & charter bus (and I might smile just a little myself), but I remember the laughs and remarks some 15 years ago when a mention of tourists coming to Nauvoo was made. We will have tourist headquarters in the Benne building right next to the hotel. There will be someone there every day to answer tourist questions, arrange lodging, etc. Anyone having tourist rooms call our headquarters." The businessmen appealed for locals to become involved financially in the endeavor, "If you can spare 50—100—200—or any more the corporation will pay 5% interest. Oh sure some will say just a donation, never get your money back, and they may be right. We also know the bank won't finance an idea, even Henry Ford had to borrow from friends when he started. We believe it will go and we need your support, moral if you don't have money, both if you do. I'll say this, if it does work out and we believe it will, it won't only make us money but will be a financial benefit to everyone in the community. Contact any of us but Kron is secretary. We need your help."[109]

Nauvoo's longtime stakeholders sensed something big was about to happen. But no one fully envisioned how it would unfold. For the meantime, the Reorganized Church desperately tried to protect its place as the caretaker and interpreter of the Mormon story in Nauvoo. Their chief rival, The Church of Jesus Christ of Latter-day Saints, actively purchased available properties, applying financial leverage to expand their presence in the city, much as they were expanding nationwide. The state of Illinois and local businesses explored ways to use Nauvoo's past to bolster the local and regional economies. In the ensuing decade, alliances formed between some of these parties set up an outsider-versus-insider conflict in Nauvoo that split the city. Throughout the 1960s and 1970s, Nauvoo was forced to decide between an agricultural or tourism-based economy and, increasingly, between a Mormon and non-Mormon identity.

# CHAPTER 4

# Nauvoo Restoration Incorporated and a Formal Latter-day Saint Presence in Nauvoo

In 1961, Reorganized Church Apostle Donald V. Lents warned his faith's First Presidency that The Church of Jesus Christ of Latter-day Saints was about to do something big in Nauvoo. "The *Mormons* are stepping up their program for the purchase of property in the area and seem, too, to be increasing the number of personnel in responsibility here in the town." Adding specific detail, Lents continued,

> I am informed that they have a full-time couple at the Heber Kimball home to tell the story. Of course at their Information Center they also have a full-time couple to answer questions and direct folk on tours of the town. They have two more full-time people at the home they call the John Taylor house. They have just purchased the Brigham Young home and report is they will renovate it and provide caretakers and guides. Within the past thirty days or so they have purchased the remainder of the old Temple lot (the area where the Catholic School and Parish Hall now stand). This gives them the complete old Temple lot . . . with the exception of the lot we own in the area.

He then concluded, "It would appear to me that careful consideration needs to be given by us as to our purpose and our plans for the future here in Nauvoo."[1]

Indeed, while earlier attention was focused on the temple property throughout the 1940s and 1950s, other land transactions Lents referred to dramatically shaped the future of restored Nauvoo. On February 23, 1938, Utah newspapers reported Wilford Wood's purchase of the John Taylor residence, together with the adjoining home for the printing office of the *Nauvoo Neighbor* and the *Times and Seasons*, Mormon-era newspapers. At the time, Wood noted that "the purchase . . . was made privately and possession of the property remains with him."[2] Fifteen years later, Wood deeded the property to the Church, which stationed a missionary couple, David and Lily Haycock, in the Taylor home. The pair began conducting tours in the *Times and Seasons* building, called a "Church Education Center," in 1953.[3] On March 17, 1956, a branch of the Church was organized in the city, serving the missionary couples and a handful of local members. Originally meeting in the Reimbold home on the temple lot that Wood had acquired in 1951, the branch relocated to the *Times and Seasons* building in 1960. Four years later, the branch moved again when the Church remodeled the old Icarian schoolhouse on the southwest corner of the temple lot into an information bureau.[4] With an organizational presence in the city, the stage was set for the dramatic expansion of restored Nauvoo, first by private individuals and later, in a more formal way, by The Church of Jesus Christ of Latter-day Saints. Their actions in celebrating a particular portion of the past, coupled with the corresponding reactions by other stakeholders in the 1960s and 1970s, shaped the future of Nauvoo.

## The Nauvoo Dream of Dr. J. LeRoy Kimball

While Latter-day Saints orchestrated the return of a Church organization to Nauvoo, Salt Lake City physician J. LeRoy Kimball likewise became interested in Nauvoo family property. More than any man, his influence over nearly fifty years shaped Mormonism's presence in Nauvoo. Visiting the area as a medical student at Northwestern University in Chicago in the 1920s, Kimball stumbled across the home of his great-grandfather, Heber C. Kimball. "I had never been to Nauvoo and I don't think that I even knew that there was a Kimball home here," Dr. Kimball later recalled. He acquainted himself with a St. Louis–area family, the Joneses, who used the Kimball home as a summer retreat, and embarked on a twenty-four-year effort to acquire it. Visiting the family every year beginning in 1932, Kimball eventually "extracted from them the promise if they ever sold the home that they would let [him] have it."[5] True to their word, when Mr. Jones died in 1954, his widow sold the property to Kimball.

"At that time I had no idea what [had] developed," Kimball recalled decades later. "I thought, here's a home, a beautiful home and I'll restore it. It'll be a good place to get away from medicine, spend two weeks."[6] Remodeling it as a summer retreat while maintaining, in part, its 1840s charm, Dr. Kimball invited

FIGURE 11. Heber C. and Vilate Kimball residence, Nauvoo, Ill., 1886.
Photograph by B. H. Roberts. Used by permission, Utah State Historical Society.

Elder Spencer W. Kimball, a fellow Heber C. Kimball descendant and Apostle
in the Latter-day Saint Church, to dedicate the home in 1960.[7] For the occasion,
Elder Kimball was accompanied by some of the faith's most prominent leaders, including President J. Reuben Clark of the Church's First Presidency and
Harold B. Lee and Delbert L. Stapley of the Quorum of the Twelve Apostles.
The words of the prayer reflected Kimball's plan to use the home as a family
retreat. "In compliance with the request of Brother and Sister Kimball, as Thy
servant," Elder Kimball prayed, "I do dedicate this lovely home, that it might be
a haven to which those who are in need of comfort, who need strengthening,
families may come when there are problems and they need the kindliness of
a father and mother and a grandfather and grandmother."[8] Ironically, Kimball
did not spend a single night in the restored residence, lodging instead at a local
hotel. "At this dedication there were a thousand people who met me and my
wife. . . . We spent that two weeks we thought as a vacation simply showing
tourists through the home." The next year, they put a couple, a Mr. and Mrs.
Perkins, in the home, as fifteen thousand guests visited.

Surprised by the interest his renovation generated, Kimball set about acquiring other historically significant properties in Nauvoo. Kimball's motivation

for purchasing properties began with a desire to protect the Heber C. Kimball home from encroaching entrepreneurial interests.[9] "After I bought the home, right across the street someone . . . was going to set up a motel," Kimball later recalled. "Well, I thought I'm not going to spend the money on this home because it cost me a lot of money to restore it. In fact, I figured I'd spen[t] $50,000 on that home to restore it and put in furniture and such as that. So I thought well, I'll buy that property and I was able to buy it. The kidd[ie] corner was the home of Porter Rockwell, so I bought that. So I bought a number of the properties around the Kimball home primarily to conserve that Kimball home," he summarized.[10] Eventually, the strategy of buying and building a buffer around historically significant properties became the model for Nauvoo's restoration.

After having protected the environs of his ancestral home, Kimball turned his attention elsewhere in the city. "People told me that more people asked about the Brigham Young home than asked about the Heber C. Kimball home or about the Joseph Smith's properties," he continued. "So I thought that will be interesting." He bought the Brigham Young home. At the same time, Nauvoo mayor Lowell Horton approached Kimball with an idea. "On the block where the Kimball home stands," Horton noted, "it's really the only remaining block which approached the original block that was set up by Joseph Smith. . . . Wouldn't it be fine to get that full block and put it back as it was, to give an idea of Joseph Smith's idea of what a block should be?"[11] Kimball was hooked. He purchased the Winslow Farr and Wilford Woodruff properties that shared the block with the Kimball home.[12] "So, then I got that idea," Kimball later recalled. "So I bought the Brigham Young home, I bought [t]his land around the Kimball home, I bought the farm home, I bought the Woodruff home, and before I knew it I had a $100,000 worth of property in Nauvoo. But I knew I had hold of an antique. I knew from experience just from the Kimball home, when you went from zero to 15,000 people that I couldn't lose."[13]

The purchases paved the way for significant expansion of the Latter-day Saint Church presence in Nauvoo, actions that would, in part, reverse the Church's 1846 exodus from the city and change the community. The expansion began when, with the assistance of longtime friend President J. Reuben Clark of the Church's First Presidency, Dr. Kimball shared what he had done with Church president David O. McKay.[14] "I told [President McKay] about Nauvoo and what I was doing," Kimball remembered. "I said there were about forty homes in Nauvoo and I just said that I hadn't gone to him then for finances, but I said I know what I'd do if I had the money. He said, 'What would you do?' And I said, 'I'd restore all of them.' Right back he said, 'You've got the money. How much do you need?' Well, I said, 'President McKay, I know it would take more than a million dollars to buy this land,' and it stood at that."[15]

With McKay's assistance, Kimball contacted experts who could move the project forward. Chief among them was Harold P. Fabian, head of the Utah State Parks system and a member of the advisory board on National Parks, Historic Sites, Buildings, and Monuments for the United States Department of the Interior. In December 1961 Kimball, Fabian, and Dr. Melvin L. Fowler, curator of North American archaeology at Southern Illinois University, stood on the site of the former Nauvoo temple and watched as a backhoe clawed at the ground, hoping to find the building's long-buried foundations. Upon success in locating one of the structure's south piers, a project was born.[16]

Kimball readily admitted that while his plan gained notoriety for the homes and businesses he acquired, Nauvoo's temple square had "always been the center of this restoration."[17] Arrangements were made for Dr. Fowler to lead a team in excavating the temple the following spring. Meanwhile, rumors quickly resurfaced around town that the Church was going to reconstruct the temple. In December 1961 the local newspaper enthusiastically reported, "The multi-million dollar project planned for this vicinity staggers the imagination, for all the eminent landmarks are to be reconstructed, the work to include recreating the environment of the Nauvoo period, 1839–1846, so that future generations may appreciate more vividly the contribution the Mormons gave to the ideas and future of America. . . . The news of the Nauvoo restoration came as an exciting Christmas gift to local citizens," the paper announced, "and now religion, education, labor, industry and commerce face a challenge in building this Nauvoo of the future."[18]

## Formation of Nauvoo Restoration Incorporated

Seeking to expand the organization beyond "a one man proposition," Kimball recommended that an organization be formed, partnering public and private interests.[19] In May 1962, Presidents Henry D. Moyle and Hugh B. Brown of the Church's First Presidency, Conrad Wirth, director of the National Park Service, A. Edwin Kendrew, senior vice president and chief historical architect for the restoration of Colonial Williamsburg, entrepreneur businessman J. Willard Marriott, and A. Hamer Reiser, member of the Utah State Parks and Recreation commission, toured Nauvoo with Kimball, Fabian, and others.[20] Their fact-finding mission aimed "to discover the possibilities for the restoring of the historic significance of Nauvoo as one of the major bases of overland migration from the Mississippi into the American West."[21] "We hope to restore the historic city so it can be a proper base from which to tell the Mormon story and of the Mormon contribution to the building of the West," Fabian announced.[22] He outlined a four-phase project, the first of which would be the temple site. "It could be left bare after the excavation project is completed, or a structure could be built on the site," Fabian revealed. Other phases included restoring homes and businesses and constructing a visitor orientation center and accommodations.[23]

A month later, Nauvoo Restoration Incorporated, a nonprofit Church-sponsored organization was formed.[24] Explaining its mission, President McKay outlined that the corporation was being created "for the purpose of restoring the residences in historic Nauvoo as they were left when the Mormons evacuated the city in 1846." He added that it would also "perpetuate in history the part played by the Mormon Pioneers in the building of the West."[25] More specifically, the foundation's articles of incorporation outlined its mission: "To acquire, restore, protect and preserve, for the education and benefit of its members and the public, all or a part of the old city of Nauvoo in Illinois and the surrounding area, in order to provide an historically authentic physical environment for awakening a public interest in, and an understanding and appreciation of, the story of Nauvoo and the mass migration of its people to the Valley of the Great Salt Lake in the area which has now become the State of Utah." Seeking a much larger connection than to Utah and Mormonism, the mission statement also outlined that Nauvoo Restoration was "to interpret and dramatize [Mormonism's exodus from Nauvoo], not only as a great example of pioneering determination and courage, but also as one of the vital forces in the expansion of America westward from the Mississippi River; to engage in historic and archaeological research, interpretation and education and to maintain, develop and interpret historic landmarks and other features of historic, archaeological, scientific or inspirational interest anywhere in the United States and particularly along the Mormon Pioneer Trail from Nauvoo, Illinois to its terminus in the Valley of the Great Salt Lake."[26] Nauvoo Restoration Incorporated, or NRI, as the entity came to be known, embarked on this ambitious endeavor for the next four decades.

While Nauvoo "residents expressed willingness to cooperate with the Church in any restoration projects that might be planned," newspaper accounts also acknowledged the potential challenges the project would create. Sensing the far-reaching effects the organization's plans might have for the city, one local newspaper urged caution. "The range of exploration . . . has not been as wide in scope as the imaginations of some citizens have soared. Unfounded rumors and surmises have stimulated some active imaginations unreasonably.

Experience will caution the practical-minded to discount these substantially."[27] Another sought to reassure readers concerned about what was happening to their rural hometown, "Restoration of the old city might be undertaken without intrusion of commercial enterprises, and a visitor orientation center or information bureau established nearby. Visitor accommodations such as shops and lodgings would be located next to, but not part of, the restored old city section."[28] Townspeople were abuzz with possibilities, as were those leading Nauvoo Restoration.

In the project's earliest days, Kimball and Fabian dreamed big, and the temple was always at the heart of their plans. In a document prepared six months prior to the board's formal organization, the pair outlined as their first objective "to restore the Mormon Temple at Nauvoo as a shrine to those whose perseverance and faith built it, and to establish and re-dedicate it as a present day place of religious worship."[29] However, as reflected in the later Articles of Incorporation, their vision did not stop with the temple. They planned "to acquire the historically important part of Nauvoo and restore it in a way designed to give visitors there a feeling of the atmosphere and way of life of Nauvoo and its people in the time when it flourished under Mormon leadership, a conception of the character of those people as shown by the homes they built and the way they lived, and an understanding of the depth of their emotions and the strength of their faith when they abandoned their Temple, their homes and their beautiful city and started on their long migration westward across the prairies to the far-off Rocky Mountains." Additionally, Kimball and Fabian anticipated "a visitor orientation center to interpret the story of Nauvoo and its people, and its contribution to the history and character of western America," together with "adequate and attractive modern visitor accommodations" in a portion of the city "not a part of the restored area but from which it will be readily accessible."[30] Not so subtly, however, all of these plans prioritized one version of one period of Nauvoo's past.

Initial implementation of the plan focused on property acquisition. In fact, at the public announcement of the formation of Nauvoo Restoration Incorporated, officials revealed that most purchases had already quietly been made. Kimball reported that "many of the residences have been purchased, and option is obtained on about three-quarters of a mile of beautiful Mississippi River front property."[31] He later explained,

> We moved right in because I was heavily involved and I could see that with the backing of President McKay, with the finances there it was basically the first thing we did was buy land because we knew what we would run [in] to. Mr. Kendrew, of course, was advising us even as early as that and he told

me instances in Williamsburg, one instance where a piece of property they later bought for $350,000 they could have bought for $7,500. So we set up a perimeter in order to protect ourselves and in order to know how to move so we could move with surety and that's what we have at the present time. So we own . . . just short of a thousand acres.[32]

Kimball further detailed how transactions were finalized. "As we were buying these homes out, frequently I would ask someone what they wanted for the home and they would say, 'Well, we've been living in this home for so many years, we don't owe any money. If you give us enough to buy a home we'll move,' and I'd say how much it cost. Well, they may say $20,000 and I'd give them $20,000 and there are a lot of these homes up on the east side that were bought and paid for from that standpoint." He then summarized the result, "There were several approaches that I made in purchasing and some people were interested in this thing as a project. Some people wanted to sell and some people sold because they got a good price, but I think that I made very few enemies because it was a rare case that I didn't give the people what they asked as far as the property was concerned."[33]

By 1964, board reports indicated that most of the desired property had been acquired. Of the $1,500,000 authorized for property acquisition, $1,134,359.18 had been expended to purchase 767 acres of land and twenty-eight of the available thirty-four Mormon homes and buildings in the area to be restored. Officials anticipated "sufficient finances to cover acquisition of the available property within the foreseeable future."[34] This financial commitment, which appears to have been backed entirely by the Church itself, represented a sizeable investment in one rural location for a faith of approximately two million members.

In these transactions, Kimball employed the assistance of Preston Kimball, a local Nauvoo attorney and distant relative. "I don't know of anyone I would rather trust [my money to] than Preston Kimball," Dr. Kimball declared in 1972. "He knew the city and he knew the flats, he knew everything I needed. He was in the bank, he was a lawyer and he was favorable towards us so that he came into the picture early and certainly I thank him more than any other single person. . . . We attempted to organize and in purchasing it, we went through one or two types of committees in order to get the land. Finally it came back to Preston and we made 130 deals here over a period of six or seven years."[35]

While property acquisition led the way, early Nauvoo Restoration work focused on the city's connection to the American westward migration more than on the Church's core doctrinal messages. Frequent reference was made to a National Park Service report touting "the movement of the Mormons to the valley of the Great Salt Lake [as] one of the most dramatic events in the history of America westward expansion," highlighting Nauvoo's role as its launching point.[36]

The makeup of NRI's original board, together with the early participants in its projects, reflected this emphasis on national prominence. President J. LeRoy Kimball was joined by Vice President Harold P. Fabian, Secretary A. Hamer Reiser, chairman of the Utah State Parks and Recreation Commission and assistant secretary to the First Presidency, with prominent Latter-day Saint businessmen David M. Kennedy and J. Willard Marriott as trustees. The connection to national historic sites was strengthened when the board added A. Edwin Kendrew, senior vice president and chief historical architect for the restoration of Colonial Williamsburg, as an adviser in 1962 and ultimately as a board member in 1965.[37] Mormons were thrilled at the breadth of the organization's board. "That such men are actively interested in restoring Nauvoo to its condition before Brigham Young and his followers were driven out in 1846 suggests fascinating possibilities," opined editors of the Utah newspaper, the

FIGURE 12. Nauvoo Restoration Incorporated officials and dignitaries, including George and Lenore Romney, Mary Firmage, J. LeRoy Kimball, J. Willard and Alice Marriott, Rowena Miller, Lenora and David Kennedy (left to right). Nauvoo Restoration Incorporated historical files. Church History Library, The Church of Jesus Christ of Latter-day Saints, Salt Lake City.

*Deseret News.* "Surely, the city's history represents one of the most dramatic pages in the great American pageant."[38] Likewise, local Nauvoo residents noted the powerful makeup of the body. At the 1969 groundbreaking for the organization's million-dollar visitor center, the *Nauvoo Independent* reported, "Never before, to our knowledge, has there been such an array of prominent personages in our city."[39]

## Historical Emphasis of NRI Projects

Early NRI projects reflected the historical and professional expertise of its board members. The most prominent of these projects were the archaeological excavations conducted in the late 1960s by J. C. Harrington, a founding member of the Society for Historical Archaeology and widely considered the father of historical archaeology, and his wife, Virginia. The Harringtons, who had gained prominence in their interpretive work at the settlement of Jamestown and in J. C. Harrington's excavations of Fort Raleigh, North Carolina, and Fort Necessity, Pennsylvania, directed the excavation of five historic sites in Nauvoo, the most significant among them being the temple lot itself.[40] Their work on the temple employed crews from Brigham Young University, the University of Utah, and Weber State College, all located in the Intermountain West, and individuals from the Nauvoo area, building on an initial survey of the site conducted by Dr. Melvin L. Fowler and Southern Illinois University in 1961 and 1962.[41] Updates on their excavations regularly appeared in local newspapers, where Salt Lake archaeologist and project field supervisor Dee F. Green emphasized its historical aspects: "When the entire [temple lot] is cleared, it should be done with the idea of preserving the wood and charcoal fragments [from the building's burning] on the floor. As a permanent display, it could be covered with glass or plastic to protect it from the elements, and at the same time allow visitors to view the remains."[42] As readers learned about the various findings, some brought forward their own artifacts from the former structure. For example, from across the river in Keokuk, Iowa, Miss Elizabeth Baur donated an original temple star stone taken from the ruins of the building by her grandparents in the 1860s. Nauvoo Restoration officials appealed for additional discoveries.[43]

During the height of her work on the temple, archaeologist Virginia Harrington answered the question, "Why archaeology at Nauvoo?" After acknowledging that archaeological explorations "give prestige to historical restorations" and also that "it makes a good show," Harrington offered more. "The most obvious reason is that archaeology provides information that is not otherwise available in spite of all the records and books and historical research." Her several examples from the Nauvoo project included knowledge gained regarding the brick-paved floor in the basement of the original Nauvoo Temple, the design of the baptismal font, the floor drain used to remove its water, and the skill (as well as the occasional lack thereof) of those who worked the massive stones that made up the building's foundations. Turning to other areas around town, Harrington noted the discovery of an older well outside the Wilford Woodruff home, the uncovering of a brick vegetable cellar adjacent to the Brigham Young home, and the full size of the Webb blacksmith shop, originally thought to be thirty feet wide but discovered to be more than double that size. Additionally, she highlighted the "information that comes from the artifacts, as we call the china and glass, the metal and stone, that are almost invariably found in the ground in association with buildings that have been lived in or otherwise occupied." For Harrington and her audience, all of this pointed to the purpose for Nauvoo Restoration, "to preserve and interpret the site so that visitors, and people generally, will better understand its importance in American history."[44]

As is clear in Harrington's response, while archaeological work on the temple drew the greatest initial attention, experts also dug in other areas. For example, in 1965 a partial exploration was conducted of the Brigham Young lot. From the Young excavation, officials learned that "the quantity of cultural material will probably be much greater than anticipated from historical records and the short span of the Mormon period." Additionally, they came to appreciate the greater digging depth necessary in their excavations due to the considerable filling done to alleviate Nauvoo's marshy conditions.

Projecting forward, researchers concentrated their efforts on standing buildings. Preparing a five-year plan, supervising archaeologist J. C. Harrington proposed conducting research in the perimeter areas immediately surrounding the Brigham Young, Wilford Woodruff, Winslow-Farr, Lucy Mack Smith, Joseph Coolidge, and Snow-Ashby homes. However, Harrington readily acknowledged, "certain auxiliary work very probably will be called for," including the construction of administrative and visitor facilities, all of which would require archaeological verification prior to construction. The fluidity of these plans later became evident, as both the Webb blacksmith shop site and the Browning home were dug, even though they were not part of the proposed schedule. Overall, Harrington's plan called for determining "the date, identification, and construction details of standing portions of the structures, or of missing elements, such as outside cellar entrances, porches, terraces, walks, and other architectural features which have a functional relation to the buildings and a bearing on their restoration." He admitted that it would "be slow, painstaking work," requiring "considerable measuring, drawing, and photographing"

FIGURE 13. Excavation of the Jonathan and Elizabeth Browning
home, Nauvoo, Ill., 1968. Courtesy of Archives and
Special Collections, Western Illinois University Libraries.

with "continuous and close supervision."[45] It involved the work of historians
to collect and analyze written records, architects to determine what features of
surviving buildings were original, and archaeologists to uncover structures.[46]

In spite of their complexity, the archaeological and restoration aspects of
the project fascinated Kimball. "We found out as we moved along that people
were more interested in the process of restoration than in the restored. So we
see there that we didn't want to cover up," he noted.[47] Kimball summarized
their methods:

The process of restoration is a tremendously complicated and costly process.
First, we had to get the land. Second, we brought in some fine historians:
Dr. Ed Lyon, my son James L. Kimball, was also involved in it so we started

collecting pictures. Then we brought in the archaeologist, Mr. Harrington . . . and later on we had another archaeologist with us to dig out the foundation because without archaeology we would have a poor restoration. . . . Then we had to bring in construction people most of which we have to and have trained right here in order to put these buildings back together.

Kimball added his philosophy: "So it's true that practically any of these buildings we could build a new building for about a third of what it's cost us to put up the old one. But I always told them that I've always looked on this Nauvoo thing just like I would a resurrection."[48] Interestingly, though public statements emphasized historical accuracy, Kimball's choice of religious terminology to explain the workings of Nauvoo Restoration reflects the reality that this was more than an historical project.

For Kimball, the goal was to bring Nauvoo back to life as it was in the 1840s. Kimball's son James summarized his father's love for the technical detail of the project. "One of my father's favorite sayings was that NRI 'is no crash program.' . . . This belief was a part of his basic philosophy and was a key factor in making the restoration of homes more accurate and authentic. Dad felt it would have been inappropriate to rebuild Nauvoo with what he called a Disneyland approach; proper historical, architectural, and archaeological research was needed to drive the final results."[49]

This commitment to bringing Mormon Nauvoo back to life led to activity all over town. Shortly after work commenced on the excavation of the temple, restoration work also began on the Brigham Young, Snow-Ashby, Lucy Mack Smith, Winslow Farr, Wilford Woodruff, and Joseph W. Coolidge properties. In 1963 the Church budgeted $375,000 for the restoration of these six properties, together with the erection of a temporary visitors' information center and offices in the city.[50] Though Church-sponsored, the projects continually emphasized Mormonism's place within the American story of the settling of the West. Charles A. Lipchow, blacksmith and guide at the Webb blacksmith shop, summarized the organization's initial approach: "We do not preach the Church at the restoration; we preach history."[51]

While they outlined an ambitious agenda, officials also recognized the limitations on their project, including the impossibility of restoring everything that was once in Nauvoo. "At Nauvoo, complete restoration will not likely be undertaken," Nauvoo's *New Independent* noted in 1962 while reporting on the organization. "Preservation and restoration of authentic Mormon homes still standing will be the first order of business. Beyond this, structures, commercial and residential, may be represented only by foundations, found still to be in place, as archaeological excavations are undertaken, or by reconstruction as original sites are established by historical research. These means of partial 'restoration' will leave to the imagination of the visitors the 'reconstruction' and re-opening of historic Nauvoo life and times which gave the city its fame."[52]

Dr. Kimball himself further clarified the project's bounds in an article for Church members. "I want all Latter-day Saints to know that the Church is not committing itself to something that is going to involve a fantastic outlay of money," he reassured concerned readers. "This complete restoration project is such that we could stop at any particular phase of our ten-phase development program and not be the loser. Each phase can stand on its own and to some degree satisfy visitors." Like the article for Navuoo readers, Kimball explained to his Church audience,

> It is not contemplated that all of the houses still standing be restored as museums or exhibition houses, but they are to be restored at least as to the exterior to form the background of a section of the city that will be representative of the City of Nauvoo as a whole. We plan to rebuild the Seventies Hall and shops of tanners, blacksmiths, wheelwrights, wagon makers, bakers, apothecary, general stores, and some of the more interesting and important of the trades that were in Nauvoo in the Prophet's time. We know the actual location of most of the shops and have photographs of some. We have a committee of experts and authorities whose role is to see that everything is done accurately.[53]

By the late 1960s, Nauvoo Restoration's plan came into greater focus. Project historian T. Edgar Lyon wrote in the Illiamo Tourist Guide,

> The Master Plan for the restoration of a portion of old Mormon Nauvoo is now in its final stages. The plan calls for a restoration of an historic area of the old city on the "Flat," that will be approximately a half-mile in length and a quarter-of-a-mile in width. Many of the old buildings will be restored to a functioning condition. It is contemplated four residences, two public buildings, and fifteen craft shops will be open where visitors can see the functioning life of the 1840's in a living museum city. In addition other period homes, restored to add atmosphere of the 1840's, will be inhabited by families employed in the craft shops and agricultural enterprises.[54]

As mentioned, in all of these early endeavors, historical accuracy occupied an important place. For example, to match the mortar used in the brick homes of Brigham Young and Wilford Woodruff, forty-three different mixes were tested with microscopic scrutiny against the buildings' original mortars.[55] Wood samples from the Brigham Young house mantel were taken to a Harvard University chemical laboratory for analysis of paint layers and primers, determining that "there seems to be no doubt the black is sandwiched between a priming coat and the graining ground color."[56] Modern amenities like electrical wiring and vents for heating and air conditioning were carefully concealed as much as possible.[57] Discussion even ensued regarding the recreation of the Brigham Young and Wilford Woodruff orchards, aligning the trees on a straight line because officials "reasoned that everything else being laid out as carefully as it was that most surely a line would have been used to carefully line up trees in an orchard."[58] However, in all of these discussions, accuracy trumped mere speculation. "I will try to clearly distinguish between the actual findings in the ground and my purely hypothetical restorations," J. C. Harrington wrote.[59]

## Tempering Expectations for the Nauvoo Temple

Meanwhile, around town, speculation concerning the project grew. As the excavation of the temple lot unfolded, temple reconstruction rumors dominated discussion. Even before the formation of NRI, one newspaper reported on the temple reconstruction, keenly aware of its priority over other historic structures. "The plans call for rebuilding the Nauvoo Temple and possibly acquiring considerable land below the hill on what is commonly referred to as the 'flat,'" the author announced.[60] However, Church leaders quickly downplayed the idea. The following May, the *Quincy Herald Whig* reported on the visit of Latter-day Saint First Presidency members Henry D. Moyle and Hugh B. Brown to the Nauvoo temple site, noting, "The church leaders said that although a final decision has not been made, the temple will probably not be rebuilt on the old foundation. A sunken garden or other development may be fashioned within the old stone walls, which extend six feet below ground level, and eventually a replica of the original temple may be built on another section of the square."[61]

By 1963, board members and Church officials internally acknowledged that plans to reconstruct the temple were on hold. The organization's original statement of purpose that had emphasized the restoration and rededication of the temple on the block "was amended and revised, because the plan of restoring the temple did not appear to be feasible under the present situation." Not giving up hope, officials cautiously began to look elsewhere in the city for the possible reconstruction of the once grand edifice. In a 1964 report, board members announced having acquired "several hundred acres in the northeast part of the Nauvoo area" where "a full temple facility could be erected, if and when the Church desires it; or a university, visitor accommodations and facilities, an orientation center with its adjacent landscaping, utilities and all that pertains to such a development, can be erected." On the temple lot itself "could be added some development . . . in accordance with instructions to be received from the First Presidency regarding its treatment." Architect George Cannon Young was contracted to draw up several possibilities.[62]

In spite of their best efforts, as archaeological excavations of the temple site progressed through the 1960s, rumors of the building's restoration persisted. In 1969, NRI manager J. Byron Ravsten answered a local newspaper about the possibility that the temple would be reconstructed: "The LDS [Church] has pledged itself to beautifying the Temple site. Whether there will be sufficient money actually to rebuild the Temple is conjectural. It would take millions."[63] Possibly because of cost, rumors circulated about a partial rebuild. Later the same year, the local *Nauvoo Independent* reported that "a partial restoration of the Nauvoo Temple . . . is planned for the near future."[64] Elaborating further on the proposal, J. LeRoy Kimball even answered questions about the temple in the Church's *Improvement Era*: "This has not been decided yet. One suggestion is to partially restore it, perhaps rebuilding only a corner of the building to the tower base. This will allow people to get an idea of the temple's grandeur, and permit them to climb to the top and see the beautiful view of the Mississippi River and the countryside about which so many visitors as well as the Saints wrote. The temple story is part of our historic presentation."[65] In October 1968 the *Improvement Era* even ran a cover story on the proposal, including an artist's rendering of the restored temple corner and the announcement that "construction on the partial restoration of the Nauvoo Temple is expected to begin in 1970. A two-year construction period is anticipated."[66]

Talk of partially restoring the temple led to one of the most unique proposals of the era. In April 1970 the Nauvoo Restoration architect's office received a letter from a young man asking for all architectural information on the original Nauvoo Temple, including estimated reconstruction costs and plans. Trying to "formulate this project in such a manner as to meet the approval of the Prophet and the Council of the Twelve," the individual proposed the joint efforts of Church youth organizations worldwide in producing a "total and accurate restoration of the Temple." By doing so, he hoped to "1) give the teen and college age youth a significant, meaningful goal for which to work, 2) to erect a living tribute to our martyred Prophet and Patriarch (one which was the hope and joy of their hearts), 3) to demonstrate to the world at large that as young Latter-day Saints we honor our past, love our Church, and possess courage and hope to face our future."[67] Praising the inquirer for his "very worthwhile aspirations to restore the Nauvoo Temple," NRI's architectural department nevertheless declined the request to have the youth of the Church rebuild the building.[68]

While initial work focused on the temple site and the historic homes themselves, Nauvoo Restoration officials anticipated an expansive Nauvoo experience and frequently referred to it as the Williamsburg of the Midwest.[69] Corporate records from the era reveal plans for hotels, restaurants, a university, golf course, amphitheater, shopping center, marina, and family recreational areas. In the Church's *Improvement Era*, Dr. Kimball announced plans to duplicate earlier riverboats and "provide short river trips for those wishing enjoyable recreation and a flavor of the past," as well as efforts to establish NRI-owned hotel accommodations. In terms of entertainment, he also outlined "many possibilities, ranging from parading a Nauvoo Legion to a dramatic production telling the story of Nauvoo. There is a natural amphitheater down by the river," Kimball continued, "one that could easily seat thousands of people. We hope to have a dramatic-musical production written that will appeal to tourists and portray the dramatic story of the rise and fall of Nauvoo."[70]

Such grand ambitions thrilled some interested groups. For their part, local residents appeared pleased at the prospects for increased entertainment and recreation in their city. When Nauvoo Restoration purchased the temple quarry, the local newspaper urged its development into a marina. "The corporation is blessed with a huge hole in the ground that appears useless," the author wrote. "However, we will presume to suggest to Nauvoo Restoration that a public recreation area with boating facilities would be of great benefit to those of this community and to the thousands of visitors who will come here to view the restoration."[71]

Groups beyond Nauvoo also became involved. For example, the National Park Service provided a grant of $15,000 to the University of Utah for historical research in the city. It also secured the cooperation of the Mississippi River Parkway Commission of the State of Illinois to ensure that the "Great River Road," then under development, would "best serve the project's interests." George B. Hartzog Jr., Director of the National Park Service, pledged "to cooperate in every way, . . . [as] it is [the Park Service's] intention to include Nauvoo in their over-all plan of development, to furnish such information as will aid in the project, and to include Nauvoo in their literature." From the State of Illinois, the Division of Tourism printed a new brochure highlighting Nauvoo, the State Engineering Department conducted a study for a possible marina, and the Department of Tourism examined statistics and tourist data.[72] Inspecting the project during a 1964 visit to Nauvoo, Illinois Governor Otto Kerner admitted, "There is a great work you are doing here. Tourism is going to grow in Illinois, and restored Nauvoo has a rightful place in the tourism picture. . . . I look forward to cooperation between the Church and the state of Illinois in this great undertaking."[73]

Practically, Kimball saw benefit from these national and regional connections. In his public discourse, he regularly emphasized the seventeen million people living within a half-day's drive of Nauvoo and the fifty million people residing within five hundred miles. Additionally, he emphasized Nauvoo's "strategic location in a section already having great historic attraction," including Abraham Lincoln's New Salem, Illinois, and Mark Twain's Hannibal, Missouri, both less than one hundred miles away. "What an attractive area for tourists!" he exclaimed.[74] Philosophically, Dr. Kimball summarized the breadth of the project's potential: "Nauvoo is a great center from which to tell many stories: The Mormon Nauvoo story, the migration story of all peoples who headed westward, the Mississippi River traffic and merchandising story, and the always enjoyable experience of seeing how people of another time lived."[75] Indeed, "there is no end to what can be done in Nauvoo," Kimball boasted.[76]

## A Tightrope of Historical Interpretation and Proselytizing

While officials wrangled with the difficulties of restoring historic structures and providing modern amenities, the young organization also wrestled to find a balance between authentic restoration and evangelizing because of its Church affiliation. The tension was especially acute because of Mormonism's well-known reputation for proselytizing. Nauvoo Restoration secretary Rowena Miller sensed the dilemma the organization faced. "It will take the wisdom of a Solomon," Miller cautioned, "to walk the tight-rope of historic interpretation proselyting you people . . . have confronting you."[77] For his part, board vice president Harold Fabian championed a historical emphasis rather than overt proselytizing in Nauvoo's restoration. Early in the project, he cautioned Church president David O. McKay, "If you undertake to restore it as a religious restoration, as a proselyting institution to get members to your church, it will not be received generally and will not have the approval of the nation. But if you will restore it as an historic restoration it must be based on all of the best things that your church has to offer and has had to offer in history and must give you all of the benefits and standing which you would not get if you tried to restore it as a religious restoration."[78] Indicating that Fabian "had no patience with the proselyting interests" of the Church, Reiser reported that "on several occasions [Fabian] mentioned the fact that the less we had to say about Joseph Smith the better it would be."[79]

For his part, Dr. Kimball envisioned using restored Nauvoo as a nontraditional means for sharing the message of his faith. "The role of the Church in restoring Nauvoo envisions a different approach to missionary work," Kimball remarked. "Our guide service is one that tourists will find informative,

educational, and inspiring, but also one that those who do not desire a proselyting approach will find acceptable. Nauvoo will be a historical place where
people will first look and then possibly listen to the gospel message."[80] Speaking
to the Rotary Club of Burlington, Iowa, NRI manager J. Byron Ravsten reassured locals about the endeavor's emphasis: "Nauvoo Restoration is a historical
and not a religious project."[81] From a national perspective, seeking to educate
about religion rather than advocate for it conformed to the prevalent debate of
the era, as courts around the country specifically, and American society generally, contentiously grappled over issues like public prayer and Bible reading. In
this way, Nauvoo's restoration was a reflection of its era.

As American society demonstrated with its own debates, implementing a
middle ground approach in Nauvoo was easier said than done. To facilitate
crowds, Nauvoo Restoration organized a guide service composed of volunteer
couples personally selected by Dr. Kimball, augmented in the summer months
by Latter-day Saint college students. Using "experience at various museum cities
and restoration projects," Restoration officials established two basic principles
for guide service. First, they sought to emphasize buildings that were unique.
Acknowledging that "the architecture of Nauvoo houses was not a new type
and made no impression on the development of American architecture" and
also that "no Nauvoo building is associated with a great historical event," officials chose to focus on the temple, which "was unique—there was only one of
its type—and has never been duplicated." Second, guides were instructed to
emphasize the people and their lives rather than the buildings. "The men who
built and inhabited these houses," officials emphasized, "were more important than their dwellings. Their personal achievements, their impact on other
people, their influence on the community and the country as a whole, their
relationship to the social, political, or religious institutions of the community,
or their influence upon a region of the country—such as the expansion of
American institutions to the Far West—should be our stock in trade, rather
than the houses in which they dwelt." Specifically applying these principles,
guides were instructed to discuss the contributions of prominent Latter-day
Saint leaders like Joseph Smith, Heber C. Kimball, and Brigham Young in the
areas of "city planning, religious leadership, [and] pioneering in the Far West.
. . . The houses are but structures in which to place the men and their families
as living people, facing problems people face today, and to indicate how they
solved their problems through their religious convictions, their ability to cooperate to a remarkable degree, and to show the cultural level they were striving
to maintain in spite of economic adversity and opposition from their neighbors
who failed to understand their motives."[82]

While early Nauvoo Restoration guides sought to implement these principles, adaptation was necessary, especially for the various groups attracted to the restoration project. In particular, the religious component of the endeavor challenged early guides. Nauvoo Restoration officials wisely observed that tourists with personal connections to Nauvoo differed significantly from other outside visitors. Latter-day Saint visitors "are very interested in the religious life of the city and the rapid growth of the city through its missionary system. Many are blood descendants of those who resided in Nauvoo. They want to hear of their ancestors even though they were not prominent in the city's history. The guide must have a treasury of information concerning people and items which are of little interest to the majority of tourists but which will give these Mormons a great thrill of pride and a vicarious feeling of participation with their ancestors in the rise and fall of Nauvoo."[83]

Though the philosophy seemed clear, finding a balance between historical tourism, missionary outreach, and appeal to those who were already Mormon proved problematic. Additionally, the Reorganized Church, who had controlled the Mormon message in Nauvoo since the 1860s by virtue of their ownership of the Joseph Smith family sites, was less-than-enthused about the emphasis on certain aspects of Nauvoo's history. For example, they were particularly troubled by the frequent rumors regarding rebuilding the Nauvoo temple, a structure and a theology about which they had long contended with their Utah counterparts. Additionally, they saw little need to emphasize Mormonism's role in the settling of the West because Reorganized Church membership generally comprised those who remained in the Midwest following the Mormon exodus from Nauvoo. Eventually, they crafted a response of their own to these prominent parts of the Latter-day Saint message in restored Nauvoo.

Interestingly, voices of concern were not limited to those outside the faith either. Within Latter-day Saint leadership itself, some questioned the historical emphasis evident in the project. After the death of Church president David O. McKay in 1970, Nauvoo took on a decidedly different focus, shifting from the historical recreation of a Midwest Williamsburg to transforming the site into a missionary tool. Restoration secretary Rowena Miller summarized the change: "The restoration was administered as an historical project, as outlined in the Articles of Incorporation, and the purpose for which the corporation was set up. With two non-members on the Board of Trustees, the corporation had a standing in the nation as an historical restoration project. . . . After the death of President David O. McKay, who had supported the corporation in all of its activities, there were some in the officialdom of the Church who did not believe in the historical approach of the restoration."[84]

McKay's immediate successors, Joseph Fielding Smith and Harold B. Lee, were among those with different views on Nauvoo Restoration's mission. As early as 1964, T. Edgar Lyon, historical consultant to the project, sensed a possible shift. "The road ahead does not look too cheery—some opposition is arising within the Church."[85] In particular, Lyon later recalled President Smith's concern—"This isn't missionary work. This is just entertaining the gentiles."[86] Lyon likewise reported President Lee's reaction: "The money that's going in back there can better be spent for helping the Church in lands where they need schools and where we can make more converts as a result of it. We can do greater missionary work there than we can back [in Nauvoo]."[87] Early guide and later Church historic sites researcher Don Enders summarized the shift in emphasis. "The Church could restore one house in Nauvoo, or pay for five full-time seminary teachers in Central America with the same amount of money."[88] These statements reflect larger trends within the Latter-day Saint Church at the time. Following decades of little growth in the Southern Hemisphere, the faith was exploding across Latin America, creating greater opportunities but straining limited resources. Additionally, Church leaders in Salt Lake City, headed by President Harold B. Lee, sought to centralize and standardize the faith's many endeavors, implementing a program called priesthood correlation. Eventually, these trends of centralized control and worldwide growth reached Nauvoo, causing significant organizational change for the restoration project.

On May 13, 1971, the Board of Trustees of Nauvoo Restoration was reorganized. While Kimball was retained, Fabian, Kendrew, Reiser, Kennedy, and Marriott were moved into advisory positions. Bringing a measure of centralization and greater Church control to the organization, Elders Mark E. Petersen and Delbert L. Stapley of the Quorum of the Twelve Apostles assumed positions on the board itself.[89] Outgoing board members sensed the change in focus for Nauvoo Restoration that would result. In his benedictory remarks, Kendrew cautioned the new board "to be very careful about [a] missionary emphasis which may offend more people than you attract," calling it "a great mistake if [the Church] lured people here on the basis of a historic site and then took the opportunity for excessive proselyting."[90] For his part, Fabian continued to champion Nauvoo's connections to the American past, emphasizing that "Nauvoo was a great story, a great American story, that of an historic movement with its origins in the religious."[91]

Transforming the restoration into a proselytizing program corresponded with the Church's biggest Nauvoo project of the era, the erection of a two-story, twenty-four-thousand-square-foot visitors' center completed in 1971. Ground for the project was broken in 1969 when, under the Church administration of

President David O. McKay, the Nauvoo project and Nauvoo Restoration were at their historical and archaeological pinnacles. Illinois's governor supplied an enthusiastic endorsement of the building. In addition, the director of the National Park Service personally attended the groundbreaking event. Church and board luminaries participated in the program, which included remarks from Harold Fabian, board vice president; David M. Kennedy, trustee and U.S. Secretary of Treasury; George W. Romney, U.S. Secretary of Housing and Urban Development; Belle S. Spafford, president of the National Council of Women and Church General Relief Society president; George B. Hartzog Jr., director of the National Park Service; Neal A. Maxwell, executive vice president of the University of Utah; and Hugh B. Brown, counselor in the First Presidency, with prayers by Harold B. Lee and Delbert L. Stapley, members of the Church's Quorum of Twelve Apostles.[92]

Though many of the same participants gathered for the building's dedication two years later, a marked shift toward greater Church control over Nauvoo's restoration had occurred. Four thousand people in attendance heard an

FIGURE 14. Church and government officials participating in the groundbreaking of the LDS Visitors' Center, May 24, 1969. Holding shovels (left to right) are Steven T. Baird, Harold B. Lee, Hugh B. Brown, A. Edwin Kendrew, A. Hamer Reiser, George B. Hartzog, David M. Kennedy, and an unknown individual. Nauvoo Restoration Incorporated historical files. Church History Library, The Church of Jesus Christ of Latter-day Saints, Salt Lake City.

address by new NRI board member, Elder Delbert L. Stapley of the Quorum of Twelve Apostles, and listened as First Presidency member N. Elder Tanner dedicated the building. The LDS *Church News* covering the event highlighted a newly formed Nauvoo Mission, signaling a major step forward toward formal proselytizing efforts for the project.[93] Though senior couples had served in Nauvoo for years, they did so under the personal invitation and direction of Dr. Kimball. While Kimball also served as the first president of the mission, calls were now processed through official Church channels in Salt Lake City. Additionally, young elders from nearby missions were transferred to Nauvoo for the busy summer seasons to complete their service. The project was clearly turning more religious.

The message of the missionaries was also revised, with greater emphasis placed on Joseph Smith and his role in the founding of the movement. Kimball explained to his missionaries, "You could explain the fact that Brigham Young was probably America's Greatest Colonizer. But as you do that, I would have the guide explain that it was Joseph Smith's idea in the first place to come to the west. I would call attention to the fact that when he was in Montrose, Iowa, he told about the saints becoming a mighty people in the midst of the Rocky Mountains." Stressing the differences between the various factions of Mormonism, Kimball continued, "I think it is very important that we emphasize the Prophet's prediction that the saints would go to the Rocky Mountains in view of the fact that the Reorganites make the claim that he did not. This pins the label of authenticity upon the Utah Church, and lets them know that Joseph Smith intended the saints to go there."[94] Understandably, emphasizing differences between the faiths in Nauvoo led to friction between them.

In addition to focusing on Joseph Smith's role in envisioning Mormonism's westward movement, Latter-day Saint officials also increased emphasis on his Nauvoo teachings. "I would, especially here at Nauvoo, emphasize the fact that Joseph Smith was the original temple builder and that Brigham Young and his associates merely carried on the program that Joseph Smith started as a temple builder," Kimball wrote to his missionary couples. "And then I would call attention to the fact that the Utah Church has continued this program." These messages, however, opened conflict with the Reorganized Church, as temple theology and westward resettlement had long been points of contention between the denominations.

Kimball summarized the shift from history to proselytizing: "You are still telling the story in terms of history, but at the same time you are satisfying the desire of the brethren to preach the Gospel."[95] Speaking to a *Church News* reporter, Dr. Kimball emphasized his understanding of and support for this new focus: "Every move in the restoration [of Nauvoo] has been done with proselyting in mind."[96] This seems to be a stark shift from Kimball's earlier views. While he always acknowledged a religious component in the project, he appears to have received and acted on the message that Nauvoo Restoration was to be more than merely a celebration of the Mormon role in American westward expansion.

Kimball's instructions to his missionaries reflect the emphasis he placed on proselyting. To one missionary couple, Kimball wrote, "If you will put it all in a historical setting and yet tell it as history but tell it also as the principles of the Gospel, you will get the idea over to the people and they will understand it. It will not be like throwing 'preaching' at them, but at the same time they will understand the message." Explaining the rationale, Kimball continued, "In this respect, you are still telling the story in terms of history, but at the same time you are satisfying the desire of the brethren to preach the Gosple [*sic*]. Keep in mind that there are many ways to approach the history of Nauvoo, but this gives you some idea of the great missionary tool that each home or shop really has!"[97]

Balancing his original historical approach with an increased emphasis on religion required great care by Kimball. His son, James, later recalled, "Over the years dad cultivated friendships with various Nauvoo merchants and town leaders keeping them informed about NRI activities. He felt that warming people was more important than warning them. Making friends was more important than conversion to the church for the second could result if the first were sincere. . . . Dad was well aware that many feared a big corporate takeover by the LDS church, and he did not wish to tread heavily on the toes of the townspeople. No one was to think that NRI was a western carpetbagger coming in to impose its will on the community."[98] In some ways, Kimball succeeded in his subtle approach. But when the temple was rebuilt at the end of the twentieth century, the underlying accusations against a wealthy, outside entity influencing local life in Nauvoo quickly resurfaced.

Some visitors appear to have responded positively to the gospel message being preached in Nauvoo. One Illinois resident wrote of having toured the city many times. Especially moved by his most recent visit, however, he praised the new emphasis: "Through the years I have read and studied extensively concerning the history of old Nauvoo. I continue to do so avidly with special interest and emphasis upon its people, their aspirations, motivations, and ultimate anguished despair and decision to move elsewhere." Touched by the story, the visitor continued, "The more I learn about these fascinating historical facts, the more impressed and involved I become. I am going to concentrate now upon Mormonism itself in order to better understand its tenets and its follow-ers' contributions to and benefits from their participation in it. I am especially impressed and intrigued with the zeal and purpose manifested so visibly by those with whom I have become acquainted."[99]

Though the change in message was difficult, results like this pleased Kim-ball, who reported to the First Presidency, "Nauvoo has met and exceeded our greatest desires as an instrument to tell the story of the Church of Jesus Christ of Latter-Day Saints." Noting that the way Nauvoo told "the American history of the westward expansion of this great country" had been "hailed as an unsurpassed eyewitness example" and that "the authenticity of the restora-tion work has been compared to that of Colonial Williamsburg for its impact and quality," Dr. Kimball nevertheless concluded, "Proud as we are of these accomplishments, we are even more excited at the prospect of the number of people that are touched not only with history and the physical restoration, but also with the spiritual restoration of the gospel."[100]

## Capitalizing on National Trends

The change toward using Nauvoo for missionary purposes rather than to cel-ebrate American westward expansion did not go unnoticed, however. A writer for the *Chicago Tribune* summarized his visit to Nauvoo, and specifically his experience in the visitors' centers itself. "Subject matter is about 50 percent history and 50 percent religion. The Mormons are active recruiters, as most Chicago householders know from the periodic visits of the polite, well-dressed young men from Utah. There is no pressure of any kind in the center tour, but you will come out knowing a lot about Joseph Smith and the principles of the religion he founded."[101]

The emphasis on Nauvoo as the City of Joseph was no more evident than in the creation of the musical theatrical production of the same name, which was first performed for visitors in 1971.[102] The pageant's author, R. Don Oscar-son, summarized its missionary potential. "The show is designed for the non-member," Oscarson noted. "It is low key; it doesn't preach . . . yet it shows Joseph going into the grove to pray and presents all the principles of the gospel."[103] The success of the pageant, coupled with ongoing restoration efforts, increased visi-tors to Nauvoo. Attendance exploded from 154,782 visitors in 1970 to 671,065 visitors in 1981, with a spike of 855,204 visitors in 1978, the year a Relief Society Monument to Women was dedicated in the city.[104]

At the same time, the Nauvoo project coincided with a larger national trend to explore America. Stifled throughout the 1930s and 1940s by the Great

Depression and the country's involvement in World War II, family vacations became "an established summer tradition" in postwar America where cars were prevalent and the highway system ever expanding. Retreating "to home and family" following the war and bolstered by "robust consumerism," Americans enjoyed "experiences prepackaged in national parks, amusement parks, or highway landscapes," all of which fit well into master plans for Nauvoo.[105]

Furthermore, the federal government sought to spur interest in celebrating America's past, in part because of periods of "low national morale" brought about by the Great Depression of the 1930s and the Cold War of the 1960s. Passing both the 1935 National Historic Sites Act and the 1966 National Historic Preservation Act, officials hoped to use "the nation's historic sites to remedy the diminishing sense of national unity."[106] Coincidentally, both the 1930s and the 1960s were significant eras for Latter-day Saint acquisition and development in Nauvoo. As a launching point for westward American expansion, the city's restoration served both Church and national interests well.

While attendance growth mirrored tourist destinations nationally, the project remained unique because of its proselytizing potential. Attempting to capitalize on the opportunity, Nauvoo Restoration officials noted that between 60 percent and 70 percent of all visitors were non–Latter-day Saints.[107] Officials hoped that those touring Nauvoo would "be more receptive to the missionary approach when called upon at their homes."[108] Nauvoo's Restoration had become what non–Latter-day Saint board members Kendrew and Fabian had sensed, a historic site for use by the Church in advancing its mission.

During the 1960s and 1970s, Latter-day Saints undertook a massive physical takeover of Nauvoo. Through the work of its nonprofit entity, Nauvoo Restoration Incorporated, the faith acquired more than half of the city's geographical footprint. Partnering with experts in American archaeology and with state and federal agencies, they initially sought to minimize Mormonism's religious message while maximizing its connections to the national narrative of westward expansion. As the project took shape, however, the approach changed when religion became the preeminent focus. The change eventually created greater conflicts in the city, as other stakeholders including the Reorganized Church as well as local residents of other faiths envisioned a different future from the celebration of Nauvoo's past. Their responses further shaped the way Nauvoo exists today.

# CHAPTER 5

# Responding to the Restoration

## Competing Visions and Unanswered Questions

During the 1960s, restoration work by teams of historians, archaeologists, and contractors was not the only construction going on in Nauvoo. While the physical walls of restored homes, pioneer shops, and a visitors' center arose across the city, metaphorical walls between the branches of Mormonism and, at times, the local residents did as well. For the two largest branches of Mormonism, Nauvoo became a key battleground as each Church sought to accurately represent their view of the faith and its history. "Wall building," as former Reorganized Church historian Richard P. Howard described it, led the two chief proponents of the Mormon story to talk "past one another, persistently and with considerable ill will" as doctrinal and historical battles emerged over the legacy of Joseph Smith and his city.[1] The era of wall building in Nauvoo was at its strongest as the Utah Church acquired properties, restored buildings, and increased its proselytizing endeavors. While Latter-day Saint property development worried Reorganized Church leadership, they were especially concerned when the project took on missionary overtones. As these projects took shape, the Reorganized Church responded vigorously. "Anything you can do, we can do better" characterized Latter-day Saint and Reorganized Church relations in Nauvoo for several decades. Meanwhile, watching it all unfold, residents of Nauvoo unaffiliated with either faith fretted over the future of their hometown.

FIGURE 15. Lucy Mack Smith and Joseph Bates Noble House,
Nauvoo, Ill., 1933. Historic American Buildings Survey, Creator.
Retrieved from the Library of Congress, https://www.loc.gov/item/il0482/.

## Reorganized Church Responses in Nauvoo

For their part, Reorganized Church officials initially debated employing a reactionary response to the Latter-day Saint projects in Nauvoo. In 1961, Reorganized Church Apostle Donald V. Lents cautioned his First Presidency that he was "not implying we should attempt to run a competitive spending program" but rather "re-emphasizing the need of careful planning and the need for some very competent personnel for assignment in the area for representation of our philosophy."[2] He was not alone in his concerns regarding competition between the faiths. In 1963 Kenneth Stobaugh, director of the Joseph Smith Historic properties in Nauvoo, wrote the Reorganized Church Presiding Bishopric, asking if they wanted to donate to a fund for comprehensive planning by the city of Nauvoo. He informed Church officials, "The Utah Church (actually Nauvoo Restoration, Inc.) has offered to give $500.00. I do not believe we are expected to give as much. They own much more land than we do, and in the future will have more places to show." Nevertheless, Stobaugh recommended some financial commitment, "as we also have a stake in the future plans of the city."[3] Bishop Walter N. Johnson responded, voicing a desire to "make a contribution to this good cause" while acknowledging, "We certainly would not want to be in a position of competing with the Utah church."[4] For the next several decades, however, reaction and competition is what occurred in Nauvoo.

One early response by Reorganized Church officials to Latter-day Saint incursion in the city was to solidify their control over properties on the southern edge of Nauvoo's flats, opting to focus their message on the Joseph Smith family sites already in their possession. Aware that the temple lot was beyond their physical and doctrinal scope, Reorganized Church leadership leveraged Latter-day Saint interest in Nauvoo to acquire important properties near their headquarters in Independence, Missouri. Owning the only parcel of the Nauvoo Temple lot not under Latter-day Saint control, in 1962 Reorganized Church leaders negotiated an exchange of their lot for four Latter-day Saint-owned parcels near the Reorganized Church Auditorium in Independence. Summarizing his feelings for the transaction, Mark Siegfried wrote to the Reorganized Church leadership, "I understand you have made a trade with the Mormons of our lot in Nauvoo for three or four tracks they own [in Independence] which are worth more to us than the little spot they are getting. [Preston] Kimball told this friend of mine the Mormons paid $25,000 for our lot. I hope they did. All we can get out of them the better it suits me."[5]

Tensions remained high in 1968 when rumors circulated that Nauvoo Restoration Inc. was conducting a survey of property along Highway 96, Nauvoo's main thoroughfare, with designs to purchase any available lots. The plans reopened wounds created by earlier contests over property. "I hope we won't have something happen on the east side of the Joseph Smith Historical Center that would parallel what has happened on the west side," Reorganized Church officials warned. "The Church's failure to buy land that (according to what I have been told) was available has resulted in the Mormon challenge to our claim to be owner of the site of the original Times and Seasons building." Additionally, some feared they "could well expect a huge sign to go up there directing northbound traffic away from our property."[6] Eventually, both parties succeeded in creating a defined line separating restored properties under the control of Utah Mormons from those in possession of the Reorganized Church.

## Developing Historical Expertise

In an effort to better utilize their facilities, Reorganized Church leaders formed a Nauvoo planning commission, charging them to study Church-owned historical property and produce "a master plan regarding additional ways the property could be developed in order to expand and update this public ministry."[7] In their findings, the commission emphasized that "the historical property needs are evident. There ha[ve] been no major improvements or additions at Nauvoo for several years." Reflecting feelings of competition, the group continued, "Presently, 'Nauvoo Restoration, Inc.' operated by the Mormon Church has a commanding lead in program development for the restoration of Nauvoo. They are the largest real estate holders and have a substantial budget for development in the next 10 years." Commission members also noted the increased efforts by the State of Illinois and the Nauvoo Chamber of Commerce to attract tourists to the area, often in collaboration with Nauvoo Restoration.

In this competitive arena, the planning commission recommended a way for the Reorganized Church to carve out its own niche. "Although the development of Nauvoo has been taken over by 'Nauvoo Restoration, Inc.,'" the report advised, "the Joseph Smith Historical Center with its properties, features, and narrative can be developed to be a superior specialty in the total effort for the restoring of Nauvoo." In light of this reality, the commission recommended the Church emphasize a historical approach to its Nauvoo sites, something that could become "the RLDS specialty." "The central idea of the development program," commissioners opined, "is to make it easy for the tourist (the public) to come to the Center and view our historical evidences and hear our story." Supporting that approach, they proposed "to be competitively equal and if not too expensive be somewhat better in the presentation of our historical evidences and story narrative. A touch of excellency in all things."[8]

By way of concrete recommendations, the commission proposed appointing a head for site development, updating audiovisual and print materials, thoroughly cleaning properties including the Mississippi River shoreline, developing a main entrance off of Highway 96, erecting signs and fencing "to give the effect that the RLDS area is separate and apart from all other developments in Nauvoo," constructing a suitable Smith family memorial to replace the gravesite, developing recreational facilities east of the Nauvoo House, building a new visitors' center, and relocating the Nauvoo branch building to the grounds west of the Mansion House. In terms of renovation and new historic site construction, officials recommended rehabilitating the Nauvoo House, transforming the Mansion House into a home atmosphere, restoring the first post office and Sidney Rigdon home, and reconstructing Joseph Smith's Red Brick Store. With their emphasis on history, commissioners believed the "historical events" associated with the store in particular "would add substantially to the total historical evidences as to the position of the church today with the original organization and its succession in presidency."[9] The

Church's First Presidency readily signed off on the recommendations. "This is an excellent report," they wrote. "We would like to see it adopted in principle and implemented subject to the availability of funds."[10]

In developing their historical specialty, Reorganized officials focused attention on the multiple generations of Smiths (Joseph Smith Sr., Joseph Smith Jr., Joseph Smith III, and their families) who had lived in Nauvoo.[11] Emphasizing the Smith family properties, the Reorganized Church contracted with Robert T. Bray from the University of Missouri to conduct archaeological excavations of the grounds. Bray and his team excavated the Joseph Smith livery stable in 1970, the Homestead's summer kitchen and the "springhouse" where the bodies and Joseph and Hyrum Smith had been secreted in 1971, the Red Brick Store in 1972, and the well and cistern belonging to Hyrum Smith in 1974. Expanding beyond these Smith family properties, the team also dug the Theodore Turley lot in 1973 as well as the site of the original *Times and Seasons* building in 1975.[12]

While these historical examinations were ongoing, officials openly resisted deviating from the historical record. When an idea emerged to "restore" the complete Nauvoo House, Reorganized Church historian Richard P. Howard opposed the idea on the grounds that it would be "restoring a building which never existed." Similarly, when someone proposed building a *Times and Seasons* building on a lot he believed to be the wrong location, Howard countered, "My immediate concern . . . is that we do not 'establish' a house of business for historic Nauvoo which did not exist in historic Nauvoo."[13] Interestingly, while the Latter-day Saint Church increasingly turned from the historical and archaeological emphasis toward a proselytizing focus in Nauvoo, the Reorganized faith sought to ground itself in historical fact. In doing so, they coopted the work championed by some of the early participants in Nauvoo Restoration Incorporated. Kenneth E. Stobaugh, Reorganized Church historical director in Nauvoo during the era, summarized, "At the Joseph Smith Historic Center, we are called upon to find historic facts and to use them, with as little bias as possible, to answer the visitors' inquiries."[14]

## Adjusting the Message at Reorganized Church Sites

An improvement in facilities led to an upgrade in presentation as well. In earlier eras, the aim of some guides was "to spoil some Mormons' vacation."[15] Confrontational dialogues included boasts about Joseph's "only wife Emma" or declarations that the Nauvoo Temple was "the last temple ever built by direct revelation from God," direct attacks aimed at baiting Latter-day Saint visitors into confrontations over polygamy and temple theology.[16] Instructions from earlier eras included giving "greater emphasis to [the] Reorganized Church, balancing this with the historical—entertainment, anti-Mormon aspects of the tour, greater emphasis to 1844 division, succession and authority of the Reorganized Church, greater emphasis to Zionic gathering, Independence, etc., greater emphasis to our possession of [the] Inspired Version, [and making the] tour predominately a Missionary-Selling experience."[17] This confrontation, Stobaugh noted, "unfortunately . . . was not a one-way street," as "similar episodes were taking place in the LDS section of Nauvoo as well."[18] Both faiths believed that Joseph Smith had been a prophet. However, each placed different emphasis on various aspects of his life while denying others, resulting, in Stobaugh's opinion, in "neither group [portraying] him . . . as he was seen by his contemporaries."[19]

These conflicts were rooted in defensiveness. Having controlled the Mormon message in Nauvoo since the Latter-day Saint exodus, the Reorganized Church rightly viewed Mormon restoration work, together with its corresponding proselytizing, as a threat to its position. Reorganized Church Apostle Donald V. Lents wrote to his First Presidency in September 1961, recommending improvements to the Reorganized Church's guide service in Nauvoo. "We need . . . to give careful attention and consideration to the type of personnel we assign to handle the guide-work. I am not referring just to the appointee personnel, but those that you might have in mind to handle the regular guide tours." Furthermore, Lents suggested an increased visual presence in the area. "I feel . . . that we need some good advertising in the area," he recommended. "A large, well-planned bill-board (similar to that used around Independence advertising the Auditorium) would be an excellent contribution to our properties."[20]

Further worried by "the increased activity of the Mormons in the area," Lents wrote again to Reorganized Church leadership two weeks later:

> We need to be very careful when we consider these couples to represent us in this ministry. It is a real public-relation contact and one where our people need to be very kind yet firm and stable. I am not suggesting that we should begin some large 'splashy' push in Nauvoo, but should just protect that which we have available. In my estimation, we are recognized as the key contact now with the historical set-up, but we certainly need to be alert to some of the moves in the town. The couples the Mormons have sent in are cultured, well-appearing people that make a fine appearance.[21]

Eventually, Lents's observation that the Reorganized Church was "recognized at the key contact . . . with the historical set-up" carried the day. As Latter-day Saint presence grew stronger in Nauvoo, Reorganized Church officials continued to develop their historical strategy among their guides. Acknowledging "it is always a struggle to understand what a historic site ought to be," Church leaders emphasized that history would be their specialty. "The Joseph Smith Historic Center," a Church publication proclaimed, "is committed to explain the Nauvoo story against the background of Hancock County, the state of Illinois, and the nation. The Joseph Smith Historic Center also is committed to carefully catalog historic artifacts, to build a reputation of integrity and professionalism."[22] Hoping to accomplish these aims while eliminating "the apologetic curtain dividing Nauvoo," in 1973 the Reorganized Church implemented an internship program in historic interpretation emphasizing Jacksonian America and Church history.[23] Students from the Church's Graceland College worked as guides at the sites while taking courses in museum interpretation, archaeological investigation, historic restoration, craft demonstration, and comparative museum techniques.[24] Church Apostle Reed Holmes summarized the intent: "We have come to understand . . . that these historic sites must not be considered as an opportunity to have a captive audience—as an opportunity to simply do our thing in apologetics for our faith, nor to consider them primarily [as] evangelistic tools. Rather, we have come to feel that it is absolutely imperative that we provide there an authentic, genuine experience of the times, the people, and the values represented."[25]

Armed with a revamped and historically focused guide program and an interest in better preserving and developing its properties, the Reorganized Church turned its attention to a master plan for all of their historic sites, with Nauvoo at the front and center. In the mid-1970s, Dr. F. Mark McKiernan, a former history professor at Idaho State University and executive director of the faith's Restoration Trail Foundation, led a multiyear study of Church historic properties. Rooted in the belief that "no site is better than the quality of its research," properties were examined based on their historical significance, architectural importance, and accessibility to the public, with stages of development ranging from designation to preservation to full restoration.[26] The resulting report recommended full restoration for the Joseph Smith Historic Site in Nauvoo, which included restoring structures and grounds to their historic period, developing interpretive and public information programs, and providing research for supportive services such as archaeological investigations. It identified as the major objective "to develop and interpret the site in ways that will bring maximum benefits to the sponsoring institution." Secondary objectives included using the site as a tool to answer questions and for institutional advertisement. These latter emphases were important because researchers reported that more than 75 percent of visitors were not affiliated with either the Reorganized Church or the Latter-day Saints and only 8 percent were members of the Reorganized Church.[27]

The study noted several unique aspects of the Church sites in Nauvoo. While the city was not on a public transportation route, nor was it near any major metropolitan area, it attracted 250,000 visitors annually, more than the faith's Kirtland Temple and Independence Auditorium combined, both of which were located near the large American cities of Cleveland and Kansas City, respectively. Additionally, the United States government had designated the entire town of Nauvoo as a national historic landmark, the highest distinction for properties in private possession. Like others interested in the city, the report's author believed "Nauvoo, Illinois, has a potential to become one of the most significant historic restoration centers in the nation."[28]

Site development in Nauvoo was not without its challenges, however. The study noted that while a quarter-million people visited the town of Nauvoo each year, only fifty thousand were touring the Joseph Smith Historic Center. Most limited themselves to the adjacent sites controlled by Nauvoo Restoration. Additionally, with only three hotels in town servicing fewer than one hundred people, "the town of Nauvoo is not equipped to house many visitors over night." Furthermore, the report noted only "two eating places in town which provide quality meals," one of which was closed on Mondays and Tuesdays and parts of the winter while the other served only breakfast and lunch. "The fact that the majority of the visitors are same day traffic is important. It would take two full days to see all of the sites in Nauvoo," the author concluded. "Thus, there is added competition between the various sites. Only one-fifth of the visitors to Nauvoo ever tour the Joseph Smith Historic Center."[29]

While the faiths contested over visitors in Nauvoo, competition was not the intent of the report's author, a welcome development for the time. In fact, McKiernan even shared a copy with Latter-day Saint officials, who reciprocated by sharing their own master plan.[30] Nevertheless, the report was influenced by the work of the Latter-day Saints and Nauvoo Restoration. It made repeated reference to the neighboring project, "the major restoration force in Nauvoo because of its massive funding." For example, assessing the Bidamon stable that had been remodeled to serve as a Reorganized Church visitors' center in the 1950s, McKiernan observed, "The nature of the structure does not compare well with the NRI Visitors Center down the street, which happens to be a 1.5 million dollar visitors center modeled after Williamsburg. Studies indicate that nearly 50% of the visitors who stop in the parking lot at the Joseph Smith Historic Center do not go in. This is an appalling loss. . . . By contrast the same study indicates that nearly all of those who stopped at the Nauvoo Restoration,

Inc., Information Center entered it. At the time of this study (1973) twice as many people visited the NRI Center as the Joseph Smith Information Center."[31] While examining potential land purchase, the study also tersely noted, "The acquisition of a few spots to make its land contiguous would be advisable if the opportunity arises at a reasonable rate. However, due to the fact that most of the Joseph Smith Historic Center is side by side with the Nauvoo Restoration, Inc., the land boundaries at Nauvoo have been set for most purposes."[32]

## Improving Reorganized Church Properties

In the face of these realities, the Reorganized Church's Nauvoo Master Plan put forward an ambitious agenda. As an initial thrust, it emphasized two major areas of focus. First, "to have credibility as a historic site," numerous changes were recommended to the buildings and surrounding property. In the Joseph Smith Homestead, "serious restoration problems" needed correcting, including fixing inaccuracies like the placement of a fireplace and the presence of nonperiod windows, wall coverings, and furnishings.[33] Similar changes were proposed to the Mansion House, Nauvoo House, Sidney Rigdon House, and other area properties, totaling nearly $50,000. In all changes and especially in any new construction, McKiernan and his team emphasized "that the policy of requiring some evidence, either historical or archaeological" be followed.[34] The second area of emphasis was the building of a new visitors' center. In his study, McKiernan forwarded several options, including reconstructing either Joseph Smith's Red Brick Store or his stable and adding therein adequate visitor facilities or erecting a new modern visitors' center. Later stages of development included reconstructing the building where the bodies of Joseph and Hyrum Smith were secreted as well as the hotel wing to the Mansion House. "The hotel wing is a vital part of the building and should be restored if the Mansion House is to be a true biographical museum," McKiernan argued. "It was very much a part of the story of Joseph Smith, Jr."[35] Altogether, the master plan called for more than a million dollars' worth of work on the Reorganized Church's Nauvoo properties.[36]

In McKiernan's analysis, one project in particular received special attention. Lobbying specifically for the Red Brick Store's reconstruction, McKiernan appended a letter to the master plan, explaining his rationale. "The Red Brick Store was an extremely significant building during the lifetime of Joseph Smith. It contained his office and was the location of the founding of the Women's Relief Society. It also was a location for the blessing of Joseph Smith III by his father as his successor." Additionally, McKiernan emphasized the historical knowledge available about the building. "The University of Missouri archaeological investigation team, which was supervised by Robert T. Bray, made a very important dig at the Red Brick Store. It is the most complete of all the Nauvoo digs and would be most helpful in a reconstruction. Material which would be on exhibit in the store if it were restored is listed in Joseph Smith's Day Book and we have a copy of that." He concluded, "In short, the building could be rebuilt and probably be the outstanding reconstruction/restoration in Nauvoo."[37]

The new master plan led to a boom in Reorganized Church building at its historic sites in Nauvoo, rivaling Latter-day Saint building of the era. Using nineteenth-century tools and methods as much as possible, the Church finished

FIGURE 16. Joseph Smith's Red Brick Store (reconstructed). Photograph by Richard Crookston. Used by permission.

work on the Homestead summer kitchen it had begun in 1973–74. However, this was merely a prelude to two much larger projects. The most visible was its own new half-million-dollar visitors' center, designed as a place where guests could have "a positive experience in a setting of peace and beauty, by preserving and interpreting Latter Day Saint heritage, inviting further exploration."[38] Dedicated on May 3, 1980, it responded to and mirrored the larger Latter-day Saint structure with theaters, a museum area, gallery, restrooms, offices, and small gift shop.

Built at the same time as its visitors' center, the most prominent Reorganized structure reconstructed was Joseph Smith's Red Brick Store, a sesquicentennial gift to the Church by approximately fifteen families donating up to $30,000 each. Meticulously "constructed with as much historical accuracy as is possible,"[39] the building matched the historical emphasis evident in other Reorganized Church projects. Its store included reproductions of items sold in Joseph Smith's time, based on his day book. Interior walls were reproduced in a rich red color, the basis for the building's name, a fact discovered from analysis of original plaster.[40] Church officials emphasized the building's economic, political, social, and ecclesiastical significance, as it was indeed the hub for "almost every major activity in the life of Nauvoo."[41] Ironically, however, though mentioning it as the site for the founding of the women's Relief Society, project plans made no mention of the building's role as site for the first temple endowment, a fact important to Latter-day Saint Church interpretation. Instead, planners repeatedly highlighted it as the site where "the blessing of Joseph Smith III took place . . . under the hands of Joseph Smith, Jr. and Hyrum Smith," establishing "him as successor to the President of the Church."[42] In the words of Reorganized Church planners and Nauvoo scholars, this "one towering incident" made the Red Brick Store "the venue in which to communicate this fundamental tenet of the RLDS faith."[43]

## An Internal Debate over the Message at Historic Sites

As the Red Brick Store project moved forward, a debate within the Reorganized Church over its potential uses ensued. Enamored of the site's proselyting possibilities, Church president W. Wallace Smith saw an opportunity to use the building to emphasize differences between the strains of Mormonism. As early as 1964, he openly admitted his desire to reconstruct his grandfather Joseph Smith's store. "We would like to get into the record," Smith wrote on behalf of his First Presidency, "the fact that we are interested in doing something towards the restoring of the brick store building at Nauvoo, looking towards placing a sign upon it which would indicate it as being the place where my father was designated as the future leader of the church."[44] A decade later, Smith's son and successor as Church president, Wallace B. Smith, likewise emphasized the site's evangelical possibilities as he invited wealthy donors to contribute to the project.

> The Red Brick Store played a significant part in the history of the church during the Nauvoo period. . . . One of the many significant events which took place in that upstairs office was the blessing of Joseph III as successor to his father in the prophetic office of the church. It is my conviction that the restoration of the Red Brick Store could provide the Reorganized Church with an important instrument for the telling of our story. The continuation of the gospel and the faith which survived the disruption in Nauvoo is an important aspect of the Reorganization and needs to be presented in the most meaningful way possible.[45]

In forwarding the project, Smith may have been considering multiple audiences, both within his own faith and beyond, in his own form of evangelism. The tone of the statement also reflects a desire to legitimize the Reorganized Church in reaction to the significant growth, in Nauvoo and around the world, of the Latter-day Saint faith.

The Smith family leadership of the Reorganized Church was not alone in seeing the site as a place for competition with its rival denomination. From the faith's Utah missionary district, John W. Bradley recommended to the Nauvoo Planning Commission an idea he believed "would be concurred in by every thoughtful church man who has ever worked in Utah." In a reconstructed Red Brick Store, Bradley proposed informational plaques discussing the original Church high council, a point of some discrepancy because of the Utah-based Church's emphasis on the Council of the Twelve Apostles as a leadership body. The information, coupled with comments by the guides, could "raise a very serious question in the minds of visiting Mormons, concerning the actions of Brigham Young following the death of Joseph Smith." Bradley hoped that this approach at a reconstructed Red Brick Store "could result eventually in the conversion of substantial numbers of Mormons."[46] In the project, Church officials saw the potential to combine their "rich heritage" with their "witnessing commission."[47]

Others wedded to the Church's historical emphasis for its sites bristled at these recommendations. In particular, Richard Howard, Reorganized Church historian, vocalized his concern and, in doing so, reflected shifting viewpoints within the faith. Learning of the plan to create "a life-size diorama in the upper office of the store, depicting the event in which Joseph Smith, Jr. and Hyrum

Smith designated Joseph Smith III to be the successor in office to the founding prophet," Howard expressed his "serious objections." This issue of successorship, and especially whether it should flow to Brigham Young as president of the Council of Twelve Apostles or Joseph Smith III as the oldest surviving son of Joseph Smith, had been one of the longest and strongest matters dividing the various branches of Mormonism. Wrestling with his feelings for several months, Howard finally wrote to Reorganized Church Apostle Paul Booth. "My concern," Howard told Booth, "is that such a course is very likely to project the image of a church so insecure about its right to exist, and so afraid of our larger Mormon competitors, that we will spend $360,000 to set up a scene designed to settle the succession question once for all."[48]

Among the "probable consequences of restoring the Red Brick Store at Nauvoo with the major aim of using it to settle the succession issue," Howard expressed concern over "a stream of minor and major disputes between LDS and RLDS people over the meaning of the Red Brick Store for Latter Day Saint history." Possibilities included instructions regarding baptism for the dead, plural marriage, sealing ordinances, and the meetings of the Council of Fifty, all of which were associated with the space and are "beliefs ... with varying intensity, close to Mormon hearts." Indeed, "what the Mormons might try to document boggles my RLDS imagination," Howard warned. Additionally, he expressed fear over "RLDS embarrassment when Mormon and secular scholars begin to publish data designed to cast doubt on the facticity of the setting apart ceremonies, not only at the store, but in other locations." Furthermore, he worried "the LDS Church will intensify its efforts to authenticate the Twelve-in-succession theory ... or [they] may simply patronize us with either total or near total neglect of the issue we are trying to raise. In either case all of our fuss over succession at an historic site will appear to the uninterested or uncommitted casual visitor to be merely a humorous, pathetic case of over-kill." In summary, Howard worried "that a dioramic setting apart scene created for the viewing of every Mormon visitor, will renew and intensify the fading century of bickering between the two churches on the question of succession." Accordingly, Howard called for "a much wider consultation over just what are our priorities and concerns at historic sites."[49]

Two months later, Howard got his wish. In November 1978 the Commission on History for the Reorganized Church took up his concerns. Before the body, Howard lobbied that "thus far the RLDS Church has yet to develop a clear image of Joseph Smith in Nauvoo at work—confronting the day-to-day issues and problems in both a secular and religious sense." In order "to appreciate the breadth and range of the total impact of Joseph Smith, Jr. on the life of Nauvoo and its environs," people need "to see him in all of his various pursuits of vocation, avocation, and interest." Emphasizing the blessing of Joseph Smith III, in Howard's opinion, would rob the faith of the opportunity to fully develop these other aspects of Joseph Smith's life because it could "unnecessarily and perhaps unwisely raise a contentious issue with Mormon visitors: the issue of prophetic succession," one that Howard believed "both churches have long ago settled." Additionally, "many aspects of the uses of the Red Brick Store in Nauvoo have minimal value to RLDS theology, polity, and history, as those uses were more nearly related to Utah Mormonism—developing as the natural extension of the Nauvoo Mormonism of 1842–1844." Calling for an interpretive program "fashioned with great deliberation and care, and, with keen awareness of the potentially divisive nuances implicit in the Nauvoo story," Howard hoped the site could "sensitize our own people to the history of Nauvoo in a most authentic way," delivering them from "disillusionment over Nauvoo, over the image of Joseph Smith, Jr. as a fallen prophet, and over the failure of the church to exemplify the earlier ideals of the Restoration movement." Additionally, he desired that the project could cease "denial of all the less-than-pleasing historical events and developments of Nauvoo, and assigning them to the later, Salt Lake City phase." In doing so, the Red Brick Store could "be instrumental in helping the RLDS membership come to a new appreciation for Nauvoo as that critically important chapter of church history that ushered in a 'sifting time.'" It might "encourage Latter Day Saints to develop the capacity to *embrace* their history."[50]

Howard and those of like mind carried the day, turning the course of Reorganized Church thought and practice for decades. Championing Howard's argument, the Commission on History made the following recommendation to Reorganized Church leadership: "An historic site restoration should not be conceived as an instrument for the advancement of any doctrine or parochial policy." Insinuating a broader, expansive vision for the faith, commissioners accentuated their position: "Any extraordinary emphasis upon the doctrine of prophetic succession in the Red Brick Store would be inconsistent with the present philosophy and practice of the church's Nauvoo interpretation programs."[51] The First Presidency responded, acknowledging "the development of ministerial resources of all kinds which are true to our historic situation and responsive to our contemporary needs and opportunities."[52] The decision was made that historic accuracy, coupled with the future of the faith, would trump proselytizing potential for historic sites in Nauvoo.

During the back-and-forth over the purpose of Church historic sites, Howard posed a provocative question to his own Church leadership: "Do we really want to revive and continue our historic warfare along the Mormon Boundary in the face of the bold, imaginative, servanthood ministries to which the Lord has called the church in recent years?" Answering his own question, Howard continued. "At the Joint Council Seminar on Church History in 1967 the conviction grew that the time had arrived for the RLDS Church to intentionally fashion its own boundaries of identity. No longer did we need to live within and against, and define ourselves in terms of, the Mormon Boundary ... I affirm," Howard contested, "that the RLDS Church does have a uniquely meaningful, beautiful witness to bear to the world of the redemption purpose of God running throughout human history."[53]

These discussions within Reorganized Church leadership over the rebuilding of the Red Brick Store presage the trajectory the faith followed in the ensuing decades, going so far as to even formally change their name to Community of Christ in 2001. Pivoting from an emphasis on the historical and theological differences that separated them from their Mormon counterparts, the faith sought instead to be a "'missional church' based in the life of Christ." In the assessment of former Church historian Mark A. Scherer, who witnessed the shift, "Restorationist positivism, expressed in incontestable claims to 'the only true church,' has been replaced by a theological ecumenism that values all religions to be of inestimable worth." As a result, while the faith's "search for community is an important tie with the institution's past, ... the Nauvoo of Joseph Smith does not model the community sought by the church's leadership and its members."[54]

## Cooperation Rather than Competition

The shift away from the Mormon boundary highlighted by the reconstruction of Joseph Smith's Red Brick Store and the internal debates about how it would be utilized marked a dramatic relationship change between the restoration efforts of the Reorganized Church of Jesus Christ and those of The Church of Jesus Christ of Latter-day Saints in Nauvoo. Ultimately, the removal of metaphorical boundaries between the branches of Mormonism in Nauvoo allowed for cooperation over the physical boundaries between their historic sites.

One area of boundary restructuring involved the location of the Reorganized Church meetinghouse, situated squarely in the heart of Latter-day Saint restoration projects in Nauvoo. As early as 1964, Church president W. Wallace Smith recognized that the state of its repair, and ultimately its location, needed to be addressed. "We are . . . interested in giving further consideration to the possibility of a new chapel in Nauvoo which would be representative of our movement as we have increasing numbers of people come there to visit," Smith wrote.[55] The failings of the old building were exacerbated by the property acquisitions of Nauvoo Restoration Incorporated later in the decade, as the organization purchased all of the lots surrounding the Reorganized Church meetinghouse, making it an island in a sea of Latter-day Saint holdings. By 1968, Reorganized Church bishop Walter N. Johnson floated the idea to construct a Nauvoo branch building on the site of the faith's historical properties, acknowledging that "the only prospective purchaser" for the old building "would be the Mormons."[56]

Though talked about, the transaction between the two faiths was slow to come to fruition. In the late 1970s the Reorganized Church Presiding Bishopric formulated a plan. "We are interested in proposing a trade of property owned by our church in Nauvoo for property owned by the Mormon church in both Nauvoo and on the Temple Lot in Independence, Missouri," wrote F. E. Hansen in 1978.

> Specifically, we are interested in trading the property owned by our church which is comprised of a cemetery and a block of land in Nauvoo, bounded by the streets of Sidney on the south, Parley on the north, Bain on the west, and Granger on the east, for the two blocks of vacant property owned in Nauvoo by the Mormon church, bounded by the highway on the east, Parley Street on the north, Hyde Street on the west, and Sidney Street on the south, together with two lots on the Temple Lot in Independence, Missouri, which are owned by the Mormon church are identified as Lots 7 and 8, both of which front on to West Lexington Street.[57]

The transaction would relocate the Reorganized Church meetinghouse squarely within its historical properties in Nauvoo, create a clean property line between the two organizations, and clear the way for future construction of the Reorganized Church temple in Independence, Missouri.

Over the next several years, modifications to the proposed transaction occurred. By 1981, different lines were being considered in Nauvoo, with efforts being made by the Reorganized Church to acquire a northern buffer for their new visitors' center in the city and as many as four lots on the temple lot in Independence, in exchange for the old Church building and the Nauvoo pioneer cemetery. Though the transactions were not finalized for several more years, the deal eventually paved the way for the construction of the Reorganized Church's Nauvoo branch building in 1988 and the beautification of the Nauvoo Pioneer Burial Ground by the Latter-day Saints in 1989. Through cooperation, clearer distinctions were drawn between the competing restoration projects.

As the various parties in Nauvoo felt their way through the city's future during the last decades of the twentieth century, it appeared that the conflicts were drawing to a close. By the end of the century, Mormon Nauvoo's two major stakeholders had clearly established their positions regarding the city's historical interpretation. At the 1989 renovation of the Carthage Jail complex and the dedication of the Old Nauvoo Burial Grounds, the Stoddard Home and Tinsmith Shop, the Riser Boot and Shoemaker Shop, and a public barn adjacent to the Jonathan Browning Home, Latter-day Saint officials announced the cessation of restoration projects in the city. Focus turned toward creating an "impressionistic view" of nineteenth-century life in Nauvoo.[58] "With the homes and shops the Church has restored over the years, plus the visitors center at Nauvoo and Carthage," Nauvoo Restoration president Loren C. Dunn declared, "there is enough of a flavor of the old city there now to give people a good idea of how it was." While Nauvoo Restoration would continue to function, its role would shift to "an operations and maintenance mode, rather than one of construction."[59] For its part, the Reorganized Church of Jesus Christ of Latter Day Saints wrapped up the era having adopted the original Nauvoo Restoration model. Specializing in historical accuracy, it emphasized Nauvoo's Smith family legacy in restored and reconstructed buildings aimed at connecting the Church to Nauvoo's founder and his family. At the same time, it tailored its message away from potentially confrontational topics that had long divided the branches of Mormonism.

A reduction in the polarization of Nauvoo set the stage for eventual cooperation. As their purposes for Nauvoo's restoration spread further apart, the Latter-day Saint and Reorganized Latter Day Saint faiths became reconciled to their proselytizing and preservation positions. By the 1990s, this allowed for mutual benefit through projects like the renovation of the Smith family cemetery and the sharing of resources in the Nauvoo Land and Records Office. Effort at goodwill and outreach eventually emerged, characterized by the message Loren Dunn delivered at the 1989 rededication of the Carthage Jail complex: "The message of the renovated Carthage complex is, we feel, one of healing and reconciliation. . . . Carthage has become more than a place of martyrdom."[60] Brochures from the era emphasize the same theme. One read, "Historic Nauvoo celebrates the accomplishments of the Latter-day Saints in establishing 'Nauvoo, the beautiful,' a place of prosperity, sacrifice, and religious refuge. It also speaks of the harmony and peace in which today's Latter-day Saints live with their neighbors."[61]

The Reorganized Church's reactionary response to Utah Mormonism's restoration project in Nauvoo, followed by an eventual resolution of the conflict, reveals the philosophical tensions that engulfed the faith during the second half of the twentieth century. Initially, leaders dug in their heels, responding with a building-for-building construction contest that drained Church coffers but seemed to produce little measurable benefit. With time, officials developing Nauvoo's historical sites convinced senior leadership within the Reorganized Church to approach both their work in Nauvoo and their interactions with others differently. Historical accuracy, devoid of denominational interpretation and strife, replaced defensiveness, bringing in its wake an era of acceptance and cooperation. Bill Russell, a scholar of the two faiths, aptly labeled the relationship that emerged between prairie and mountain Mormonism as "clearer differences, closer friends," the result of their overlapping interest and proximity in restored Nauvoo.[62]

## Residents of Nauvoo React to the Restorations

Though the two branches of Mormonism achieved a measure of reconciliation in Nauvoo by the late 1980s, they were not the only groups reevaluating their place in the city as a result of the restoration explosion. Long-time residents of the city unaffiliated with either faith expressed frustration over the lack of transparency and local involvement that had overtaken their hometown. In 1970, Elmer Kraus, area businessman and president of the Nauvoo Chamber of Commerce, remarked, "We are not a part of the big plan. Never was the community invited to share in their plans. . . . To date . . . the community has not been shown the Mormon's master plan for Nauvoo. And in back of it all they keep saying 'Look what we are doing for you.' But I'm afraid," Kraus continued, "that they are just doing it for themselves." He confessed he "was happy to see the restoration of these old homes" and that "the Midwest is fortunate that this is being done on a quality basis. They are doing a splendid job." However, Kraus nevertheless concluded, "I think we should try to help and still keep our identity. But no one likes to be pushed around, or ignored."[63] Nauvoo resident James W. Moffitt expressed similar concern regarding the marginalization of local interests: "I don't see any reason why Nauvoo can't maintain some of its own identity, along with something this massive. Nauvoo has a lot of history besides just the Mormon history. The Indian lore, the Icarians, the wine industry, the cheese industry—I mean, it's full of history. And I like to hope it can maintain its own identity along with the Mormons."[64]

Influential residents went so far as to act on their desire to celebrate Nauvoo's diverse history with a production of their own, the Grape Festival pageant, regularly performed at a Labor Day weekend festival in the city since the 1930s. Also known as the wedding of the wine and the cheese after two important industries in the community, the spectacle begins with the story of early Native American settlements in the region, followed by the Catholic, Icarian, and German settlings of western Illinois. Originally run by a local group called the Unity Club, the pageant is now performed biennially by the Nauvoo Historical Society. While the Mormon story is included because, as one official noted, "history doesn't change," the emphasis on Nauvoo's past does change from year to year depending on the theme of the event. Significantly, leaders emphasize two hundred years of Nauvoo's past rather than a single decade from the mid-nineteenth century.[65] Performed at the end of the regular tourist season, the pageant seems to mark a symbolic reclaiming of the city by the local community following the bustling summer crowds interested primarily in Nauvoo's Mormon past.

In spite of efforts like the Grape Festival pageant to celebrate their past, Nauvoo residents were forced to mourn the loss of physical reminders of their diverse story. For example, sentimental feelings for history that was other than Mormon were evident in the razing of the Catholic parish hall in 1964. Taken down to clear the temple lot property, the local newspaper reminisced about the building's place in Nauvoo's social life, including its use for athletic contests, banquets, pageants, blood drives, band concerts, graduation exercises, community celebrations, and funeral services. "The words, 'To be held in the Parish hall,' became a very familiar phrase," the author noted. "[It] had a colorful existence. . . . As the poet said, 'You may break, you may shatter the vase as you will, but the scent of the rose clings 'round it still.'"[66] Similar sentiments repeatedly surfaced across town as non-Mormon sites were cleared to make way for renovation or reconstruction of earlier 1840's-era Mormon structures.

Many of these tensions stemmed from the lack of information regarding plans by The Church of Jesus Christ of Latter-day Saints. Early on, officials had "deemed [it] wise to limit publicity given out until after the property acquisition phase of the project [was] more nearly complete."[67] However, the lack of information bred concern among the local population. This frustration was reflected in the town's 1970 "Contemporary Planning in Nauvoo, Illinois" report, which focused on zoning and future development within the city. "One significant problem that plagued the planning program from its inception," the study noted, "was the reluctance of Nauvoo Restoration, Inc. to freely discuss its plans for the Mormon holdings (the area comprising one-half of the corporate limits). . . . Reports in nationally circulated publications, however, have stated that Nauvoo Restoration planned to develop motels, restaurants and other facilities for tourists. This naturally concerned local influentials who also have plans relative to facilities that would provide services needed by tourists that would be attracted to the area."[68] Nauvoo residents felt left out of their city's resurgence.

Outside observers of the restoration of Nauvoo picked up on the controversy brewing within the city. In 1970 the *St Louis Post-Dispatch* questioned, "Could the community keep its identity in the wake of the saintly steam roller?"[69] The same year, a *New York Times* article covering the project reported, "There is ample evidence that The Church of Jesus Christ of Latter-day Saints is gaining momentum in its effort to turn Nauvoo into what church leaders call 'the Williamsburg of the West.' The non-Mormon merchants and civic leaders of Nauvoo watch all this with a mixture of approval at the thought of economic gains from visitors to the restoration and some apprehension that the Mormon plans, still not specifically outlined, will direct this potential bonanza into church-owned enterprises rather than local establishment." The article reported rumors that "the corporation is planning to ring the original Mormon area with motels, a shopping center and a golf course," adding that "older residents have bridled at . . . announcements by the Utah Mormons that the church's return to Nauvoo would rejuvenate a slumbering river village." It cited businessman Elmer Kraus—"We are well aware of Nauvoo's role in the history of the Mormons. But after they left, Nauvoo had an interesting history of its own, including the reorganized Mormons, and we have managed to maintain a modest prosperity here since the Utah Mormons left. . . . There is definitely a big change around here already," Kraus optimistically continued. "We know the village will never be like it was, but we think we'll all manage to live together hopefully to everybody's advantage."[70]

Little did Kraus know, nearly thirty years after he expressed concern that his village would "never be like it was," one stunning announcement made in faraway Salt Lake City in 1999 insured it never would be. For the meantime, Nauvoo Restoration's extreme focus on the city as it existed from 1839 to 1846 brought financial benefit to some but alienated others. Each year during the summer, residents learned to coexist with thousands of tourists extremely interested in the city's past, yet all too often expressing little regard for its present or future. Common complaints centered on the lack of information regarding the restoration's plans, coupled with the frustration that the only story that seemed to matter in Nauvoo was the Mormon one. In the picking and choosing of what matters to a community by what it opts to memorialize, local residents felt like decisions were made affecting their daily lives without either their input or their consent. These concerns were exacerbated when, at the end of the twentieth century, the largest restoration project Nauvoo ever witnessed—and, ironically, one that had been long rumored but never implemented—caught everyone by surprise.

# CHAPTER 6

# The Reconstructed Nauvoo Temple

## Crown Jewel of the Restoration

Concluding his faith's general conference on Sunday, April 2, 1999, Latter-day Saint Church president Gordon B. Hinckley stunned the assembled congregation with an announcement that rocked community relationships in Nauvoo. "I feel impressed to announce that among all of the temples we are constructing, we plan to rebuild the Nauvoo Temple," Hinckley declared. Outlining how the development had come about, together with a brief overview of the Church's plans, Hinckley continued, "A member of the Church and his family have provided a very substantial contribution to make this possible. We are grateful to him. It will be a while before it happens, but the architects have begun their work. This temple will not be busy much of the time; it will be somewhat isolated. But during the summer months, we anticipate it will be very busy. And the new building will stand as a memorial to those who built the first such structure there on the banks of the Mississippi."[1]

## Community Reaction to the Temple Announcement

Response among stakeholders in Nauvoo was swift. Watching the conference via satellite feed, Latter-day Saint Church members assembled in the city reacted audibly to the news. "There was a moment of shock, and then there was actually some applause," reported Durrell N. Nelson, Nauvoo stake president, the Latter-day Saint ecclesiastical head in the region. "Then everyone caught themselves quickly, and for most of the rest of the meeting there was crying."[2] He added, "We were not able to completely contain ourselves."[3] Speaking of the interest even among local news reporters covering the announcement, Nelson continued, "One lady from a news station, as she left, said, 'I think I'm as excited as you people.'"[4]

Though Nelson said he did not anticipate community opposition to the reconstruction of the temple, response was varied. By 1999, Latter-day Saint Church membership made up approximately 10 percent of Nauvoo's population of 1,227, and the faith itself owned much of the city, primarily in the Nauvoo Historic District.[5] From a religious standpoint, Colleen Ralson, a former Latter-day Saint turned Baptist who operated the Nauvoo Christian Visitors Center, was surprisingly optimistic about the announcement. "I'll just have more opportunity to witness to the Lord. This place will be like a Mecca for Mormons."[6] From an economic perspective, business owners hoped for a boom from what the *Chicago Tribune* expected would be one million visitors a year.[7] "It will be great for business," remarked bookstore owner Estel G. Neff, expressing optimism that those visiting the temple during Nauvoo's slower winter months "would help even things out during the year."[8] Real estate agent Wayne Marting noted an immediate uptick in interest in property. "We're getting a lot of calls already. I'm not Mormon, but I'm excited by the temple." As a father of school-age children, Marting also expressed a desire that the project would bring an influx of young families.[9]

Tom Wilson, Nauvoo's mayor, was more cautious. Realistically, he resigned himself to the reality. "You've got to have some kind of industry, and [religious tourism is] our industry. If [the Mormons] hadn't come back, we might be like a lot of other Midwestern towns—dried up."[10] However, "we want to keep our small-town atmosphere—kind of laid back," Wilson wished.[11] City clerk Carol McGhghy echoed the worry: "We here at City Hall knew nothing about it. It's kind of a mixed emotion around here. Of course, if you're a member of the church you're ecstatic. A lot of people, though, want Nauvoo just the way it is."[12]

While President Hinckley's announcement caught many by surprise, the temple site itself was actually a decade-long issue of focus for those leading Nauvoo Restoration. Early in the 1990s, negotiations ensued between the Latter-day Saint Church and the State of Illinois to transfer an original Nauvoo Temple sunstone, long located in the local state park, to a safer, climate-controlled location on the temple grounds. Later, significant revision was made to Nauvoo site presentations used for guest tours, especially of the temple lot, to "bring the physical settings and their interpretation up to the spiritual level of the central message."[13] Philosophically, restoration leaders rationalized, "In all the structures, sites and holdings of NRI, we have nothing that was owned, or lived in by the Prophet [Joseph Smith]. All of those sites belong to the RLDS." Shifting attention to the temple lot, Latter-day Saint officials continued, "However, the real focus and purpose of Nauvoo is found in the Temple thru the fullness of the gospel and the ordinances as provided in the Temple. It would seem to us that the Temple Site should in reality be the main focal point of all the restored work in Nauvoo, for it represents the greatest degree of sacrifice by the Saints and was certainly the central purpose of Nauvoo. Everything done in Nauvoo was to build the Temple in order to restore these sacred ordinances of salvation and exaltation." Officials lamented the fact that, in spite of an emphasis on the temple, the lot itself needed significant work. "Currently the Temple Site

FIGURE 17. Nauvoo Temple Lot prior to the reconstruction of the temple. A Nauvoo sunstone is featured in the left of the photograph, with a model of the temple at the center and the iconic Nauvoo city water tower in the background. Nauvoo Restoration Incorporated historical files. Church History Library, The Church of Jesus Christ of Latter-day Saints, Salt Lake City.

is probably in the poorest condition of any of our sites in Nauvoo. . . . The site needs to be totally renovated and restored so that it becomes a fitting memorial to the prophet and the principles and ordinances that were restored thru him."[14] Of course, the Church took the plan to beautify the Nauvoo Temple grounds one giant step further, authorizing much more than a renewal of the Nauvoo Temple site by announcing the building's reconstruction.

Reconstruction of the temple was also in line with a change in the focus of Nauvoo for the Church. Recognizing limitations with using historic Nauvoo as a proselytizing tool, especially because of the high concentration of members visiting the city, officials increasingly considered the potential Nauvoo presented for those already in the faith. In doing so, leaders reflected an aspect of what was termed, at the time, the "threefold mission of the church," one prong of which included "perfecting the Saints."[15] From this perspective, reconstructing the temple, with its corresponding rites of worship for faithful members, fit well, for only faithful Latter-day Saint members would be able to enter the building once it was completed and dedicated.

Writing of the restoration's various purposes, including its potential for individuals who were already members of the Church, Nauvoo Restoration Incorporated president H. Burke Peterson remarked in 1993, "As an Area Presidency and as the Officers and members of the Board of Directors of NRI, we have been instructed very clearly that, different from other visitors centers, the visitors center at Nauvoo is not seen as, nor should it be set up as a visitors center the primary purpose of which is to generate referrals and provide proselyting opportunities. In fact, the First Presidency has reminded us of the sacred nature of the entire Nauvoo Restoration project." Clarifying that purpose, Peterson continued, "In the counsel we have received, we have come to understand that the destiny of Nauvoo is to become a sacred monument to the Prophet Joseph Smith and those stalwart, faithful Saints who suffered and sacrificed so much that we might have a fullness of the gospel." He concluded, "We do not perceive the principal value of Nauvoo to be that of a proselyting tool, but rather, as a sacred, historical site where the fullness of the gospel was restored—a place where members of the Church may feel the spirit of the people who lived there and be strengthened in their desires, efforts, and convictions by an increased understanding and recognition of the faith, testimony, and dedication of the people who built this beautiful city."[16] Six years after Peterson made these observations, the Church's announcement that it would rebuild the Nauvoo Temple became the most public expression that the Nauvoo Restoration project was intended for Church members and especially as a memorial to Joseph Smith as much as it was for proselytizing purposes.

## The Sisters of St. Benedict and the Nauvoo Temple

Construction of the temple, however, could never take place without the cooperation of an important party in Nauvoo unaffiliated with the Mormon faith tradition. Indeed, directly north of the Nauvoo Temple lot, the city's skyline was dominated by Saints Peter and Paul Church, a building that had marked Catholicism's presence in the region since 1873 and served as a visible symbol of other narratives in Nauvoo. West of the lot, the presence of a second Catholic group, the Sisters of St. Benedict and their St. Mary's Academy, impeded any possible reconstruction of the Nauvoo Temple.

Though the presence of the school hindered earlier reconstruction, Mormons and Catholics had peaceably coexisted in Nauvoo since the days of Joseph Smith. In fact, Catholicism in the area predated the Mormon arrival, with traveling priests visiting what was called "the head of the rapids" on the Mississippi as early as 1820. During Nauvoo's earlier Mormon period, Catholic leaders had celebrated mass in the Mansion House, the Seventies Hall, and even a portion of the Mormon temple.[17] At the time of the exodus, interactions between the two faiths increased, as back-and-forth negotiations ensued between Latter-day Saint leaders and Catholic officials from Quincy, Illinois, Chicago, Illinois, and Cincinnati, Ohio, interested in purchasing properties, including the temple. While the sale never materialized, a formal Catholic parish was organized in September 1848 when Father Griffith was installed as Nauvoo's first resident Catholic pastor.[18] Catholic presence in Hancock County steadily increased throughout the mid-nineteenth century as German immigrants, among others, bolstered the local economy. In 1867 the cornerstone was laid for the imposing Saints Peter and Paul Church, which celebrated its first mass six years later on August 3, 1873.[19]

While the Catholic church marked an imposing visible presence for the Nauvoo skyline, the entity that dominated the city throughout the twentieth century and most influenced Mormon-Catholic relations had its beginnings when five Catholic sisters relocated from Chicago to Nauvoo in 1874. Opening a convent and school in the old Mormon arsenal building west of the temple lot, the Sisters of St. Benedict created a compound that expanded to encompass the equivalent of six city blocks surrounding Wells Street.[20] The St. Mary's Academy, a boarding school for approximately 150 girls in its prime, operated from 1874 until its closure in 1997.

Perched on the hill overlooking the restoration battle that engulfed Nauvoo's flats, the St. Mary's Academy finally fell victim to it in the 1990s, paving the way for the temple's reconstruction. Sister Roberta Bussan, longtime member of the

FIGURE 18. Nauvoo, Illinois, looking northeast toward St. Mary's Academy, 1907. George Edward Anderson glass plate negative collection: Illinois sites, Nauvoo, Illinois, Church History Library, The Church of Jesus Christ of Latter-day Saints, Salt Lake City.

Benedictine community that ran the St. Mary's Academy, noted, "The reality in Nauvoo was the restoration projects had really grown and there wasn't any sense of competition, it was just that it was hard to be known for who we were. We were kind of overshadowed by . . . the Mormon Church."[21] Sandwiched between the historic Nauvoo properties to the west and the vacant temple lot to the east, it was inevitable that the Catholic school would eventually feel the squeeze of Latter-day Saint restoration.

An opportunity to acquire the property presented itself when boarding school enrollment declined and the Benedictine Sisters chose to close the academy in June 1997. Bussan, academic dean of the school when it closed, recalled, "We came to a conclusion after a year of thoughtfulness about it and discussion and prayer as a community that we had fulfilled our missions. . . . Really the need for our kind of school had diminished so it was the right time for us to close." Primary factors in the decision to close the school included costly repairs projected for the institution's buildings and the acknowledgment that "the nature of the student and family looking for a boarding school had changed."[22]

Deciding to shift the emphasis of their ministry away from education, the Sisters of St. Benedict recognized the need for a new facility and, most likely, the need to relocate away from Nauvoo. Announcing their intent to sell their property, the Sisters were contacted by Latter-day Saint officials less than twenty-four hours later. Negotiations ensued, and in October 1998 The Church of Jesus Christ of Latter-day Saints purchased the property, an 18.5-acre parcel of land that included the monastery, school, residence hall, heating plant, and baseball diamond, for a reported $6 million.[23] Sister Bussan continued, "We were very fortunate that the LDS Church wanted the property. We would never have been able to do anything without selling."[24]

An agreement was made that the Catholic sisters could remain on site for another thirty months, as late as March 2001, as they prepared for their eventual relocation to what would be a newly constructed monastery one hundred miles upriver in Rock Island, Illinois.[25] Sister Ruth Ksycki, prioress of the St. Mary Monastery, noted that reaction to the sale was mixed. "The closing of the high school precipitated a lot of decisions," she later declared. "For the year after we closed, we looked into ways we might use the high school. There was no way we could have utilized it." Comparing it to "the things of life," she summarized, "It's just like a family that has to pick up and move."[26] She acknowledged, "I think most people are understanding of our situation." Speaking specifically of the decision to sell their facilities to the Latter-day Saints, she continued, "We know they take good care of their property. It certainly makes it a little bit easier. . . . They've been respectful," Ksycki concluded. "We've had a very good relationship with them."[27]

While the Sisters of St. Benedict and Latter-day Saint Church officials reported good feelings, the decision to close the school and sell the property was not without controversy in Nauvoo itself. In fact, though Latter-day Saints speak of the nuns in "glowing and affectionate terms," the *Chicago Tribune* noted that this was, in part, because "without the nuns' property, it would have been difficult to rebuild the temple at its original site."[28] Reporting on the transaction, the paper observed that the Sisters' decision to sell to the Latter-day Saints "stunned the town." "A lot of bitterness has had to do with that," one business owner commented. Another longtime resident more bluntly summarized his feelings: "They sold us out."[29] Ksycki acknowledged that some non-Mormon businessmen even sought to counter the transaction with an offer of their own, but an alternate sale never came to fruition.[30] Bussan recalled, "You kind of find out who your true friends are. There was a lot of distaste selling to the

Mormons. But religious communities like mine all across the United States are saddled with huge buildings. . . . We have always considered it a blessing that we were able to sell everything."[31] Among others, the Nauvoo Historical Society wished the sisters well in their relocation, "Our love and respect and a piece of our very hearts will go with them."[32]

## Constructing the Edifice

As the sale of the property of the St. Mary's Academy paved the way for the temple, construction quickly moved forward. Within days of the reconstruction announcement, architects and construction specialists descended on the city. "I know there are concerns here that need to be addressed, particularly on how a building of this size would impact the community," Nauvoo Restoration employee and local Latter-day Saint ecclesiastical leader Durrell Nelson told the Nauvoo Chamber of Commerce. While specific details were yet to be announced, "the anticipation is that it will be built on the same site, with an appreciation of the history involved," Nelson continued. "I feel there is no intention to tear down the monastery. My own feelings are that it will be used in conjunction with the temple."[33]

Though the Church owned the property and actively moved forward with its planning, the city still required a permit before they could break ground and begin construction. The issuing of the permit became more of a controversy than some originally imagined. On October 2, 1999, six months after his earlier announcement regarding the temple's reconstruction, Latter-day Saint Church president Gordon B. Hinckley publicly announced to the Latter-day Saint general conference audience the plan to break ground later that month for the temple. Officials expressed hope to take advantage of fewer tourists during the winter season to begin excavation.[34] Anticipating a more drawn-out construction schedule, the announcement again caught Nauvoo's residents by surprise. "When we first heard about this project, we were told that it would begin in the spring of 2000," Nauvoo city councilman John McCarty remarked. "Now we heard that a ground breaking was scheduled for this month."[35] When the paperwork for a permit was submitted on Monday, October 11, the council quickly balked. Meeting the next day, they voted 4–2 to deny the permit. "Everything was dropped on us in the last 24 hours," McCarty explained.[36] "It's just too much to try and figure a long-range plan out in this short of time," he added. "I can't see where they couldn't be patient. They're putting something here that's going to be here for a long time."[37] The opposition seems to have surprised the Church as well. "We didn't expect it or anticipate it," remarked Keith Stepan, managing director of the Church's temple construction department.[38]

The community and its leaders appear not to have opposed the idea of reconstructing the temple itself, or the Mormon Church generally. Rather, they wanted time to explore the building's impact on their community. In this way, the response mirrored earlier feelings about Nauvoo Restoration; most merely wanted additional information. "We had some local papers trying to dig up a story about anti-Mormon sentiment," council member McCarty reported. "All six of us [on the City Council] want to see it done," he continued. "Everyone sees great possibilities with it. It will do nothing but enhance the town. We just want to make sure Nauvoo doesn't get buried in the process."[39] The delay centered on the impact temple construction would have on the city's infrastructure, especially on its roads and water and sewer lines. However, Illinois state law did not permit towns the size of Nauvoo, with a population of little more than one thousand residents, to assess construction impact fees. Though the Church initially offered the community $235,000 as a good-faith recognition of the project's impact, city officials questioned if that would be sufficient. With state aid for road repair based on population and hotel tax revenue earmarked for tourism development, officials on both sides recognized that compromise would be required to offset the impact of the building and the corresponding increase in visitors.[40] City coffers were further pinched by the reality that the Latter-day Saint Church owned nearly half of the city, much of which was tax-exempt.[41] "We've got to do some negotiating and get some information," Mayor Wilson concluded.[42]

City officials scrambled to organize a public hearing regarding the issuing of the building permit. After securing the opinions of townspeople, the majority of whom favored going forward, the council reconvened to consider the matter. For its part, the Church increased its offer of financial aid, promising a one-time cash payment of $380,000, to be used for increased traffic control, police, and fire protection associated with the temple's construction. They also submitted a $91,440 processing fee for necessary water, sewer, electrical, and storm-water runoff improvements, agreed to provide the services of a city-planner for two years, and promised to revisit traffic and parking issues over a three-to-five-year period, agreeing to work in good faith to mitigate whatever problems may arise. In total, the city received $471,440 in cash, with thousands more in services, to offset the impact of the temple construction. "We're proud of the council for getting some money out of it," remarked newspaper editor Kathy Wallace.[43] "Legally, they didn't have to give us a dime," councilman John McCarty noted. "There wasn't much more we could have asked for."[44] Voting 5–1 in favor of the agreement, the city council approved the building permit.

On October 24, 1999, just six months after reconstruction was announced, an estimated five thousand people gathered for a groundbreaking ceremony for the Nauvoo Temple. Included in the number were representatives of the Benedictine Sisters, whose sale of their school facilitated construction; city officials who, only five days earlier, had officially granted the construction permit; and anxious community members worried over the impact the building would have on their quality of life. The Latter-day Saint Church was represented by President Gordon B. Hinckley, Elder Henry B. Eyring of the Church's Quorum of Twelve Apostles, and Elder Donald L. Staheli, area president for the Church's North America Central Area Presidency. Ecstatic members from the faith's four geographical regions (called stakes within Latter-day Saint terminology) composing the proposed Nauvoo temple district rounded out the congregation.

At the event, Hinckley reminisced about his father's plan in 1939 to rebuild the temple. "I count it something of a strange and wonderful coincidence that I've had a part in the determination of rebuilding this temple," Hinckley shared. Addressing local concern regarding the thousands of visitors who would come to Nauvoo because of the temple, Hinckley continued, "This building, in my judgment, will do more for Nauvoo than anything that has happened here in a long time."[45] He also sought to reassure nervous townspeople. "Don't worry about it. We'll work it out."[46] In particular, he invited them to examine the building, when completed, in a public open house prior to the building's dedication and subsequent closure to those not of the faith. "We hope all the people of Nauvoo will come to look it over carefully. We have nothing to hide."[47] Joined by Nauvoo mayor Tom Wilson and other dignitaries, Hinckley and the party then turned over the first shovelfuls of dirt. They also invited those in attendance to do the same, with hundreds lining up for more than an hour for the opportunity.[48]

The project was a collaboration between architects and building companies familiar to the Church and local contractors. While Legacy Construction, a consortium of Utah-based Jacobsen, Oakland, and Layton construction companies, served as the building's general contractor, most of the subcontract work involved local workers. Reporting on the excavation work, Nauvoo's newspaper noted that all contractors working on the site were local workers. The Church had also contracted with an area craftsman, Charles Allen, to construct the building's more than 130 windows.[49] Fort Madison's Ready Mix Concrete company provided the eight thousand cubic yards of concrete, while Jazz Concrete Pumping from Burlington, Iowa, delivered it on the site.[50] Additionally, officials repeatedly emphasized plans to use stone quarried from the same areas around Nauvoo as the original temple. This idea was eventually scrapped when stone from one quarry was deemed unsuitable and two other area quarries were under water from higher water levels along the Mississippi River than in the 1840s. In

FIGURE 19. Nauvoo Temple under reconstruction, ca. 2001.
Nauvoo Restoration Incorporated historical files. Church History Library,
The Church of Jesus Christ of Latter-day Saints, Salt Lake City.

its place, stone similar in appearance was acquired from Alabama, with carvers
from Idaho, Indiana, Pennsylvania, and Canada crafting the decorative stones.[51]
Eventually, the building was constructed of reinforced concrete faced with
limestone imitating the original.[52] In total, an estimated twenty-five hundred
workers both from the West and from the area surrounding Nauvoo worked
on the structure, providing a boon to the region's economy.[53]

Throughout the project, designers sought balance between historical accuracy and modern functionality. In this way, unlike other restored structures
around Nauvoo that emphasized historical accuracy inside and out, the exterior
of the temple closely aligned with the footprint and look of the original building while the interior reflected several facilities needed for modern religious
worship. This included the elimination of some rooms present in the earlier
structure as well as the addition of others never included but now utilized in
the modern structure. To accomplish their task of blending the original with
the contemporary, a research team led by Glen M. Leonard, director of the
Latter-day Saint Museum of Church History and Art, gathered as much historical detail on the original temple as possible.[54] Architect Roger Jackson of
Salt Lake City's FFKR Architects pored over hundreds of journal accounts,

letters, and diaries, examined surviving photographs of the exterior and the original architectural drawings, studied surviving stone fragments, and reviewed archaeological excavation reports in an effort to recreate the earlier structure.[55] While they sought to imitate a nineteenth-century edifice, builders were also challenged to incorporate modern amenities, including electrical outlets and switches, plumbing, and duct work. "We're trying to meet the modern requirements within a historically sized and scaled fixture . . . so we have to shoehorn all that in," Jackson noted.[56] In particular, Jackson and his associates were challenged to accurately reconstruct the building's east side, for which no drawings or photographs of the original existed. "My biggest fear and my biggest hope," Jackson later reported, "is that some day someone will find a photo of that east side. It's my fear because we may have gotten it wrong. It's my hope because we may have gotten it right."[57]

## Contending for the Legacy of Nauvoo

As the temple rose from the ground adjacent to the town's iconic water tower, concern around Nauvoo seemed to rise with it. "I wish they never dreamed this temple crap up," one local resident remarked. "[Nauvoo] is going to be nothing but a tourist trap. It just gets worse, worse and worse. Soon it will be nothing but Mormons. I hate to put it that way, but it's true."[58] Another remarked, "Tension. There is tension. They think this is their town. It ain't."[59]

Conflict over "whose city it was" underscores the differing views regarding Nauvoo's past and, by implication, its future. "In the collective Mormon consciousness," noted one reporter, "the clocks in Nauvoo stopped ticking when the wagons started rolling West. For Mormons, Nauvoo is not a bustling little town. It is a sacred place frozen in time." On the other hand, for Nauvoo residents unaffiliated with the faith, Nauvoo is "home, . . . not merely a stage for nostalgia."[60] For them, Nauvoo as home includes the farms where they earn a livelihood, the coffee shop where they exchange local tales, and the schools where they educate their children and cheer local heroes, none of which are visited by most Mormon tourists. "It's our town, as far as we're concerned," commented former Mayor Dale Bruegger. "And as far as the Mormons are concerned, it's their town."[61] John McCarty, a city council member who ultimately voted in favor of the building permit, nevertheless remarked, "We felt, hey, you're going to take away our quiet little town. But the church never had a concept of that. They were just going to get their temple."[62] Joan Kraft, the lone city council member who voted against the building permit, summarized the perspective, "[The Mormons] were here for seven years [in the 1840s]. I have been here 48 years. People out there (in Utah) are not even aware that people live here, thrive here, raise their families here."[63] Getting at the heart of the matter, Kraft added, "They have such little respect for what belongs to us, for our heritage, our roots. They're only concerned about their heritage."[64]

While some worried about preserving Nauvoo's rural identity, others found fault with the terms of the offer accepted by the city council. "If you've got to put a road in, $300,000 doesn't amount to nothing," complained Nauvoo resident Douglas Knowles.[65] Councilwoman Kraft also worried about the Church-provided city planner. "It's a conflict of interest for an LDS missionary to be our city planner," she noted. "I only hope we don't turn into a little Williamsburg. This is a real town."[66] Still others vented frustration over the perceived ability by the Latter-day Saint Church to pay any price. "They want to take back Nauvoo, and since they can't do it with guns, they are doing it with money," one resident remarked.[67]

While tensions simmered, others within the community came to the defense of the Church and its temple project. "It goes against the grain here to prevent people from using their own land," summarized newspaper owner Jane Langford.[68] "They've got every right to worship the way they want," added Jim Moffitt. "It's their religion. I'm not against the Catholics for having Rome, and . . . this is just as important to them."[69] Chamber of Commerce president Steve Sanders adopted a pragmatic approach. "It's the hand the community has been dealt. The county needs it. Hancock County needs an economic boost. This is what has been offered to us."[70] He added, "It's a very conservative town. Some people are not happy with what is happening. I have heard the word cult. But as a businessman, it's the best thing that ever happened to me."[71] Ginger Reese, director of Nauvoo Tourism, exhibited outright enthusiasm. "This is like their Jerusalem. You can't help but get excited about that."[72]

The differing viewpoints eventually attracted the attention of outside observers. In April 2000, a dozen *Time* magazine reporters, editors, and photographers descended on the city as part of a two-week tour down the Mississippi River exploring America's heartland. One of the authors noted, "Hamlets all along the Mississippi are searching for a picturesque and salable past. But Nauvoo is the uneasy recipient of a double bounty: a town with two histories and two identities."[73] Special-projects editor Barry Seaman summarized, "I think this is going to be a very interesting story coming down the pike on how this town either absorbs the temple or is overwhelmed by it. And I don't know which."[74] He was not alone; the residents of Nauvoo openly wondered the same. Religion reporter David Van Biema noted that Nauvoo was different from other tourist destinations. "You can go to a lot of re-creations of historic this and historic that.

135

But you can't go to a lot of re-creations that have so much meaning to a group of people."[75] As far away as Pennsylvania, the *Philadelphia Inquirer* also reported on the changes expected in the city, noting that land prices had doubled since the announcement of the temple and in anticipation of an expected doubling in visitors.[76] The temple project drew the kind of national attention the founders of Nauvoo Restoration always hoped their Williamsburg of the Midwest would generate.

The Church and its leaders actively worked to allay local concerns. "I know there are people in the community who really wish we weren't here, but I don't think there are very many of them. They're good, hardworking folks who would probably just [wish] their lives weren't disturbed," opined Nauvoo Restoration director R. J. Snow.[77] Kenneth Godfrey, an instructor for a Brigham Young University study program in Nauvoo that regularly brought students to the area for religious and historical studies, added, "While there are some in Nauvoo who resent the Mormons and their temple, I have only met those who have been kind, considerate and full of trust."[78]

Both parties hit a few speed bumps along the way, including the quiet reassignment of the Church-provided city manager and an investigation of the mayoral race over public allegations that some Latter-day Saints were barred from registering to vote. However, most residents appear to have eventually accepted the project, even if they never openly embraced it. Following a building moratorium growing out of the temple construction, the city formalized its zoning ordinances, something former planning commission and council member Karen Ihrig called "good for everyone involved." Ihrig added, "I think that Nauvoo is in a position that it can have rules and regulations, without being completely restricted. This is just more organized. The people of Nauvoo want to protect what they have and make an organized move into the future. This ordinance allows for that."[79] As a result, the reconstruction of the Nauvoo Temple led the community to formalize procedures for preserving local control.

## Healing Wounds through the Temple Dedication

By late 2001, construction had progressed enough for plans to be finalized for the building's dedication. Learning from the reaction to the announcement regarding the temple's construction, all parties were more cooperative as they prepared to celebrate its completion. Church officials announced a public tour period beginning in May 2002, complete with special media events and "Neighbor Days" for residents of Iowa's Lee and Illinois' Hancock Counties.[80] Dedicatory services would follow, with thirteen sessions from June 27 through June

30.[81] Response was swift and positive. Within weeks of the announcement, tickets for all of the weekend tour dates were reserved. Many of the available weekday slots were also quickly reserved, until more than 350,000 open house tickets were distributed, with a maximum capacity of six hundred visitors per hour.[82] Officials reported that visitors from Illinois made the highest number of reservations, followed by residents of Utah and Iowa, with inquiries coming from every state in the United States, every Canadian province, and more than seventy other countries.[83] Reassuring concerned visitors about what they would see, Church spokeswoman Ann Orton emphasized, "You can see all of the temple. There aren't any secret places."[84]

Additional construction around town prepared for the expected onslaught of hundreds of thousands of visitors, together with the corresponding change of life created by an operating Latter-day Saint temple. In November 2001 the city's firehouse was lifted five feet off the ground so crews could pour a new foundation and enlarge the building in order to accommodate a new aerial fire truck. Serving the temple as well as area hotels and other large buildings, the $435,000 truck was made possible by a state grant, donations from the Latter-day Saint Church and a local grain-elevator company, and financing from a local bank.[85] South of the temple, a two-hundred-space, two-level parking garage with public restrooms took shape. Down the hill on the flats, twenty-four buildings containing sixty apartments were built to house the faith's senior missionaries who would service the temple.

With Nauvoo only having 150 hotel rooms, area communities got in on the action as well. Nearby Fort Madison advertised its available three hundred rooms for visitors, Quincy marketed its eight hundred rooms, and Western Illinois University in Macomb opened up a block of vacant dormitory space.[86] In the end, area hotels and even local campgrounds reported being at nearly 100 percent occupancy for the entirety of May and June 2002.[87] "I think we're really fortunate to be a neighbor of Nauvoo," remarked Fort Madison Convention and Visitors Bureau Director Mardie Smith. "I have had phone calls from as far away as Alaska and Hawaii."[88] Area schools also became involved, with the Keokuk School District providing buses to shuttle visitors between Keokuk and Nauvoo. "We want to make them feel like they're in their living room," remarked Keokuk tourism director Kirk Brandenberger. However, with Keokuk located fifteen miles away and across the river, Brandenberger recognized his town's limitations, adding, "The reason they're staying in Keokuk is because they can't stay any closer to Nauvoo."[89]

As the open house ensued, both Church and community representatives praised the relationship they had developed. It "started out real bad," Nauvoo

Alderman Bob Soland said about the surprise announcement that the temple would be rebuilt.[90] However, he praised the work of construction managers and Church officials for improving the relationship dramatically. "This was an ambitious project for a small town like Nauvoo," Church representative Donald L. Staheli told more than one hundred journalists who toured the building during one media event. "And with all that is involved, we have found the relationship between the community and the Church to be excellent."[91] David E. Sorensen, executive director of the Church's temple department, added, "We couldn't have asked for more cooperation. We are associated with building temples all around the world and I don't think there has been one temple where we have had more cooperation from the local city fathers than we have had in Nauvoo, along with a great feeling of harmony, mutual tranquility and respect."[92] Church president Gordon B. Hinckley echoed the praise for his faith's relationship with the city of Nauvoo, "The mayor and the city council have been very cooperative. We have worked with them in an effort to do everything we can to ameliorate any problems that might arise."[93]

The Church and the community sought to preserve these feelings during the difficult time of hosting hundreds of thousands of visitors for the open house. Hinckley challenged those visiting Nauvoo:

> I hope that when people gather there for the public showing and for the dedication and subsequent to that, that there will be an attitude of courtesy and forbearance, respect and kindness one toward another. Inevitably when you bring that many people together you have some inconvenience. I hope that we all rise above it, that we will be neighborly and good, and treat one another with the greatest deference as we gather together in this historic city on the Mississippi River. . . . We hope that courtesy will prevail in everything that goes on, that there will be respect and appreciation one for another, patience. All of these qualities will be required and we hope that they will shine forth.[94]

For its part, the city reciprocated. Though the mayor acknowledged, "The open house is going to be a big mess," he added, "but we're as ready as we can be." City council member John McCarty pleaded, "We all need to try and show our new guests that are coming what Nauvoo is all about. Show them our history, show them our pride and show them some patience. Let's not add to the problems."[95]

Though entrepreneurs reported smaller-than-expected crowds initially, business picked up as the open house period progressed and the formal dedication of the temple approached. "Visions of just a mob of people and cars lined up to Quincy aren't going to happen, but it's a lot of people," remarked Tim Reinhardt, vice president of Nauvoo State Bank.[96] "This town looks like a small Branson, [Missouri,] in the afternoon," added the local grocer.[97] While area businesses reported record sales, Chamber of Commerce president Steve Sanders longed for more. "I wanted them to stay in town longer and spend more money and time in the Nauvoo area. Did we fail there? Yes."[98]

In addition to catering to the tourists, business owners also openly acknowledged a desire to remember resident patrons. "One thing we want local people to know is we want to take care of the local people. We reserved some space for them, and we hope they keep coming," remarked hotel and restaurant owner Dan Kraus. "We want to make sure they know that we will make every effort to see they're taken care of."[99] Law enforcement acknowledged the strain brought on by the hundreds of thousands of visitors. "I talked to the St. Louis and Denver, Colo., police departments about what they did [during similar Latter-day Saint temple open houses]," commented police chief Jerry Floyd. "They have more than 100 police officers. I said I have two, and they just laughed." At Church expense, Floyd added three additional officers for the open house.[100]

As the seven-week open house came to a close, Church officials reported a total of 331,849 visitors touring the temple, an average of 7,607 per day, or 565 per hour.[101] Mission officials boasted receiving 2,086 missionary referrals from the event, though "we had to dig for them," remarked Samuel Park, Nauvoo Mission president, "because the visitors were primarily Church members. We had to look underneath and over and around for those who were not LDS."[102] In this regard, the temple reconstruction reflected the reality that the Nauvoo project was no longer merely a historical recreation or an evangelizing tool. Even more than it had before, the Nauvoo Temple made the city a focus for those who were already Latter-day Saint.

When the open house concluded on June 22, Church officials turned their attention to the events of the building's dedication on June 27, the 158th anniversary of the martyrdom of Church founder Joseph Smith. "I chose the date [and] the same hour of the day when Joseph and Hyrum [Smith] were murdered in Carthage. We dedicate this structure as a memorial to them," remarked Church president Gordon B. Hinckley, adding, "I intend to say at the dedication service that with us today is an unseen audience and that Joseph Smith will be in that audience, Hyrum Smith will be in that audience."[103]

Speaking of its significance, Elder Donald L. Staheli, president of the faith's North American Central Area, which included Nauvoo, noted, "This is one of the most significant events in our 172-year history and a defining moment for us as a people."[104] More than twelve hundred people assembled in the temple itself for the first of the thirteen dedicatory services, with another one thousand people gathered in the nearby Church meetinghouse and hundreds of others milling around on the streets surrounding the temple grounds.[105] An estimated two million others participated via direct satellite feed to approximately twenty-three hundred Church meetinghouses across seventy-two countries in North and South America, Europe, and Asia.[106]

Emotionally affected by the occasion, Hinckley reflected on his feelings for Joseph Smith, the members including his grandfather who built the original temple, and his father's earlier efforts to have it reconstructed. In the prayer itself, he also prayed for the modern community of Nauvoo and the city's future as a Church historic site. "Bless this city of Nauvoo, which came to be known as the City of Joseph. May it shine with a renewed luster as the home of a Temple of God. May this sacred house stand as a memorial to him who lived here and was buried here, Joseph Smith, the great prophet of this dispensation, and his brother Hyrum, whom he loved."[107]

While the dedication highlighted the day in Nauvoo for Latter-day Saints, other activities surrounding it reflected the nature of faith and community relationships in the City of Joseph. Because the dedicatory services were limited only to Church members, other events of the day included a number of activities geared toward the local community. The morning began with a cover-stone ceremony, which included sealing a time capsule in the temple's southeast cornerstone. As many as four thousand people gathered to watch Hinckley and other dignitaries place several building-related artifacts in the capsule, including copies of the faith's scriptures, historic news articles, books authored by Hinckley, histories of Hancock County and the temple, and tools used in its construction.[108] Important, too, was the fact that the Church leaders and prominent temple donors who sealed the stone were joined by the mayors of Nauvoo, Quincy, Keokuk, and Fort Madison. "We're very proud of the accomplishments in Nauvoo and western Illinois, and we're proud to have been a part of it," remarked Fort Madison Mayor Joe Kowzan.[109] Following the ceremony, Hinckley led a forty-five-minute press conference where he shared his familial connections to Nauvoo, personal feelings about the temple's construction, and outlook for the faith's future in Nauvoo. "Contrary to all the predictions that were made when we were driven out of here," he declared, "we have come back with strength and membership, capacity to do that which we believe deserved to be done here."[110]

Later that afternoon, Hinckley met with officials from the Community of Christ (known as the Reorganized Church until 2001) at the graves of Joseph, Emma, and Hyrum Smith for a memorial service, visibly demonstrating the relationship between the two faiths that share a common heritage in Nauvoo.

The occasion brought the heads of the two Churches together for the first time in more than a decade. In tones that were markedly different from earlier messages of contestation over how Nauvoo should be preserved and interpreted, the pair outlined hope for a cooperative future in the city. Calling his tour of the reconstructed Nauvoo Temple "truly a breathtaking experience," Community of Christ president Grant McMurray noted, "We are together on this day because we share an important slice of history. We share a foundation in our respective faith journeys."[111] Latter-day Saint president Gordon B. Hinckley added, "I think we have a good relationship or I hope we do. I feel nothing but kindness in my heart toward them. . . . It has been a great privilege of gathering together with our friends in the Community of Christ."[112]

In addition to the Church presidents, the directors of each faith's respective historic sites in Nauvoo openly praised the relationship developed through Nauvoo's restoration. R. J. Snow, manager of Nauvoo Restoration, called their association "excellent. We have warm friendships. We try to support their activities and they're generous to support us. We don't discuss things doctrinal. There's more that links us together than takes us apart."[113] Joseph Smith Historic Site director Joyce Shireman echoed the feeling from a Community of Christ perspective: "We have a really good working relationship here in Nauvoo." Speaking specifically of the temple, she added, "It's part of our shared heritage. . . . We wish them well. It's a lovely building."[114]

The reconstruction of the Nauvoo Temple, a project long viewed as the pinnacle for Nauvoo's restoration, revealed how far relationships had progressed between the branches of Mormonism in Nauvoo. Adversarial when the idea was floated six decades earlier, the Reorganized Church and the Latter-day Saint Church vied for control of the lot for more than twenty years until the Utah faith eventually reassured their rival that reconstruction was not imminent. Years later, after living and laboring alongside each other in Nauvoo, one would control but both could celebrate the return of Nauvoo's Temple to a bluff overlooking their shared space. For the community, the project also laid bare festering wounds inflicted by the restoration project over the years. Grievances over impact, information, and influence helped the parties recognize a need for greater communication and cooperation. Though much still needs to be done, those emphasizing Nauvoo's Mormon story learned from the temple's construction to work with and value Nauvoo's many other histories while residents of the city reconciled themselves to the reality that their iconic Nauvoo water tower would share its aerial view with the now iconic Nauvoo Temple spire. A project with the potential to divide the faith and community in Nauvoo had brought many of the parties together.

# Epilogue

## The Future for Faith in Nauvoo

"Hello mayor, we've changed your town," quipped Latter-day Saint Church president Gordon B. Hinckley as he greeted Nauvoo mayor Tom Wilson the morning of the dedication of the Nauvoo Temple.[1] While clearly referring to the reconstructed sacred building being celebrated that day, the observation summarized the dramatic transformation of Nauvoo as a result of its twentieth-century restoration boom. As a town, modern Nauvoo was forever changed because of Mormonism's return.

Furthermore, while restoration changed the town, lessons learned from the experience may also have changed the major branches of Mormonism as well. During much of the twentieth century, it appeared that the presence of prairie Mormon and mountain Mormon Churches in Nauvoo exacerbated conflicts between the faiths, making it seem that they would, in the words of Reorganized Church historian Richard Howard, "forever be separated by a common wall of enmity." However, their proximity in the city and creating their own preservation missions eventually fostered coexistence, if not compromise.

Living and working with each other broke down decades of disagreement, discord, and distrust as the faiths acted to preserve their sometimes-competing histories in a shared space. With time, the interpretive possibilities for the City of Joseph, coupled with the divergent paths taken by the two faiths, led to the replacement of what Howard called "a wall of hostility and exclusiveness . . . [with] an illuminating window."[2] Like siblings that mature, find their separate paths, and reconcile better as adults than they ever did as youths, Latter-day Saint and Reorganized Mormonism seem comfortable with their chosen paths, both in Nauvoo and beyond. Nauvoo's restoration may have helped facilitate what historian Richard Moore call "two churches with a common origin which have developed into substantially different religious entities."[3]

The administration of the sites in Nauvoo across the twentieth century reflects the development of these identities. From his perspective, Howard summarized the change that occurred over time at both Latter-day Saint and Reorganized Church historic sites. "I have noticed through the years a heightened cordiality between Mormon visitors to our official historic sites and RLDS docents guiding them through. Where once tension and animosity prevailed—sometimes marked by hostile verbal exchanges—more often than not both parties are experiencing the pleasures of friendliness and openness to one another." Howard added a revealing anecdote. "One RLDS member told me recently, 'I no longer sign other peoples' names and addresses to the guest books in Mormon visitors' centers. I sign my own, and look forward to the missionaries' visit.'"[4]

## Community Relationships in Nauvoo

Looking ahead for both faiths in Nauvoo, following the massive temple recon-struction project, renovation and restoration appear to have slowed across the City of Joseph. For the Community of Christ, building projects like the temple in Independence, Missouri, dedicated in 1994, and a state-of-the-art spiritual formation and visitors' center at the Kirtland Temple, completed in 2007, seem to have diverted limited renovation budgets away from Nauvoo. Additionally, fiscal factors beyond their ideological control, including a budget crisis that led to massive layoffs of Church staff worldwide over the past decade, have further undermined prospects for additional projects. In a personal interview with the author, one Community of Christ official doubted that new construction might occur. Hoping at least for a modernization of the present visitor center in Nauvoo as well as a more historically accurate restoration of the Joseph Smith Homestead, he longed for a proactive approach to historical site preservation, frustrated by the reactionary stance taken in the past by some within his faith.

From the Latter-day Saint perspective, one similarly wonders about the future of restoration work in Nauvoo. With the temple complete and numer-ous historically significant buildings restored, much of the Nauvoo narrative is told by the existing impressionistic patchwork in place. Focus appears shifted from renovation to maintenance and public relations. In 2018, Church leaders announced a long-anticipated master plan for their sites in Nauvoo, "designed to feature core messages, integrate historical landscapes, increase authenticity, and improve guest experiences" prior to Nauvoo's bicentennial in 2039. Some additional restoration and reconstruction is anticipated, including of properties designed to better inform visitors about the construction and purpose of the original Nauvoo Temple. These include the homes of temple architect William Weeks, temple laborer William Gheen, Church Apostle Orson Hyde, and businessman and bishop Edward Hunter. However, "the greater emphasis," senior curator for historic sites Steven Olsen remarked, will be to improve existing homes and other structures so that they are more accurate. "The landscape itself may not radically change, but the visitor experience will hopefully become much more meaningful."[5] Additionally, the faith now grapples with internally overlapping bureaucratic layers in Nauvoo, as three major Church departments operate within the city. With differing priorities, the Church's temple department directs the affairs of the modern Nauvoo Temple, its missionary department oversees proselytizing and guide services, and the historical department involves itself in site development, preservation, and interpretation. Each brings a different perspective, shaping a complex future for restored Nauvoo while making it unlikely that any one entity within the faith will dominate the future of the site.[6]

Regardless of the direction either faith takes with its historic sites, community building may be the greatest need in Nauvoo moving forward. Scattered throughout the history of the twentieth-century restoration of Mormon Nauvoo are repeated cries from residents unaffiliated with either faith for a voice in the telling of their town's story. These cries include calls from local residents to celebrate their own rich history of Icarian settlement, German immigration, and Midwestern farm life that gets tossed aside too often because of its irrelevance to 1840s Mormon Nauvoo. This call for a celebration of Nauvoo's multiple pasts was reflected in a six-week traveling exhibit sponsored by the Smithsonian Institution that occupied Nauvoo in late 2012. Emphasizing more than just the Mormon story of the city, displays within the "Journey Stories" exhibit, as it was called, also highlighted the Icarians, Germans, and Catholics as groups who built Nauvoo in hopes for a better life. Similarly, local residents recently developed an award-winning self-guided walking tour of Nauvoo's business district from the 1850s through the 1960s. Chronologically removed from the Mormon era and geographically located away from the religious sites generally emphasized in town, the placards and informational brochures likewise offer hope for a way for locals to preserve and celebrate Nauvoo's many histories.

Indeed, residents hope for a louder, more recognized voice in shaping their town's future. As early as 1970, Nauvoo residents lamented the lack of community involvement and secrecy associated with Nauvoo's Latter-day Saint restoration. Following a master planning effort for the city of Nauvoo, a community committee observed, "Officers of [Nauvoo Restoration Incorporated] and its staff did discuss their tentative plans with the planning firm, but evidently only under the condition that the consultant not disclose what he was told."[7] Confidentiality, coupled with the lack of input from local citizens, gave rise to frustrations with what was happening to their community. David A. Knowles, one of Nauvoo's mayors during the early historic restoration, vocalized the concern: "The problem with the Mormon Nauvoo Restoration, Inc., is that it

FIGURE 20. Removal of the girls' infirmary, one of the buildings of the St. Mary's Academy, ca. 2002. Nauvoo Restoration Incorporated historical files. Church History Library, The Church of Jesus Christ of Latter-day Saints, Salt Lake City.

145

was super secret. Dr. Kimball said that the NRI 'was not going to be a big deal. We are just buying a few houses, putting them together, and remodeling them, making them look good.' Maybe this is what he had in mind at the particular time," Knowles concluded, but a change in the plan clearly created "a lot of animosity."[8]

As visitors multiplied and construction boomed, this animosity slowly simmered around Nauvoo. Though quietly talked about in homes, across store counters, and in private gatherings, the divide caused by the restoration was openly revealed during the temple construction. A series of more than twenty-five interviews with longtime Nauvoo residents conducted as the temple was being built exposed local frustrations. Summarizing what some in town felt, one resident noted, "I would say the majority of the population of Nauvoo wished that this never happened. . . . They'd just as soon not have the Mormon influx and keep the town the way it was. It's changing their town. They lived here because they liked this quiet little community, and also it's a natural thing to have a fear of the unknown. Here's this large influx come in, and they're afraid of it."[9] A second account revealed, "The city is split right now. There's a handful of people that are against any kind of growth. Those are the ones you hear: the loudest ones. They're not really anti-Mormon as much as they don't want to change their way of life. It could be the largest Jewish group you've ever seen, and move into Nauvoo and take over and build some massive synagogue, and have two hundred thousand Jews coming in here, and that would bother them. It's just the impact of the people. It's not as much the Mormon Church as it is the change of life."[10] A third respondent commented, "It seems to me that for whatever reason, the Church has an abundance of money, and what it really wants to do, it has the money to do it. Mormons are well organized, well-schooled. The plans were put in place, and maybe the plans have been in place for years that they would return to Nauvoo, rebuild the temple, and restructure the flats the way it was back in 1839 to 1847."[11]

While the sample size for these interviews is small, so too is the town of Nauvoo, where it appears that the return of Mormonism has been met with mixed feelings. Within the adherents to the mission of Joseph Smith, restoration has, at times, caused division, contention, and competition. For some residents, it has brought economic prosperity but also unwelcome change. For others, the anticipated revival of the city has been more bust than boom, adding to the acrimony. The feeling of pending prosperity that accompanied the reconstruction of the temple in the early 2000s has evaporated. The economic downturn of 2008 forced plans for new hotels never to come to fruition. Across town, the foundations of homes for an expected flood of new residents sit incomplete.

Along the main drag of Mulholland Street, a host of businesses are shuttered. Religiously themed Nauvoo is a witness, as historian Hal Rothman famously warned, that tourism is a "devil's bargain."[12] Indeed, it is ironic that the twentieth century renovation of the City of Joseph would not only restore the town to its 1840s' character, but it would also bring back some of the 1840s' enmity. Forwarding a message of inclusion, creating a place of intersection rather than division, but coupling it all with a dose of economic realism for a tourism-based economy, may be Nauvoo restoration's next and greatest hurdle.

Faith leaders in Nauvoo sense this need for bridge building in the community. In 2012 the *Catholic Post*, the newspaper for the diocese of Peoria, of which Nauvoo is a part, noted, "In recent years, Catholics, Mormons, and other faith communities in this area have been laying more 'delicate foundations' in the forms of relationships, friendships, and moves to foster greater dialogue and understanding of beliefs." The article continued, citing Father Tony Trosley, Nauvoo's parish priest, "No matter what the political climate, it's our role to set up such a relationship that we can engage in open exposition and discussion of our teachings. That's been the approach here."[13] His words echo those of Gordon B. Hinckley, then counselor in the Latter-day Saint First Presidency, delivered as he dedicated the remodeled Carthage Jail complex in 1989. Hinckley's message suggests hope for a brighter future for the Church in Illinois through its historic sites. "Ours is the duty to forgive and put behind us the troubles of the past. Ours is the obligation to rise above old animosities. . . . [The site should be] a place hallowed and sacred to which people of all faiths may come and learn."[14]

FIGURE 21. Nauvoo's religious skyline, including the Saints Peter and Paul Catholic Church (left) and the Nauvoo Temple of The Church of Jesus Christ of Latter-day Saints (right). Photograph by Scott C. Esplin. Used by permission.

## Nauvoo Restoration, Mormonism, and Commemoration across America

Stepping back for a broader view of it, the restoration of Nauvoo is also an American story. As a religiously themed experience, Nauvoo offers lessons on faith tourism, contested space, and commemoration. Though "the embrace of tourism triggers a contest for the soul of a place," as historian Hal Rothman argued, it is unfortunate that the restoration of a religious site like Nauvoo, long associated with the salvation of souls and founded on the pursuit of peace, would engender such a conflict.[15] However, "American sacred space has been produced from the beginning out of multicultural relations and intercultural conflict," noted religious studies professors David Chidester and Edward Linenthal. "Clearly, these conflictual relations persist in the present."[16] The experiences of faith relations and the local community in Nauvoo support this assertion, adding a contested-space case study to the American narrative of memorial sites. Sadly, "conflict and sacred space in America go hand in hand."[17]

As a national story, the restoration of Nauvoo reveals the anxieties that enveloped America during the mid-twentieth century. Hoping to reclaim a carefree, celebratory past, private and public groups partnered to build a place in the rural Midwest where American exceptionalism, human achievement, and pioneer fortitude could be celebrated in the face of social upheaval, division, and discord. By employing selective memory and "historical amnesia," twentieth-century America overlooked a long history of conflict with Mormonism's nineteenth-century story to create a "usable past" that would serve its present needs.[18]

Capitalizing on an environment increasingly friendly to its past, The Church of Jesus Christ of Latter-day Saints also used the project to restore Nauvoo as a way to shape its public image. The city was the headquarters for Mormonism in the 1840s, the setting for one of its greatest tragedies, and the scene of its most dramatic physical return. Nauvoo's restoration, originally intended as an attraction for those unfamiliar with the faith's history and beliefs, has been extended to include the majority of the city's visitors who already know and believe the Latter-day Saint story celebrated there. Thus, commemoration served a social function for Mormonism, both for those outside the faith and for those already firmly entrenched in its practice. The story of the Latter-day Saint return to and restoration of Nauvoo, therefore, reveals much about the faith. Restoring homes, businesses, and eventually the Nauvoo Temple itself became a way for it to say, in a tangible way to a region it had fled more than 150 years earlier, that Mormonism had survived, that it mattered, and that it was now in Nauvoo to stay. The permanence with which the Church has planted itself in the city, most dramatically by the imposing temple presiding on the hill over the restored area below, represents a blend between preserving and reconstructing its past. While the outside mirrors the original, the interior has been manipulated to serve the needs of the present. Similarly, in restored Nauvoo, the faith chooses which stories to highlight in ways that speak as much about the future of the faith and the needs of its members as they do about its past.

The tension created by Mormonism's return, first with its closest religious relative, the Reorganized Church, and eventually with the remainder of the citizens of Nauvoo themselves, also reveals the cost of commemoration. As minority landholders in a town dominated by the late-returning western organization, both the Reorganized Church and the townspeople of Nauvoo were left trying to find a way for their story to matter in a town hyperfocused on seven brief Mormon years from the 1840s. The Reorganized Church of Jesus Christ of Latter Day Saints sees in Nauvoo the cradle of its reorganization, the town that nurtured its founding family and where it most closely battled its religious rival, but where it now holds on to a past that feels distant from its present or its future. The way the Church first dug in its heels, matching brick-for-brick the building boom across old Nauvoo, only to abandon course and change their tack, reflects the broader changes this faith experienced during the twentieth century. "Historically we denied we were Mormons, but we couldn't shake the label," observed longtime scholar of the faith Bill Russell. "In recent decades," Russell continued, "the Utah church has become more conservative while we have taken a giant step to the left in our theology."[19] Giant steps in a different direction are reflected in the approach the Reorganized Church has taken with its historical holdings in Nauvoo. The resolution of the conflict created by the restoration of Nauvoo lays bare the realities the Church underwent as it transformed from being the Reorganized Church, rooted in a historically reactionary founding, to become Community of Christ, an outward-focused faith dedicated to forming Christian communities around the globe.

For those in Nauvoo unaffiliated with either faith, their town on a bend of the Mississippi River in western Illinois bears little resemblance to the rural home of their parents and grandparents. These stakeholders seem to have paid the highest personal price for the activities that transformed Nauvoo from a midwestern German rural community with a well-known blue cheese industry, local wines, and a Catholic boarding school into a tourist haven for throngs of enthusiastic, religiously observant Mormons and those interested in learning about their narrative. Locals with the will to persist find ways to celebrate

Nauvoo's non-Mormon past, all the while wondering if the tourism bargain they made—or, at times, was made for them—was worth it. Too often, they find their city made over into a stage for costumed actors in a historical drama, with their lines in the play or their ability to direct its acts cut from the script.

In its future, modern Nauvoo can tell, and even celebrate, these diverse stories. In 1973 Nauvoo's longtime resident historian Ida Blum outlined the layers of historical complexity that shaped her home. "When Nauvoo fell into decay after the Mormons left, it became one of the nation's richest compost heaps. Anyone coming here will learn an unparalleled chapter in American history."[20] An important part of that chapter is the interaction between faiths and residents in Nauvoo in the twentieth century, including the competition and compromise evident in the rebuilding of Nauvoo's sacred spaces. The unfinished portion is how these same groups are learning to work together for the future of Nauvoo.

# Appendix

## Chronology of Restoration Projects in Nauvoo/Carthage

### Church of Jesus Christ of Latter-day Saints Projects

| Year | Building or Site |
| --- | --- |
| 1903 | Carthage Jail acquisition |
| 1933 | Relief Society monument dedication |
| 1937–62 | Nauvoo Temple site acquisitions |
| 1952 | Relief Society monument moved to temple site |
| 1956 | Nauvoo LDS Branch organized |
| 1960 | Heber C. Kimball Home dedication |
| 1961–62, 1966–69 | Nauvoo Temple excavation |
| 1962 | Nauvoo Restoration Incorporated organized |
| 1969 | LDS meetinghouse dedication |
| 1970 | Wilford Woodruff Home dedication |
| 1971 | Nauvoo Visitors' Center dedication; City of Joseph Pageant first performed |
| 1973 | Seventies Hall, Brigham Young Home, Joseph Bates Noble-Lucy Mack Smith Home, Jonathan Browning Home and Workshop, Webb Wagon and Blacksmith Shop dedications |
| 1978 | Relief Society Monument to Women and Statutory Garden dedication |
| 1979 | Nauvoo LDS Stake formed |

| Year | Building or Site |
| --- | --- |
| 1982 | Nauvoo Temple site renovation, Cultural Hall, Scovil Bakery, William Weeks Home, Lyon Drug and Variety Store, Ivins-Smith (John Taylor) Home, Printing Complex (*Times and Seasons* Printing Building and Post Office), Snow-Ashby Duplex, Coolidge Home, Simeon Dunn Home, William Gheen Home, Henry Thomas Home, Vinson Knight Home, Raymond Clark Store, Chauncey G. Webb Home, Winslow Farr Home, Hiram and Sarah Granger Kimball Home dedications |
| 1989 | Carthage Jail block renovation, Old Nauvoo Burial Grounds, Stoddard Home and Tinsmith Shop, Riser Boot and Shoemaker Shop, Browning Barn dedications |
| 1991 | Pendleton Log Home and Schoolhouse construction |
| 1997 | Land and Records Office opens |
| 1999 | Patty Sessions Log Cabin dedication |
| 2002 | Nauvoo Temple dedication |

## Reorganized Church of Jesus Christ of Latter Day Saints Projects

| Year | Building or Site |
| --- | --- |
| 1908–19 | Homestead, Mansion House, Smith Family Cemetery, and Red Brick Store site deeded to Church |
| 1909 | Nauvoo House acquisition |
| 1918 | Homestead, Mansion House, and Nauvoo House preservation begins, first caretakers assigned |
| 1921 | Nauvoo RLDS Branch formed |
| 1923 | Nauvoo reunion begins |
| 1928 | Reburial of Joseph, Emma, and Hyrum Smith |
| 1953–56 | Homestead and Mansion House renovations |
| 1959 | Nauvoo House renovation |
| 1960 | Camp Nauvoo created |
| 1969 | Levee built to protect properties from Mississippi River |
| 1970–75 | Excavations of the Joseph Smith Stable, Red Brick Store, Theodore Turley Home, Hyrum Smith Home, "Springhouse," and original *Times and Seasons* Building; Homestead summer kitchen reconstruction |
| 1980 | Red Brick Store and RLDS Visitors' Center dedications |
| 1988 | New RLDS meetinghouse; "Springhouse" reconstruction |
| 1991 | Smith Family Cemetery rededication |

Sources: NRI historical files; Bingham, "Packaging the 'Williamsburg of the Midwest.'" For building projects lasting several years, dates represent the year the structure was formally dedicated. Additionally, the names of some buildings have been changed at times, reflecting different occupants and presentation purposes (see the Printing Complex as an example).

# Notes

## Acknowledgments

1. Stark, "Rise of a New World Faith," 19.

## Introduction

1. Buckingham, in Pratt, *Illinois as Lincoln Knew It*, 66.
2. Personal interview with the author.
3. Rothman, *Devil's Bargains*, 11.
4. Doss, *Memorial Mania*, 27.
5. Rugh, *Are We There Yet?*, 2–5.
6. Olsen and Dallen, "Tourism and Religious Journeys," 1–3.
7. Savage, "History, Memory, and Monuments."
8. Shackel, "Introduction," 10.
9. Kammen, *In the Past Lane*, 214; Bodnar, *Remaking America*, 13.
10. Shackel, "Introduction," 10.
11. Misztal, *Theories of Social Remembering*, 127.
12. Shackel, "Introduction," 3.
13. Bodnar, *Remaking America*, 43.
14. Doss, *Memorial Mania*, 2.
15. Olick, "Genre Memories and Memory Genres," 381.
16. Mitchell, "Monuments, Memorials, and the Politics of Memory," 443.
17. Rothman, *Devil's Bargains*, 12.
18. VanSledright, *In Search of America's Past*, 79.

19. Kammen, *Mystic Chords of Memory*, 3.

20. Shackel, "Introduction," 10–11.

21. Ibid., 6.

22. Bodnar, *Remaking America*, 170.

23. Ibid., 177.

24. Rugh, *Are We There Yet?*, 2–5.

25. Bodnar, *Remaking America*, 177.

26. Ibid., 173.

27. Doss, *Memorial Mania*, 57

28. Savage, "History, Memory, and Monuments."

29. Kenney, *Wilford Woodruff's Journal*, 9:74.

30. Alexander, *Mormonism in Transition*, 3, 14.

31. Eliason, "Cultural Dynamics," 161.

32. Flake, "Re-placing Memory," 71.

33. Marty, "Foreword," xiii. In his essay "Muslims and Mormons in America," Marty summarized Mormonism's position: "Attacks on them are vicious, as they have been since founder-prophet Joseph Smith was assassinated and his successors were in constant conflict with non-Mormon Americans. Yet they also return not attack for attack but show up in surveys as super-Americans, super-patriots, and super-loyalists. They like it here."

34. Flake, *Politics of American Religious Identity*, 172.

35. Ibid., 176.

36. Arrington and Bitton, *Mormon Experience*, 184.

37. Flake, "Re-placing Memory," 80. Supporting this view, Latter-day Saint Apostle Francis M. Lyman declared at the dedication of the monument to Joseph Smith's birth in Sharon, Vermont, "And now we come back. The west and the east meet here on this blessed occasion. . . . We want your friendship; and you have ours." *Proceedings at the Dedication*, 17.

38. Doss, *Memorial Mania*, 59–60.

39. Moore, "LDS Misconceptions," 2.

40. Scherer, "Answering Questions," 73.

41. Ibid., 73, 76.

42. Cited in Russell, "LDS Church and Community of Christ," 189.

43. Scherer, "Answering Questions," 77.

## Chapter 1. The Mormon City in Decline

1. Kane, *Mormons*, 3–6.

2. Buckingham, in Pratt, *Illinois as Lincoln Knew It*, 63–64.

3. Black, "How Large Was the Population of Nauvoo?," 91–94.

4. Bennett, *We'll Find the Place*, 5.

5. Bennett, *Mormons at the Missouri*, 5.

6. "History, 1838–1856."

7. McBride, *House for the Most High*, 177.

8. "Epistle of the Twelve," 779.

9. Brigham Young, in Roberts, *History*, 7:386.

10. Brigham Young, August 18, 1844, in ibid., 7:256.

11. Morley, "Brief History."

12. Sessions, *Diaries*, B-41.

13. Smith, *Intimate Chronicle*, 183.

14. John B. Hardin, W. B. Warren, S. A. Douglas, and J. A. McDougal to the First President and High Council of the Church of the Latter-day Saints, October 2, 1845, in Roberts, *History*, 7:450.

15. Smith, *Intimate Chronicle*, 184.

16. Letter of Irene Hascall, October 29, 1845, cited in Bennett, *Mormons at the Missouri*, 15.

17. Brigham Young, February 8, 1846, in Roberts, *History*, 7:580.

18. Kenney, *Wilford Woodruff's Journal*, 3:49.

19. Brown, "Perfect Estopel," 62–63.

20. Kimball, *On the Potter's Wheel*, 155.

21. Brown, "Perfect Estopel," 64–65.

22. Historian Richard Bennett summarized the challenges these individuals faced. "In addition to selling Church properties, including the temple . . . they were responsible for paying outstanding Church debts, contesting legal actions, helping the poor and destitute still languishing behind, and keeping a watchful and caring eye on Emma Smith, widow of the Prophet, and her immediate family as well as her mother-in-law, Lucy Mack Smith.

They also represented the private business concerns of many former citizens. Properties were to be sold at the best price possible and the proceeds credited either against past debts or toward future purchases. . . . Misunderstood and unappreciated by their own people, whose property values plummeted as the city emptied, and distrusted by the anti-Mormons, who viewed them contemptuously as the last vestiges of an evil empire, the trustees inherited a lose-lose situation. Almost everyone with Nauvoo property and improvements got far less than they needed or deserved—no more than one-eighth the value and often far less than that at sale. Ill feelings inevitably developed." (*We'll Find the Place*, 318–19).

23. *Hancock Eagle* (Nauvoo, Ill.), May 13, 1846, cited in Brown, "Perfect Estopel," 69.

24. *Hancock Eagle* (Nauvoo, Ill.), May 15, 1846, cited in ibid., 70.

25. Watson, *Manuscript History*, 399.

26. John S. Fullmer to George Fullmer, September 2, 1847, John S. Fullmer Letterpress Book, LDS Church Archives, cited in Leonard, *Nauvoo*, 593.

27. Brown, "Perfect Estopel," 74.

28. Brigham Young to Joseph Young, March 9, 1846, in Watson, *Manuscript History*, 74–75.

29. Journal History of the Church, November 5, 1847, 1, Church History Library, Salt Lake City; see also Roberts, *History*, 7:617.

30. Kenney, *Wilford Woodruff's Journal*, 3:356–57.

31. *Journal of Charles Peabody*, June 2, 1848, Journals and Diaries Collections, vol. 1, Missouri Historical Society, St. Louis, Mo., cited in Bennett, *We'll Find the Place*, 25.

32. Joseph Smith III, cited in *Memoirs*, 43–44. As townspeople flocked to the structure in a failed attempt to extinguish the flames, Smith stood guard near the Smith family properties, including the Mansion House and Red Brick Store, fearing they may suffer a similar fate.

33. *Nauvoo Patriot*, cited in Roberts, *History*, 7:617–18, note; see also McBride, *House for the Most High*, 350.

34. *Keokuk Register*, September 21, 1848, taken from News Clippings 2, no. 18, 2; cited in Colvin, *Nauvoo Temple*, 263.

35. Young, *Journal of Discourses*, 8:203.

36. Snow, *Biography*, 112–13. Snow also visited Carthage, where he dramatically captured his hatred for the place. "Shortly after leaving Nauvoo, I visited another place of painful interest in the history of the Saints. If, on ordinary occasions, words are too weak to convey the feelings of the soul, where shall I find language to portray the thoughts that agitated my mind as I entered Carthage? There, but a few years before, was a scene over which my breast alternately glows and chills with horror and indignation. There an infamous mob were imbruing their hands in the blood of our beloved Prophet and Patriarch, Joseph and Hyrum. . . . Over that guilty place there seemed to hang the gloom of death, the emblem of the deed committed, and the foreshadowing of righteous retribution! Although fatigued and hungry, nothing could induce me to eat or drink among that cursed and polluted people" (113).

37. Brown, "Perfect Estopel," 78.

38. Vallet, *Icarian Communist in Nauvoo*, 15–18. Vallet's account, written in 1886, is a reminiscent treatise on his experience as a youth in the Icarian community and his warning against communal endeavors as a panacea (13–14, n1). For a basic overview of the Icarian experiment, see Nordhoff, *Communistic Societies*, 333–39. For a more extended examination of the group and its teachings, see Piotrowski, *Etienne Cabet*.

39. *Charter and By-Laws*, 8.

40. Vallet, *Icarian Communist in Nauvoo*, 19.

41. Ibid., 20. Vallet reports the sale at $1,000, while deeds and other accounts indicate it was $2,000. Vallet also indicates that the citizens of Nauvoo donated $500 toward the $1,000 purchase price as a donation to the Icarian community.

42. Dourg, "Destruction of the Temple."

43. Vallet, *Icarian Communist in Nauvoo*, 22–23.

44. P. Dourg, Secretary of the Icarian Community, reported, "The same evening the masons . . . acknowledged and declared that the southern and eastern walls would soon fall down, and that, to avoid any serious accident, it was better to destroy them. The next morning the General Assembly . . . met on the Temple Square, and unanimously resolved: first, that the demolition was urgent, for the safety both of the members of the Colony themselves, and of the inhabitants and foreigners whom curiosity might bring to the spot. Second, that by unfixing the walls, stone by stone, they might preserve some good ones.

But as this operation would take up much time, occasion much work, and expose them to many fatigues and dangers, and considering the lives of men as much more valuable than money, they decided to use some other means. Those means having been discussed and agreed upon, they set at work immediately, and the walls were pulled down." Dourg, "Destruction of the Temple."

45. Blum, *Nauvoo*, 24–26; Vallet, *Icarian Communist in Nauvoo*, 24.

46. Vallet, *Icarian Communist in Nauvoo*, 27.

47. Ibid., 27.

48. Piercy, *Route from Liverpool*, 63.

49. Vallet, *Icarian Communist in Nauvoo*, 33.

50. Piotrowski, *Etienne Cabet*, 135.

51. Vallet, *Icarian Communist in Nauvoo*, 36. While Mormons and Icarians shared some ideas relative to communal life, their religious differences were stark. Chapter III, section 14 of the Icarian constitution stated, "Religion. The Icarian Community adopts as its Religion—the Religion of Christianity in its primitive purity, and it fundamental principle of Fraternity of Men and of Peoples." *Charter and By-Laws*, 17. In practice, Vallet described the place and function of religion for the Icarians: "The Icarians had no form of religion—no ceremonies. The majority were agnostics, some atheists, theists, others spiritualists. They all revered Christ as a great philosopher and philanthropist, and admired his moral teachings. Cabet, on Sundays, held a course of lectures on true Christianity. Leaving the miraculous and supernatural apart, he tried to demonstrate that Christ's moral teaching was perfect and based on communism, because Jesus and his disciples had everything in common among themselves and were not allowed to own anything in private—Apostles, chap. 2 and 3; that to reserve and keep for private use any portion of wealth was condemned, as shown in Ananias' case—Apostles, 5; the renouncement of accumulated wealth, and that the only true happiness consisted in loving one another—being one in soul and spirit. Those lectures were very attractive and well attended, being delivered by a forcible and eloquent orator. It is so easy to preach morality to others. When the Icarians compared the theory with the practice; when they seen how far they were from the mark, they began to think, and like many others that are not Icarians are asking: 'where are the Christians?'" (31).

52. Piotrowski, *Etienne Cabet*, 135.

53. Vallet, *Icarian Communist in Nauvoo*, 37.

54. Federal Writers' Project of Illinois, *Nauvoo Guide*, 40.

55. Ourth interview.

56. Smith, cited in *Memoirs*, 39.

57. Blum, *Nauvoo*, 27.

58. Following the death of her husband and the departure of most of the Mormons from Nauvoo, Emma Smith appears to have informally participated with this Methodist congregation, including being married to Lewis Bidamon by the Methodist preacher, possibly in the Seventies Hall. However, she never formally united with the faith. Newell and Avery, *Mormon Enigma*, 246–48; Nauvoo Tourism Office, "Nauvoo German—Icarian History."

59. Ibid.

60. Ourth interview.

61. Ihrig and Shurts, "1200 Mulholland." Nauvoo church records also record more than 130 German-born members among their congregations. Minert, *German Immigrants*, 315–322.

62. Blum, *Nauvoo*, 28. The Kaufmann home was built in 1843 by Joseph Coolidge, a Latter-day Saint.

63. Griffith and Griffith, *Historic Nauvoo*, 38–39.

64. "Nauvoo's Historic Business District."

65. Piercy, *Route from Liverpool*, 62–63.

66. J. M. Davidson, "Nauvoo: The Past and Present of That City: Visits of 1846 and 1864," *Carthage Republican*, February 25, 1864, cited in McBride, *House for the Most High*, 364.

67. J. C. Rich to Edward Hunter, December 25, 1869, NRI historical files, Nauvoo, Ill.

68. Young, "In the Wake of the Church."

69. Roberts, "Nauvoo in Winter," 3.

## Chapter 2. Nauvoo as a Reorganized Church Foothold

1. Smith, *Intimate Chronicle*, 137.

2. Newell and Avery, *Mormon Enigma*, 200.

3. Smith, *Intimate Chronicle*, 136.

4. Spencer and others to Emma Smith.

5. See Shireman, "Joseph Smith, Jr."; for full details, see Newell and Avery, *Mormon Enigma*, 258–59.

6. Romig, *Emma's Nauvoo*, 8–10.

7. Newell and Avery, *Mormon Enigma*, 237–38.

8. Smith, *Memoirs*, 39.

9. Cited in Newell and Avery, *Mormon Enigma*, 243.

10. Bidamon had the tile of Major from his service in the Illinois Militia and was generally called by this title rather than by his given name. Smith, *Memoirs*, 41–42.

11. Newell and Avery, *Mormon Enigma*, 246.

12. Smith, cited in *Memoirs*, 42.

13. Ibid., 240.

14. Edmund C. Briggs, "A Visit to Nauvoo in 1856," *Journal of History* 9 (October 1916): 446–62, cited in Newell and Avery, *Mormon Enigma*, 269.

15. "Mormon Conference," 102.

16. For a discussion of these tensions, see Newell and Avery, *Mormon Enigma*, 272–73.

17. Smith, cited in *Memoirs*, 65.

18. Statement of Joseph S. Jemison, August 29, 1940, cited in Linda and Avery, *Mormon Enigma*, 276.

19. Berry, "Mormon Settlement in Illinois," 93.

20. William R. Hamilton, cited in ibid., 99.

21. Tapfield King, Journals, 99.

22. Ibid., 92.

23. J. C. Rich to Edward Hunter, December 25, 1869.

24. Launius, *Joseph Smith III*, 128–30. The other Smith brother, Frederick G. W., died in April 1862, before formally aligning with the faith.

25. Newell and Avery, *Mormon Enigma*, 284–88.

26. Page, "Manuscript on Nauvoo, Illinois."

27. Launius, *Joseph Smith III*, 128.

28. Emma Smith Bidamon to Joseph Smith III, October 22, 1866, Community of Christ Archives, cited in Newell and Avery, *Mormon Enigma*, 290–91.

29. Shireman, "Joseph Smith, Jr." At the encouragement of Emma while on her deathbed, Lewis Bidamon married Charles's mother Nancy Abercrombie a year after Emma's passing. Upon his death, a portion of the Riverside Mansion was deeded to her. Newell and Avery, *Mormon Enigma*, 303, 306.

30. Page, "Manuscript on Nauvoo, Illinois."

31. Cited in ibid., 18–19.

32. Heman C. Smith to E. L. Kelley, October 17, 1905, cited in Richard P. Howard, "The Nauvoo Heritage of the Reorganized Church," *Journal of Mormon History*, 16 (1990), 49.

33. Charles E. Bidamon to Heman C. Smith, December 30, 1905. The revelation in question appears to be the instruction, canonized in Latter-day Saint scripture as Doctrine and Covenants section 124, directing the construction of a boarding house in Nauvoo called the Nauvoo House.

34. Heman C. Smith to Charles E. Bidamon, May 19, 1906.

35. Charles E. Bidamon to Heman C. Smith, promissory note.

36. Charles E. Bidamon to Joseph F. Smith, May 26, 1909.

37. Heman C. Smith to Charles E. Bidamon.

38. Mary Dean Hancock to C. A. Skinner, October 13, 1947.

39. While the Church received the Red Brick Store lot from Frederick M. Smith, the building itself was razed a generation earlier when, in 1890, the brick was used for the Hudson Meat Market, part of what is today the Hotel Nauvoo. See "History of the Community of Christ in Nauvoo, IL."

40. Shireman, "History."

41. *History of the Reorganized Church*, 7:193.

42. Ibid., 7:223.

43. Page, "Manuscript on Nauvoo, Illinois."

44. Layton, "Sunday in Nauvoo," 443.

45. Burtons, "Another Sunday at Nauvoo," 494.

46. Burton, "Sister Emma Burton at Nauvoo," 433.

47. Burton, "Historic Nauvoo," 489.

48. Ourth interview.

49. Thomas, "Nauvoo Branch Organization," 221–22.

50. Burton, "Old Nauvoo," 795.

51. Smith, "Work in Nauvoo District," 109.

52. Smith, "Things Moving in Nauvoo District," 125.

53. Bennett, "Weirdest Place in Chicagoland."

54. Rothman, *Devil's Bargains*, 11.

55. Bennett, "Faded Mormon Glories."

56. For additional details, see Bernauer, *Still "Side by Side."*

57. Page, "Manuscript on Nauvoo, Illinois."

58. For a discussion of the tension between Emma Smith and Brigham Young over the bodies of Joseph and Hyrum Smith, see Brown, *In Heaven as It Is on Earth*, 301–2.

59. While some in Nauvoo feared the remains of Joseph and Hyrum Smith might be washed away by the rising waters of the Mississippi River, others may have been reacting to rumors circulating in Utah, particularly among Fundamentalist Latter-day Saint groups, that the bodies had been secretly relocated to Utah. Both the mainstream Latter-day Saint and Reorganized Churches refuted this claim. See Hales, *Modern Polygamy*, 165.

60. William O. Hands, cited in Bernauer, *Still "Side by Side,"* 15.

61. Samuel O. Bennion to President Heber J. Grant and Counselors.

62. Frederick M. Smith, cited in Bernauer, *Still "Side by Side,"* 18.

63. Joseph Fielding Smith, *Kansas City Times*, February 1, 1928, cited in Smith, *Doctrines of Salvation*, 1:200–201.

64. Bernauer, *Still "Side by Side,"* 20.

65. Frederick M. Smith, cited in ibid., 19.

66. Ibid., 21.

67. Walter Johnson papers, P 67, folder 48, Historic Properties: Nauvoo Correspondence, 1921–1943, Community of Christ Archives, Independence, Mo.; Walter Johnson papers, P 67, folder 49, Historic Properties: Nauvoo Correspondence, 1944–1952, Community of Christ Archives, Independence, Mo. During the 1940s, Reorganized Church officials worked to acquire both a bed and a spinning wheel from descendants of the Isaac Hale family. Rebuffed in the endeavor, Mrs. Isabelle Pittman responded to the Presiding Bishopric of the Reorganized Church, "I have a few things that have been in the family for years and I do not care to part with them and see no reason for doing so. No Hale (Emma included) belonged to the Mormon Church." Isabelle Pittman to C. A. Skinner.

68. See "Preservation and Development of General Church Properties at Nauvoo."

69. Ibid.

70. Federal Writers' Project of Illinois, *Nauvoo Guide*, 11–12.

71. Rothman, *Devil's Bargains*, 12.

72. Federal Writers' Project of Illinois, *Nauvoo Guide*, 12–13.

73. Bennett, "Faded Mormon Glories."

## Chapter 3. Latter-day Saint Re-Interest in Nauvoo

1. Taylor, *Journal of Discourses*, 23:61–62.

2. Burton, "Visit to Nauvoo and Carthage."

3. "Utah Mormons Visit Nauvoo."

4. "Visit City of Nauvoo."

5. "Conference in Nauvoo, Illinois."

6. Ibid.

7. Ibid.

8. Ibid.

9. "Utah Mormons Visit Nauvoo."

10. "Conference in Nauvoo, Illinois." A similar conference of elders from the Iowa and Illinois conferences of the Church was held in the Nauvoo the following year. See "Grand Conference."

11. "In Nauvoo."

12. "Grand Conference."

13. "Utah Mormons Visit Nauvoo."

14. Cannon, "Long Shall His Blood."

15. "Meeting of First Presidency and Apostles."

16. Journal History of the Church, September 24, 1903, 4, Church History Library, Salt Lake City.

17. "Meeting of First Presidency and Apostles."

18. "Grand Conference"; Brown, "Nauvoo's Temple Square," 24.

19. "Conference in Nauvoo, Illinois." Admission fees are no longer collected at Latter-day Saint historic sites. A nominal preservation fee is collected by Community of Christ at the Joseph Smith Historic Site in Nauvoo, causing some resentment among a small number of visitors. Blythe, "Emma's Willow," 415.

20. Cannon, "Long Shall His Blood," 6.

21. Bennett, "Faded Mormon Glories." The blood stain on the floor is more likely from Hyrum Smith than from his brother Joseph.

22. Cannon, "Long Shall His Blood," 7.

23. Smith, "To the Relief Society."

24. Julia A. F. Lund, "Relief Society Monument Unveiled in Nauvoo," *Relief Society Magazine* 20, no. 9 (September 1933), 507–8.

25. Lund, "Relief Society Monument," 508–10.

26. "LDS Relief Society Memorial Dedicated."

27. Ibid.; Lund, "Relief Society Monument," 511.

28. L. F. P. to M. Ray Carmichael.

29. Scott, Memorandum.

30. DeLapp to the First Presidency, May 14, 1952.

31. DeLapp to the First Presidency, June 24, 1952.

32. DeLapp to Bertha A. Hulmes, July 9, 1954.

33. Wilford Wood (1893–1968) was a Salt Lake–area businessman who purchased several significant Church historic sites and artifacts, many of which were later donated to the LDS Church. In addition to his acquisition of portions of the Nauvoo Temple lot, Wood acquired the town's *Times and Seasons* building, the John Taylor home, and the Snow property. Beyond Nauvoo, he purchased a portion of the Martin Harris farm in Palmyra,

New York, the Newel K. Whitney store in Kirtland, Ohio, the Liberty Jail in Liberty, Missouri, and property in Adam-ondi-Ahman in Missouri. See Kurki, "Wood, Wilford C."

34. Wood to G. L. DeLapp, July 8, 1952.

35. Kammen, *In the Past Lane*, 214; Bodnar, *Remaking America*, 13.

36. Brown, "Nauvoo's Temple Square," 19–21.

37. "Mormon Temple Site Sold."

38. M. C. J., "Church Acquires Nauvoo Temple Site."

39. Brown, "Nauvoo's Temple Square," 18.

40. "Mormons Are to Increase Holdings Here."

41. Hinckley, "Nauvoo Memorial," 461.

42. Ibid., 460.

43. Ibid., 511.

44. First Presidency to Lane K. Newberry, April 9, 1938, cited in ibid., 460.

45. "To Rebuild Old Temple."

46. Federal Writers' Project of Illinois, *Nauvoo Guide*, 13.

47. "Nauvoo—A State Park?"

48. "State, Church, and Civic Leaders." Ironically, this description largely matches the eventual restoration of Nauvoo, without state involvement. The neighboring 143-acre Nauvoo State Park, without most of the historic homes or the temple lot, opened in 1950. Blum, *Nauvoo*, 54–55.

49. "State, Church, and Civic Leaders."

50. Smith, Personal notes.

51. Hinckley, "Nauvoo Memorial."

52. Smith, Personal notes.

53. See Dahl and Norton, *Modern Perspectives*.

54. "Nauvoo Greets 700 Mormons"; "Marked Route Guides Tourists."

55. "Nauvoo Greets 700 Mormons."

56. Smith, Personal notes.

57. "Nauvoo," draft of document.

58. "Monument Is Urged."

59. Cannon, *Centennial Caravan*, 2.

60. The centennial caravan was one of several ways Utah and the Mormons celebrated the pioneer centennial. Other events during that summer of 1947 included a month-long performance of the 1930 Church production, "The Message of the Ages," in the Salt Lake Tabernacle, dedication of the This Is the Place Monument, issuance of a centennial stamp, and a two-hour-and-fifteen-minute flight by a U.S. Army jet named the "Mormon Trail Blazer" from Omaha to Utah to demonstrate one hundred years of transportation improvements. See Haddock, "Celebrating."

61. Cannon, *Nauvoo Panorama*, 75–77.

62. George B. Everton, in Cannon, *Centennial Caravan*, 60–62.

63. Cannon, *Centennial Caravan*, 60–64.

64. Spencer W. Kimball, "Remarks Given by Spencer W. Kimball in Carthage, Illinois Radio Station WCAZ," July 13, 1947, in ibid., 187.

65. Illinois House of Representatives, Resolution no. 53.

66. Pykles, "Josephites, Brighamites, and Bureaucrats."

67. "What Is Nauvoo Restoration, Incorporated?"

68. Kornman to Walter Johnson, September 13, 1950.

69. Johnson to Harold Smith, September 23, 1950.

70. Kohlman to G. Leslie DeLapp.

71. Brown, "Nauvoo's Temple Square," 22.

72. Scott to the Presiding Bishopric, June 28, 1952.

73. Scott to the Presiding Bishopric, September 5, 1952.

74. DeLapp to M. W. Siegfried, November 16, 1954.

75. Brown, "Nauvoo's Temple Square," *BYU Studies* 41, no. 4 (2002): 22.

76. Skinner to the Presiding Bishopric, January 23, 1950.

77. DeLapp to the First Presidency, January 27, 1950.

78. Skinner to G. Leslie DeLapp, February 2, 1950.

79. Allen, "Nauvoo's Masonic Hall," 48–49.

80. Arline Mulch to Wilford Wood, April 26, 1954, in *Arline Mulch v. Wilford C. Wood*.

81. Wood to Arline Mulch, April 29, 1954.

82. *Arline Mulch v. Wilford C. Wood*. This is not the only instance of Wood's claiming divine guidance in procuring Latter-day Saint artifacts and properties, or of his using creative, if not controversial, tactics to secure a transaction. See Haws, "Wilford Wood's Twentieth-Century Treks."

83. "Masonic Temple Cornerstone."

84. *Arline Mulch v. Wilford C. Wood*.

85. Martin to Adam S. Bennion.

86. Allen, "Nauvoo's Masonic Hall," 49.

87. Sister Mary Paul to Wilford Wood, August 16, 1952.

88. Wilford Wood to Sister Mary Paul, August 23, 1952.

89. Stobaugh to Bishop DeLapp, February 28, 1962.

90. First Presidency to the Presiding Bishopric, March 30, 1962.

91. DeLapp to the First Presidency, March 23, 1962; see also DeLapp and Stobaugh (telephone conversation), May 2, 1962.

92. The four properties in Independence were located at 909 West Kansas Street, 429 South Grand Street, 322 South Grand Street, and 412 South Grand Street. They were appraised at $22,250.00. The Nauvoo lot appraised at $11,500.00. Olson to G. L. DeLapp, November 20, 1962.

93. First Presidency to the Presiding Bishopric, March 28, 1962. See also DeLapp to the First Presidency, March 23, 1962.

94. Siegfried to G. Leslie DeLapp, June 11, 1962.

95. Delapp to Mark H. Siegfried, June 20, 1962.

96. Mackay, "Brief History," 245.

97. Nauvoo Mission Report.

98. Stobaugh, "Development of the Joseph Smith Historic Center," 36.

99. Johnson to R. H. Fishburn, August 3, 1956.

100. Johnson to Charles Kornman, September 9, 1950.

101. Johnson to M. L. Draper, August 23, 1955.

102. Stobaugh, "Development of the Joseph Smith Historic Center," 36.

103. Kendrew to Lewis E. Scott, May 12, 1952.

104. Booton to Lewis E. Scott, July 31, 1952; Lewis E. Scott to Joseph F. Booton, August 8, 1952.

105. Ettinger to Walter N. Johnson, May 4, 1950.

106. "Division of Visitors."

107. Cited in Siegfried to the First Presidency, August 31, 1953.

108. Fishburn to Walter N. Johnson, July 22, 1956.

109. "Horton's Standard Service." Though unnamed in the advertisement, Nauvoo Mayor Lowell Horton appears to be the author and fourth entrepreneur referenced. Lewis E. Scott wrote to Reorganized Church officials, asking if they wanted to "be in this corporation to be sure that we get the proper publicity and that our story is properly told." Church officials responded, "I think not. Our job is to improve & control our own property. Also to control guides & parties going thru."

## Chapter 4. Nauvoo Restoration Incorporated and a Formal Latter-day Saint Presence in Nauvoo

1. Lents to the First Presidency and Presiding Bishopric, September 25, 1961.

2. "Buys Nauvoo Historic Site."

3. "Historic Nauvoo Buildings."

4. Brown, "Nauvoo's Temple Square," 24–25.

5. Kimball, "Interview and Memoir," 11.

6. Ibid.

7. The Kimball home, the first structure "restored" in old Nauvoo, contains elements that are beyond the building's 1840s simplicity. Restorations like this, with "nonperiod, overly elegant furnishings," became a source of conflict for Nauvoo Restoration officials. See Lyon, *T. Edgar Lyon*, 281.

8. "Dedicatory Prayer."

9. For a discussion of this and other issues related to Nauvoo's restoration, see Pykles, *Excavating Nauvoo*, 58–60.

10. Kimball, "Interview and Memoir," 13.

11. Ibid.

12. Kimball, "J. LeRoy Kimball," 7.

13. Kimball, "Interview and Memoir," 13.

14. Kimball, "J. LeRoy Kimball," 8–9.

15. Kimball, "Interview and Memoir," 13.

16. Harrington and Harrington, *Rediscovery of the Nauvoo Temple*, foreword.

17. Kimball, "Interview and Memoir," 22.

18. Blum, "Mormons Plan to Re-Build."

19. Kimball, "Interview and Memoir," 14.

20. "LDS Weighs Restoring of Nauvoo."
21. "City Co-operation a Necessity."
22. "LDS Weighs Restoring of Nauvoo."
23. "Church Officials Study Historic Nauvoo Sites"; Kimball, "Outline."
24. The board of Nauvoo Restoration Incorporated was formed on June 28, 1962. Its Articles of Incorporation were filed with the State of Illinois on July 27, 1962. "Report of Progress," 10.
25. "LDS Church Forms Corporation".
26. "What Is Nauvoo Restoration, Incorporated?"
27. "City Co-operation a Necessity."
28. "Church Officials Study Historic Nauvoo Sites."
29. Kimball, "Outline." While the document is signed by Dr. Kimball, a later 1964 report states that the document was "drafted by Mr. Fabian in consultation with Dr. Kimball" prior to its presentation to the Church's First Presidency on January 4, 1962. "Report of Progress."
30. Kimball, "Outline."
31. "LDS Church Forms Corporation."
32. Kimball, "Interview and Memoir," 15.
33. Ibid., 17.
34. "Report of Progress."
35. Kimball, "Interview and Memoir," 16.
36. "What Is Nauvoo Restoration, Incorporated?"; Kimball, "Outline."
37. Miller to J. Alan Blodgett, July 6, 1981; see also Pykles, *Excavating Nauvoo*, 89.
38. "New Look at Nauvoo."
39. "Over 1500 Watch Ground Breaking."
40. Pykles, *Excavating Nauvoo*, 1–2.
41. Harrington and Harrington, *Rediscovery of the Nauvoo Temple*, acknowledgments.
42. Green, "Interior Partitions Found." For extensive details regarding the archaeological work on the Nauvoo Temple, see Harrington and Harrington, *Rediscovery of the Nauvoo Temple*.
43. "Old Mormon Temple Star Stone."
44. Harrington, "Why Archaeology at Nauvoo?"
45. Harrington, "Nauvoo Restoration Incorporated."
46. Crellin, "Archaeological Excavations," 2.
47. Kimball, "Interview and Memoir," 17.
48. Ibid., 18. Kimball described his comparison between the Resurrection and the restoration of homes in Nauvoo. "When we get up, we'll take up our bodies again and you want your own body, and when Nauvoo came up we needed to do it accurately and properly, and not so that when a building was restored, that as near as we could humanly do it, it was as it was when it was here a 125 years ago. That's been the model that we've followed and we've had fine men who have helped us do that."
49. Kimball, "J. LeRoy Kimball," 10.

50. "Report of Progress."

51. "Abandoned Mormon Village."

52. "Nauvoo Restoration, Inc. Organized."

53. Kimball, "Era Asks about Nauvoo Restoration," 14, 17–18.

54. Lyon, "Illiamo Tourist Guide."

55. Nauvoo Restoration Incorporated, "Mortar Analysis."

56. Perry to Rex L. Sohm, May 27, 1968.

57. Kendrew to Rex Sohm, April 10, 1967.

58. Baird to J. Byron Ravsten, April 24, 1969.

59. Harrington to Rex Sohm, March 19, 1968.

60. Blum, "Mormons Plan to Re-Build."

61. "Team Will Uncover Nauvoo Temple Foundations."

62. "Report of Progress," 16, 22–23. George Cannon Young was a respected Salt Lake City architect with expertise in restoration work. Prior to contracting with NRI, he had worked on the restoration of the Beehive House in Salt Lake City and the Brigham Young home in St. George, Utah.

63. Maffitt, "Nauvoo to be Williamsburg of Midwest."

64. "Nauvoo Restoration, Inc., Announces."

65. Kimball, "Era Asks about Nauvoo Restoration," 14.

66. Todd, "Nauvoo Temple Restoration."

67. Reed to NRI Architects Office, April 8, 1970.

68. Sohm to Michael W. Reed, April 20, 1970.

69. Maffitt, "Nauvoo to be Williamsburg of Midwest."

70. Kimball, "Era Asks about Nauvoo Restoration," 16–17.

71. "Nauvoo Restoration Buys Quarry."

72. "Report of Progress," 4–5.

73. "Governor Hails Nauvoo Project."

74. Kimball, "Era Asks about Nauvoo Restoration," 16–17.

75. Ibid.

76. Frederick, "Historic Mormon Town."

77. Miller to Rex Sohn, April 26, 1967.

78. Harold P. Fabian, "Mr. Fabian's Remarks at the Presidential Dinner," April 20, 1965, cited in, Pykles, *Excavating Nauvoo*, 139–40.

79. A. Hamer Reiser, cited in Pykles, *Excavating Nauvoo*, 147–48.

80. Kimball, "Era Asks about Nauvoo Restoration," 16.

81. Maffitt, "Nauvoo to be Williamsburg of Midwest."

82. "Two Basic Principles for Guide Service."

83. Ibid.

84. Miller to J. Alan Blodgett, July 6, 1981.

85. T. Edgar Lyon to William E. Berrett, November 13, 1964, in Lyon, *Teacher in Zion*, 280.

86. T. Edgar Lyon, cited in Pykles, *Excavating Nauvoo*, 152–53.

87. T. Edgar Lyon, quoted in Pykles, *Excavating Nauvoo*, 152–53.

88. Quoted in Lyon, *T. Edgar Lyon*, 280.

89. Pykles, *Excavating Nauvoo*, 158–59; see also Miller to J. Alan Blodgett, July 6, 1981.

90. A. Edwin Kendrew, "Remarks by A. Edwin Kendrew," May 22, 1971, cited in Pykles, *Excavating Nauvoo*, 160.

91. Minutes of the Annual Meeting of the Members and Board of Trustees on Nauvoo Restoration, Incorporated, May 22, 1971, 3, cited in Pykles, *Excavating Nauvoo*, 161.

92. Ogilvie to J. LeRoy Kimball, May 11, 1969; Hartzog to J. LeRoy Kimball, May 1, 1969; "Program," in "Nauvoo Information Center Groundbreaking."

93. "Nauvoo Mission Unique."

94. Kimball to missionary couple, ca. 1971.

95. Ibid. This approach was not original to Kimball. Rather, it appears he patterned it from a letter sent by Mark E. Petersen to Delbert L. Stapley, summarizing a meeting between Kimball, Petersen, and Stapley. See Petersen to Delbert L. Stapley, July 7, 1970; see also Pykles, *Excavating Nauvoo*, 163–64.

96. Avant, "Nauvoo's Impact."

97. Kimball to missionary couple, n.d.

98. Kimball, "J. LeRoy Kimball," 9–10.

99. Bright to Director, Visitors Information Center, October 13, 1982.

100. Kimball to President Spencer W. Kimball and Counselors, April 23, 1982.

101. Mabley, "Mormons of Nauvoo."

102. The original City of Joseph pageant ran nearly every year through 2004. Beginning in 2005, a new show has been performed each summer in the outdoor theater. Oscarson, "City of Joseph."

103. Avant, "Play Beckons."

104. "Nauvoo Restoration."

105. Rugh, *Are We There Yet?*, 2–5. Rugh's work is an excellent analysis of American vacation trends from the 1950s through the 1970s.

106. Pykles, *Excavating Nauvoo*, 10.

107. NRI historical files, Nauvoo, Ill.

108. Nauvoo Restoration Inc., "Mission Handbook."

## Chapter 5. Responding to the Restoration

1. Howard, "Mormon-RLDS Boundary," *Journal of Mormon History*, 11, 18. Howard's article is an excellent summary of the changing nature of LDS and RLDS relationships. While discussing the walls created in the nineteenth and early twentieth centuries over succession, polygamy, and property ownership, Howard highlights windows that emerged between the faiths in the last half of the twentieth century, especially through the sharing of historical documents and cooperation at common historic sites, including Nauvoo.

2. Lents to W. W. Smith, December 26, 1961.

3. Stobaugh to W. N. Johnson, October 23, 1963.

4. Johnson to Kenneth Stobaugh, October 31, 1963.

5. Siegfried to G. Leslie DeLapp, June 11, 1962.

6. Sartwell to Walter N. Johnson, March 8, 1968.

7. Sartwell to the First Presidency, January 23, 1968. Leonard W. Stiegel, Florence S. Ourth, Larry McKiernan, and Gerald L. Sooter served on the committee.

8. "Nauvoo Planning Commission's Report."

9. Ibid.

10. First Presidency to the Presiding Bishopric, January 30, 1968.

11. Lachlan Mackay, interview by author, August 16, 2007.

12. McKiernan, "Historic Site Development," 111–12. The "springhouse" was the structure under whose foundation the bodies of Joseph and Hyrum Smith were found in 1928. Reconstructed in 1988, it is sometimes called the "beehouse" or the "martyry."

13. Howard to Reed M. Holmes, April 7, 1969.

14. Stobaugh, "Historic Site."

15. Stobaugh, "Getting a Foothold Again."

16. Ibid.

17. Stobaugh, "Historic Site."

18. Stobaugh, "Getting a Foothold Again."

19. Stobaugh, "Historic Site."

20. Lents to the First Presidency and Presiding Bishopric, September 25, 1961.

21. Lents to the First Presidency and Presiding Bishopric, October 4, 1961.

22. "Joseph Smith Historic Center."

23. Stobaugh, "Development," 39.

24. McKiernan, "Historic Site," 139–40.

25. Cited in Stobaugh, "Development," 39.

26. See Historic Properties: Administrative: Historic Sites Development, 1976, RG 26, folder 16, Community of Christ Archives, Independence, Mo.

27. McKiernan, "Historic Site," 26–33.

28. Ibid., 25.

29. Ibid., 33, 36–37.

30. McKiernan to Kenneth Stobaugh, December 18, 1978.

31. McKiernan, "Historic Site," 26, 41–42.

32. Ibid., 122.

33. Ibid., 69.

34. Ibid., 81.

35. Ibid., 89.

36. "Nauvoo Master Plan."

37. McKiernan to Paul W. Booth, February 9, 1977, in McKiernan, "Historic Site," 122.

38. Program for the "Joseph Smith Historic Center Service of Dedication," cited in Bingham, "Packaging," 141.

39. "Restoration . . . Red Brick Store," 3.

40. Stobaugh, "Getting a Foothold Again."

41. "Restoration . . . Red Brick Store," 5.

42. Ibid., 6.

43. Pykles, *Excavating Nauvoo*, 180–81.

44. First Presidency to the Presiding Bishopric, June 5, 1964.

45. Smith to Wilmer Andes, September 26, 1977.

46. Bradley to Leonard W. Stigel, August 10, 1967.

47. Pearson to the Presiding Bishopric.

48. Howard to Paul Booth, September 29, 1977.

49. Ibid.

50. Howard, "Values."

51. Flanders, Commission on History meeting, motion.

52. First Presidency to Paul W. Booth, February 3, 1978.

53. Howard to Paul Booth, September 29, 1977.

54. Scherer, "Answering Questions," 77.

55. First Presidency to the Presiding Bishopric, June 5, 1964.

56. Johnson to the First Presidency, February 9, 1968.

57. Hansen to T. Bennett, September 21, 1978.

58. "Nauvoo's Rich Past."

59. "Church Dedicates Visitors Center."

60. Van Orden, "Hallowed, Sacred Site," 8.

61. Nauvoo Restoration Incorporated, "Historic Nauvoo."

62. Russell, "LDS Church and Community of Christ," 17–190.

63. "Rebuilding at Nauvoo," 6.

64. James W. Moffitt, interview by Jayson Edwards, October 2001, in Dahl and Norton, *Modern Perspectives*, 180.

65. Marilyn Candido, interview by Scott C. Esplin, November 1, 2017.

66. Blum, "Parish Hall, Old Landmark, Being Razed."

67. "Report of Progress," 17.

68. Kirchner, "Contemporary Planning in Nauvoo."

69. "Rebuilding at Nauvoo."

70. King, "Utah Mormons Restore Historic Village."

## Chapter 6. The Reconstructed Nauvoo Temple

1. Hinckley, "Thanks to the Lord."

2. Lloyd, "Historic Nauvoo Temple," 3.

3. Swensen, "News Elicits Cheers and Tears."

4. Lloyd, "Historic Nauvoo Temple," 4.

5. Anderson, "Temple Building."

6. Kloehn, "Nauvoo's Prospects on Rise."

7. Ibid.

8. Fidel, "Nauvoo Expects Temple."

9. Ibid.

10. Kloehn, "Nauvoo's Prospects on Rise."

11. Fidel, "Nauvoo Expects Temple."

12. Anderson, "Temple Building."

13. Leonard and Enders, "Proposal."

14. "Nauvoo Temple Site Restoration."

15. The threefold mission of the Church was introduced by Church president Spencer W. Kimball in a Latter-day Saint general conference in April 1981. In addition to perfecting the Saints, the other two aspects included proclaiming the Gospel and redeeming the dead through ordinances performed in Latter-day Saint temples. Kimball, "Report of My Stewardship."

16. Peterson, Rector, and Doxey to L. Aldin Porter, June 29, 1993.

17. Cannon, *Nauvoo Panorama*, 64. Givens and Givens, *500 Little-Known Facts*, 231.

18. "Walk through Sts. Peter and Paul," 1.

19. Ibid.

20. Ihrig-Gilbert and Shurts, "Sisters of St. Benedict," 1.

21. Roberta Bussan, interview by Scott C. Esplin, July 7, 2014.

22. Ibid.

23. According to records of the transaction filed with Hancock County. Heinzmann, "When the Saints Go Marching In"; "St. Mary Monstery [*sic*], Academy Sold;." In her interview, Roberta Bussan revealed that "the LDS Church bought the buildings at their market value and then they made another donation to us towards finishing out the monastery." This was done to "bring the cost of the original buildings around to what their real value was. Let's say the first negotiation really probably sold for less than it should have." Roberta Bussan, interview by Scott C. Esplin, July 7, 2014.

24. Roberta Bussan, interview by Scott C. Esplin, July 7, 2014.

25. Martin, "LDS Church Buys Nauvoo Catholic Monastery."

26. Heinzmann, "When the Saints Go Marching In."

27. Martin, "LDS Church Buys Nauvoo Catholic Monastery."

28. Heinzmann, "When the Saints Go Marching In."

29. Ibid.

30. Ibid.

31. Roberta Bussan, interview by Scott C. Esplin, July 7, 2014.

32. Simmens, "St. Mary's."

33. See "Utah Architect Visits Nauvoo." St. Mary's Academy facilities were used for several years to house Brigham Young University's Semester in Nauvoo program. However, in 2002 several buildings, including the chapel and monastery, were demolished. Other structures, such as the school's auditorium, continued in use after the dedication of the Nauvoo Temple. By 2007, they too were removed. Martin, "Former Monastery Will Be Torn Down"; Swearingen and Endres, "Items Too Numerous to Mention."

34. Martin, "Temple News Rocked Nauvoo."

35. Stack, "Temple Put on Hold."

36. Martin, "No Permit for Temple."

37. Martin, "LDS May Have to Wait."

38. Martin, "No Permit for Temple."

39. Stack, "Temple Put on Hold."

40. Hughes, "Mormon Temple."

41. Ibid.

42. Martin, "No Permit for Temple."

43. Van Biema, "Invasion of the Saints."

44. Martin, "Nauvoo Clears Way."

45. Lloyd, "Rebuilding a Magnificent Temple."

46. Martin, "New Beginning in Nauvoo."

47. Martin, "Full Circle for Nauvoo Temple." Hinckley's invitation to tour the completed temple referred to the open-house period, when completed Latter-day Saint temples are open to the public for tours. Following a temple's dedication, only faithful members of the Church can enter the structure.

48. Lloyd, "Rebuilding a Magnificent Temple."

49. "Nauvoo Temple Construction Is 'On Schedule'"; Husar, "Nauvoo Firm Gets Opportunity."

50. Martin, "Temple Fueling Nauvoo Economy."

51. Lloyd, "Commanding Presence"; Martin, "First Temple Sunstone Placed."

52. Lloyd, "Rebuilding a Magnificent Temple."

53. Moore, "New Centerpiece Rises."

54. Hart, "Nauvoo Illinois Temple."

55. Moore, "Resurrecting a Temple"; Jackson, "Designing and Constructing," 207–13.

56. Moore, "Resurrecting a Temple."

57. Park, "Rebuilding the Dream."

58. Egan, "Tensions on the Rise."

59. Ibid.

60. Ibid.

61. Ibid.

62. Ibid.

63. Ibid.

64. Egan, "After 154 Years."

65. Egan, "Tensions on the Rise."

66. Ibid.

67. Van Biema, "Invasion of the Saints."

68. Ibid.

69. Egan, "Tensions on the Rise."

70. Martin, "Nauvoo Temple Construction."

71. Cawthon, "New Temple Is a Monument."

72. Ibid.

73. Van Biema, "Invasion of the Saints."

74. Martin, "Time Magazine Does Nauvoo."

75. Ibid.

76. Cawthon, "New Temple Is a Monument."

77. Egan, "After 154 Years."

78. Godfrey, "Volunteers."

79. Dutton, "Zoning Should Help Nauvoo."

80. Sheridan, "Response." In total, the open-house period spanned seven weeks.

81. Officials originally announced ten dedicatory sessions but added one extra session each on Friday, Saturday, and Sunday to accommodate crowds. Husar, "Mormon President to Help."

82. Moore, "Nauvoo Temple Open House."

83. Martin, "Nauvoo Temple Tickets"; Petroski, "S.E. Iowa Set"; Martin, "More Tickets Made Available"; Husar, "Mormon President to Help."

84. Martin, "Nauvoo Temple Tickets."

85. Martin, "Nauvoo Firehouse."

86. Sowby, "Nauvoo, Nearby Towns"; Martin, "Nauvoo Gears for Tourist Flood."

87. Richardson, "Hotel Business Booming."

88. Martin, "Nauvoo Gears for Tourist Flood."

89. Martin, "Keokuk Hopes for a Good Impression."

90. Moore, "Good Will."

91. "Journalists Visit."

92. Hart, "Yearning Is Fulfilled."

93. "Interview with Church President Gordon B. Hinckley about the Nauvoo Illinois Temple," *Meridian Magazine*, May 3, 2002.

94. "Interview with Church President."

95. Martin, "Spirit Here Is Amazing."

96. Husar, "Businesses Glad."

97. Ibid.

98. Moore, "Yearning for Old Nauvoo."

99. Husar, "Nauvoo Businesses Bustling."

100. Husar, "Ready or Not."

101. Lloyd, "Reminiscent of 1846."

102. Ibid.

103. Husar, "Time Capsule Sealed Away."

104. Moore, "Nauvoo Temple Dedication."

105. Ibid.

106. Husar, "Time Capsule Sealed Away"; "Temple Broadcast a Pioneering Milestone."

107. "This Magnificent Structure."

108. Swensen, "Nauvoo History"; "Historic Artifacts Include Tools."

109. Martin, "Nauvoo Temple Now Official."

110. Fountain, "Mormons Return."

111. Martin, "Church Leaders."

112. Ibid.

113. Heaps, "Nauvoo 'Beautiful' Once Again."

114. Martin, "Once Feuding Saints."

## Epilogue

1. Martin, "Nauvoo Temple Now Official."

2. Howard, "Mormon-RLDS Boundary," 11, 18.

3. Moore, "LDS Misconceptions," 18.

4. Howard, "Mormon-RLDS Boundary," 14–15.

5. Husar, "LDS Church Outlines Project."

6. The different priorities of these departments were evident in the construction of the Nauvoo temple housing in 2002. Some with strong feelings for historical preservation expressed concern over the rush with which the housing was erected, eliminating the possibility for significant archaeological exploration of the area.

7. Kirchner, "Contemporary Planning in Nauvoo."

8. David W. Knowles, interview by Andrew Wahlstrom, September 28, 2001, in Dahl and Norton, *Modern Perspectives*, 109–10.

9. James W. Moffitt, interview by Jayson Edwards, October 2001, in Dahl and Norton, *Modern Perspectives*, 184.

10. John McCarty, interview by Jayson Edwards, November 24, 2001, in Dahl and Norton, *Modern Perspectives*, 156.

11. David W. Knowles, interview by Andrew Wahlstrom, September 28, 2001, in Dahl and Norton, *Modern Perspectives*, 109–10.

12. Rothman, *Devil's Bargains*.

13. Dermody, "Catholics, Mormons in Nauvoo."

14. Gordon B. Hinckley, cited in Van Orden, "Hallowed, Sacred Site," 8.

15. Rothman, *Devil's Bargains*, 11.

16. Chidester and Linenthal, *American Sacred Space*, xiii.

17. Catherine L. Albanese and Stephen J. Stein, "Foreword," in Chidester and Linenthal, *American Sacred Space*, x.

18. VanSledright, *In Search of America's Past*, 79; Shackel, "Introduction," 10.

19. Russell, "LDS Church and Community of Christ," 177–78.

20. Ida Blum, cited in Dennis, "Old Nauvoo Anew," 17.

# Bibliography

## Manuscript Collections and Unpublished Sources

"Abandoned Mormon Village Reconstructs Its Busy Past." Journal History of the Church, July 9, 1972, 1. Church History Library, Salt Lake City.

*Arline Mulch v. Wilford C. Wood*. Complaint. Circuit Court of Hancock County, Illinois, in Nauvoo, Illinois P 22, folder 69. Community of Christ Archives, Independence, Mo.

Baird, Steven T., to J. Byron Ravsten, April 24, 1969, NRI historical files, Nauvoo, Ill.

Bidamon, Charles E., to Heman C. Smith. December 30, 1905. Papers of Lewis C. Bidamon, Huntington Library, San Marino, Calif.

Bidamon, Charles E., to Heman C. Smith. Promissory note. May 24, 1906. Papers of Lewis C. Bidamon, Huntington Library, San Marino, Calif.

Bidamon, Charles E., to Joseph F. Smith. May 26, 1909. Papers of Lewis C. Bidamon, Huntington Library, San Marino, Calif.

Blum, Ida. "Parish Hall, Old Landmark, Being Razed." NRI historical files, Nauvoo, Ill.

Booton, Joseph F., to Lewis E. Scott. July 31, 1952. Historic Properties: Administrative: National Council Historic Sites, 1952, RG 26, folder 1. Community of Christ Archives, Independence, Mo.

Bradley, John W., to Leonard W. Stigel. August 10, 1967. Frederick M. Smith Papers, Nauvoo Notes and Correspondence: F. Ourth and M. Siegfried, P 120, folder 45. Community of Christ Archives, Independence, Mo.

Bright, Richard E., to Director, Visitors Information Center. October 13, 1982. NRI historical files, Nauvoo, Ill.

Burton, Thomas H. "Visit to Nauvoo and Carthage." Journal History of the Church, July 25, 1901, 7. Church History Library, Salt Lake City.

Bussan, Roberta. Interview by Scott C. Esplin. July 7, 2014.

"Buys Nauvoo Historic Site." Journal History of the Church, February 27, 1938, 4. Church History Library, Salt Lake City.

Candido, Marilyn. Interview by Scott C. Esplin. November 1, 2017.

"Church Dedicates Visitors Center Complex in Carthage." June 27, 1989. NRI historical files, Nauvoo, Ill.

"Church Officials Study Historic Nauvoo Sites." *Deseret News-Telegram*, May 5, 1962, in Journal History of the Church, May 5, 1962, 4. Church History Library, Salt Lake City.

"City Co-operation a Necessity." *Nauvoo Independent*, in Journal History of the Church, May 10, 1962, 6. Church History Library, Salt Lake City.

Community of Christ. Historic Properties: Administrative: Historic Sites Development, 1976, RG 26, folder 16. Community of Christ Archives, Independence, Mo.

"Conference in Nauvoo, Illinois." Journal History of the Church, October 3, 1905, 9–10. Church History Library, Salt Lake City.

"Dedicatory Prayer on the Home of Dr. and Mrs. J. LeRoy Kimball." NRI historical files, Nauvoo, Ill.

DeLapp, G. L., and Kenneth Stobaugh. Telephone conversations (transcription). May 2, 1962. Historic Properties, RG 26, folder 191. Community of Christ Archives, Independence, Mo.

DeLapp, G. L., to M. W. Siegfried. November 16, 1954. Historic Properties: Nauvoo: Correspondence and Miscellaneous, 1945–1954, RG 26, folder 186. Community of Christ Archives, Independence, Mo.

DeLapp, G. L., to the First Presidency of The Church of Jesus Christ of Latter-day Saints, June 24, 1952, Historic Properties file, RG 26, folder 186. Community of Christ Archives, Independence, Mo.

DeLapp, G. Leslie, to Bertha A. Hulmes. July 9, 1954, Historic Properties: Nauvoo: Correspondence and Miscellaneous, 1945–1954, RG 26, folder 186. Community of Christ Archives, Independence, Mo.

DeLapp, G. Leslie, to Mark H. Siegfried. June 20, 1962. Historic Properties, RG 26, folder 191. Community of Christ Archives, Independence, Mo.

DeLapp, G. Leslie, to the First Presidency. January 27, 1950. Historic Properties: Nauvoo: Correspondence and Miscellaneous, 1945–1954, RG 26, folder 186. Community of Christ Archives, Independence, Mo.

DeLapp, G. Leslie, to the First Presidency. March 23, 1962. Historic Properties, RG 26, folder 191. Community of Christ Archives, Independence, Mo.

DeLapp, G. Leslie, to the First Presidency. May 14, 1952. Historic Properties: Nauvoo: Correspondence and Miscellaneous, 1945–1954, RG 26, folder 186. Community of Christ Archives, Independence, Mo.

"Division of Visitors to Nauvoo Historic Properties, July 1–31, 1955." Historic Properties: Nauvoo: Reports, 1949–1952, RG 26, folder 187. Community of Christ Archives, Independence, Mo.

Ettinger, Cecil R., to Walter N. Johnson. May 4, 1950. Historic Properties: Nauvoo: Correspondence and Miscellaneous, 1945–1954, RG 26, folder 186. Community of Christ Archives, Independence, Mo.

First Presidency to Paul W. Booth. February 3, 1978. RG 30-4, folder 10. Community of Christ Archives, Independence, Mo.

First Presidency to the Presiding Bishopric. January 30, 1968. Historic Properties: Administrative: World Conference File, 1968–1976, RG 26, folder 15. Community of Christ Archives, Independence, Mo.

First Presidency to the Presiding Bishopric. June 5, 1964. Historic Properties: Administrative: World Conference File, 1968–1976, RG 26, folder 15. Community of Christ Archives, Independence, Mo.

First Presidency to the Presiding Bishopric. March 28, 1962. Historic Properties, RG 26, folder 191. Community of Christ Archives, Independence, Mo.

First Presidency to the Presiding Bishopric. March 30, 1962. Historic Properties: Nauvoo: LDS Property Exchange, 1962, RG 26, folder 191. Community of Christ Archives, Independence, Mo.

Fishburn, Edwin Robert, to Walter N. Johnson. July 22, 1956. Historic Properties: Nauvoo: Sidney Moore Correspondence, 1956, RG 26, folder 188. Community of Christ Archives, Independence, Mo.

Flanders, Robert T. Commission on History meeting. Motion, November 12, 1977, RG 30-4, folder 10. Community of Christ Archives, Independence, Mo.

"Governor Hails Nauvoo Project." *Deseret News-Telegram*, May 4, 1964, in Journal History of the Church, May 4, 1964, 3. Church History Library, Salt Lake City.

"Grand Conference and Visit of Prest. Smith in Nauvoo." Journal History of the Church, September 29, 1906, 10. Church History Library, Salt Lake City.

Hancock, Mary Dean, to C. A. Skinner. October 13, 1947. Walter Johnson Papers, P 67, folder 48, Historic Properties: Nauvoo Correspondence, 1921–1943. Community of Christ Archives, Independence, Mo.

Hansen, F. E., to T. Bennett. September 21, 1978. RG 26, folder 25. Community of Christ Archives, Independence, Mo.

Harrington, J. C. "Nauvoo Restoration Incorporated Proposed Archaeological Program, 1966–1970." February 17, 1966. NRI historical files, Nauvoo, Ill.

Harrington, J. C., to Rex Sohm. March 19, 1968. NRI historical files, Nauvoo, Ill.

Harrington, Virginia S. "Why Archaeology at Nauvoo?" Address to the Nauvoo Historical Society, July 16, 1968, NRI historical files, Nauvoo, Ill.

Hartzog, George B., Jr., to J. LeRoy Kimball. May 1, 1969. NRI historical files, Nauvoo, Ill.

"Horton's Standard Service" [1952]. Historic Properties: Nauvoo: Correspondence and Miscellaneous, 1945–1954, RG 26, folder 186. Community of Christ Archives, Independence, Mo.

Howard, Richard P., to Reed M. Holmes. April 7, 1969. Historic Properties: Nauvoo: Planning, 1968–1969, RG 26, folder 204. Community of Christ Archives, Independence, Mo.

Howard, Richard, to Paul Booth. September 29, 1977. RG 30-4, folder 10. Community of Christ Archives, Independence, Mo.

Howard, Richard. "Values in Restoring the Red Brick Store." Distributed to members of the Commission on History, November 18, 1977. RG 30-4, folder 10. Community of Christ Archives, Independence, Mo.

Illinois House of Representatives. Resolution no. 53, April 27, 1949, Illinois State Archives, Springfield, Ill.

"In Nauvoo." Journal History of the Church, December 28, 1907, 1–2. Church History Library, Salt Lake City.

Johnson, W. N., to Charles Kornman. September 9, 1950. Historic Properties: Nauvoo: Correspondence and Miscellaneous, 1945–1954, RG 26, folder 186. Community of Christ Archives, Independence, Mo.

Johnson, W. N., to Harold Smith, September 23, 1950, Historic Properties: Nauvoo: Correspondence and Miscellaneous, 1945–1954, RG 26, folder 186. Community of Christ Archives, Independence, Mo.

Johnson, W. N., to Kenneth Stobaugh. October 31, 1963. Historic Properties: Nauvoo: Miscellaneous, 1963, RG 26, folder 196. Community of Christ Archives, Independence, Mo.

Johnson, W. N., to M. L. Draper. August 23, 1955. Historic Properties: Nauvoo: Reports, 1949–1952, RG 26, folder 187. Community of Christ Archives, Independence, Mo.

Johnson, W. N., to R. H. Fishburn. August 3, 1956. Historic Properties: Nauvoo: Sidney Moore Correspondence, RG 26, folder 188. Community of Christ Archives, Independence, Mo.

Johnson, W. N., to the First Presidency. February 9, 1968, RG 29-3, folder 61. Community of Christ Archives, Independence, Mo.

Johnson, Walter, Papers. P 67, folder 48, Historic Properties: Nauvoo Correspondence, 1921–1943. Community of Christ Archives, Independence, Mo.

Johnson, Walter, Papers. P 67, folder 49, Historic Properties: Nauvoo Correspondence, 1944–1952. Community of Christ Archives, Independence, Mo.

"Joseph Smith Historic Center Service of Dedication: Red Brick Story and Visitors Center" (dedication, Nauvoo, Ill., May 3, 1980). RG 26, folder 264. Community of Christ Archives, Independence, Mo.

Journal History of the Church. November 5, 1847, 1. Church History Library, Salt Lake City.

Journal History of the Church. September 24, 1903, 4. Church History Library, Salt Lake City.

Kendrew, A. Edwin, to Lewis E. Scott. May 12, 1952. Historic Properties: Administrative: National Council Historic Sites, 1952, RG 26, folder 1. Community of Christ Archives, Independence, Mo.

Kendrew, A. Edwin, to Rex Sohm. April 10, 1967. NRI historical files, Nauvoo, Ill.

Kimball, J. LeRoy, to missionary couple. Circa 1971. NRI historical files, Nauvoo, Ill.

Kimball, J. LeRoy, to missionary couple. N.d. NRI historical files, Nauvoo, Ill.

Kimball, J. LeRoy, to President Spencer W. Kimball and Counselors. April 23, 1982. NRI historical files, Nauvoo, Ill.

Kimball, J. LeRoy. "Interview and Memoir." October 22, 1972. Oral History, University of Illinois at Springfield.

———. "An Outline for the Restoration of Nauvoo." December 11, 1961. NRI historical files, Nauvoo, Ill.

King, Hannah Tapfield. Journals. Church History Library, Salt Lake City.

Kirchner, Charles. "Contemporary Planning in Nauvoo, Illinois." March 20, 1970. NRI historical files, Nauvoo, Ill.

Kohlman, L. W., to G. Leslie DeLapp. April 24, 1951. Historic Properties: Nauvoo: Correspondence and Miscellaneous, 1945–1954, RG 26, folder 186. Community of Christ Archives, Independence, Mo.

Kornman, Charles, to Walter Johnson. September 13, 1950. Historic Properties: Nauvoo: Correspondence and Miscellaneous, 1945–1954, RG 26, folder 186. Community of Christ Archives, Independence, Mo.

"LDS Church Forms Corporation to Restore Historic Nauvoo." *Deseret News-Telegram*, June 28, 1962, in Journal History of the Church, June 28, 1962, 4. Church History Library, Salt Lake City.

"LDS Relief Society Memorial Dedicated." Journal History of the Church, September 24, 1933, 6–7. Church History Library, Salt Lake City.

"LDS Weighs Restoring of Nauvoo." *Salt Lake Tribune*, May 4, 1962, in Journal History of the Church, May 3, 1962, 5. Church History Library, Salt Lake City.

Lents, Donald V., to the First Presidency and Presiding Bishopric. October 4, 1961. Community of Christ Archives, Independence, Mo.

Lents, Donald V., to the First Presidency and Presiding Bishopric. September 25, 1961, Historic Properties, RG 26, folder 191. Community of Christ Archives, Independence, Mo.

Lents, Donald V., to W. W. Smith. December 26, 1961, RG 26, folder 191. Community of Christ Archives, Independence, Mo.

Leonard, Glen, and Don Enders. "Proposal to Upgrade Historic Nauvoo." July 30, 1993. NRI historical files, Nauvoo, Ill.

L. F. P. to M. Ray Carmichael. February 9, 1939. Walter Johnson Papers, P 67, folder 48, Historic Properties: Nauvoo Correspondence, 1921–1943. Community of Christ Archives, Independence, Mo.

Lyon, T. Edgar. "Illiamo Tourist Guide," January 10, 1968, NRI historical files, Nauvoo, Ill.

Mackay, Lachlan. Interview by Scott C. Esplin. August 16, 2007.

Martin, Harold, to Adam S. Bennion. Collection of Church Historical Materials, MS 8617, microfilm #10, as transcribed in Hollist Collection, MSS 6760, box 1, folder 5. Special Collections, Harold B. Lee Library, Brigham Young University, Provo, Utah.

McKiernan, F. Mark. "Historic Site Development Master Plan: Section Two Nauvoo." Community of Christ Archives, Independence, Mo.

McKiernan, Mark, to Kenneth Stobaugh. December 18, 1978. Historic Properties: Administrative: Mark McKiernan Correspondence, 1978–1979. Community of Christ Archives, Independence, Mo.

"Meeting of First Presidency and Apostles." Journal History of the Church, May 21, 1903, 7. Church History Library, Salt Lake City.

Miller, Rowena J., to J. Alan Blodgett. July 6, 1981. NRI historical files, Nauvoo, Ill.

Miller, Rowena, to Rex Sohn. April 26, 1967. NRI historical files, Nauvoo, Ill.

"Monument Is Urged for Smith Graves." *Keokuk Daily Gate City*, n.d, 10, in Lynn Smith Papers: Nauvoo, Ill.: Centennial, 1939, P78-3, folder 111.

Morley, Cordelia. "Brief History of Patriarch Isaac Morley and Family." Church History Library, Salt Lake City.

"Mormons Are to Increase Holdings Here." Journal History of the Church, October 29, 1937, 5. Church History Library, Salt Lake City.

"Mormon Temple Site Sold." Journal History of the Church, February 26, 1937, 5. Church History Library, Salt Lake City.

"Nauvoo." Draft of document for *Saints' Herald* in 1939. Historic Properties: Nauvoo: Miscellaneous, 1939, 1950, RG 26, folder 185. Community of Christ Archives, Independence, Mo.

"Nauvoo—A State Park?" Journal History of the Church, February 26, 1938, 5. Church History Library, Salt Lake City.

"Nauvoo Master Plan: Cost Analysis." Historic Properties: Nauvoo: General Correspondence, 1976–1978, RG 26, folder 254. Community of Christ Archives, Independence, Mo.

Nauvoo Mission Report. [1952]. Historic Properties: Nauvoo: Reports, 1949–1952, RG 26, folder 187. Community of Christ Archives, Independence, Mo.

"Nauvoo Planning Commission's Report for the Development of the Joseph Smith Historical Center." Nauvoo, Ill., January 20, 1968, RG 26, folder 15. Community of Christ Archives, Independence, Mo.

"Nauvoo Restoration." NRI historical files, Nauvoo, Ill.

Nauvoo Restoration Inc. "Historic Nauvoo." 1991. NRI historical files, Nauvoo, Ill.

Nauvoo Restoration Inc. "Mission Handbook." Circa 1971. NRI historical files, Nauvoo, Ill.

Nauvoo Restoration Inc. "Mortar Analysis for the Restoration of the Brigham Young and Wilford Woodruff Red Brick Houses, Nauvoo, Illinois." October 5, 1966. NRI historical files, Nauvoo, Ill.

"Nauvoo Temple Site Restoration." October 8, 1993. NRI historical files, Nauvoo, Ill.

"New Look at Nauvoo." *Deseret News-Telegram*, May 5, 1962, 10A, in Journal History of the Church, May 5, 1962, 1. Church History Library, Salt Lake City.

Ogilvie, Governor Richard B., to J. LeRoy Kimball. May 11, 1969. NRI historical files, Nauvoo, Ill.

Olson, C. L., to G. L. DeLapp. November 20, 1962. Historic Properties, RG 26, folder 191. Community of Christ Archives, Independence, Mo.

Ourth, Florence. Interviewed by Norma Hiles, February 20, 1975, NRI historical files, Nauvoo, Ill.

Page, James C. "Manuscript on Nauvoo, Illinois." P 22, folder 69, p. 17. Community of Christ Archives, Independence, Mo.

Pearson, Russell W., to the Presiding Bishopric. January 12, 1976. Historic Properties: Administrative: General Correspondence, 1974–1976, RG 26, folder 14. Community of Christ Archives, Independence, Mo.

Perry, Lewis F., to Rex L. Sohm. May 27, 1968. NRI historical files, Nauvoo, Ill.

Petersen, Mark E., to Delbert L. Stapley. July 7, 1970. NRI historical files, Nauvoo, Ill.

Peterson, H. Burke, Hartman Rector Jr., and Graham W. Doxey, to L. Aldin Porter. June 29, 1993. NRI historical files, Nauvoo, Ill.

Pittman, Isabelle, to C. A. Skinner. Walter Johnson Papers, P 67, folder 49, Historic Properties: Nauvoo Correspondence, 1944–1952. Community of Christ Archives, Independence, Mo.

"Preservation and Development of General Church Properties at Nauvoo." Walter Johnson Papers, Historic Properties: Nauvoo Correspondence 1921–1943, P 67, folder 48. Community of Christ Archives, Independence, Mo.

"Program." In "Nauvoo Information Center Groundbreaking," May 24, 1969. NRI historical files, Nauvoo, Ill.

Pykles, Benjamin C. "Josephites, Brighamites, and Bureaucrats: The Role of the Churches and the State in the Restoration of Nauvoo." Unpublished paper presented at the 2009 Mormon History Association annual conference, Springfield, Ill.

Reed, Michael W., to NRI Architects Office. April 8, 1970. NRI historical files, Nauvoo, Ill.

"Report of Progress and Development by the President to the Board of Trustees of Nauvoo Restoration, Incorporated." June 25, 1964. NRI historical files, Nauvoo, Ill.

Rich, J. C., to Edward Hunter. December 25, 1869. *Deseret Evening* News, January 7, 1870. NRI historical files, Nauvoo, Ill.

Sartwell, Wilbur K., to the First Presidency. January 23, 1968. Historic Properties: Administrative: World Conference File, 1968–1976, RG 26, folder 15. Community of Christ Archives, Independence, Mo.

Sartwell, Wilbur K., to Walter N. Johnson. March 8, 1968. Historic Properties: Nauvoo: Planning, 1968–1969, RG 26, folder 204. Community of Christ Archives, Independence, Mo.

Scott, Lewis E. Memorandum. Historic Properties: Nauvoo: Correspondence and Miscellaneous, 1945–1954, RG 26, folder 186. Community of Christ Archives, Independence, Mo.

Scott, Lewis E., to Joseph F. Booton. August 8, 1952. Historic Properties: Administrative: National Council Historic Sites, 1952, RG 26, folder 1. Community of Christ Archives, Independence, Mo.

Scott, Lewis E., to the Presiding Bishopric. June 28, 1952. Historic Properties: Nauvoo: Correspondence and Miscellaneous, 1945–1954, RG 26, folder 186. Community of Christ Archives, Independence, Mo.

Scott, Lewis E., to the Presiding Bishopric. September 5, 1952. Historic Properties: Nauvoo: Correspondence and Miscellaneous, 1945–1954, RG 26, folder 186. Community of Christ Archives, Independence, Mo.

Shireman, Joyce A. "History of the Community of Christ." Nauvoo Community Lecture Series, March 4, 2003. Community of Christ Archives, Independence, Mo.

———. "Joseph Smith, Jr. and His Illinois Legacy, 1844–Present." Fifth Annual Conference on Illinois History, Springfield, 2003, 6–7. Community of Christ Archives, Independence, Mo.

Siegfried, Mark H., to G. Leslie DeLapp. June 11, 1962. Historic Properties, RG 26, folder 191. Community of Christ Archives, Independence, Mo.

Siegfried, Mark H., to the First Presidency. August 31, 1953. Historic Properties: Nauvoo: Correspondence and Miscellaneous, 1945–1954, RG 26, folder 186. Community of Christ Archives, Independence, Mo.

Sister Mary Paul to Wilford Wood. August 16, 1952. Cited in "Nauvoo Temple Scripts," 1992. NRI historical files, Nauvoo, Ill.

Skinner, Clarence A., to G. Leslie DeLapp. February 2, 1950. Historic Properties: Nauvoo: Correspondence and Miscellaneous, 1945–1954, RG 26, folder 186. Community of Christ Archives, Independence, Mo.

Skinner, Clarence A., to the Presiding Bishopric, January 23, 1950, Historic Properties: Nauvoo: Correspondence and Miscellaneous, 1945–1954, RG 26, folder 186. Community of Christ Archives, Independence, Mo.

Smith, Heman C., to Charles E. Bidamon. May 19, 1906. Papers of Lewis C. Bidamon, Huntington Library, San Marino, Calif.

Smith, Heman C., to Charles E. Bidamon. September 15, 1909. Papers of Lewis C. Bidamon, Huntington Library, San Marino, Calif.

Smith, Lynn. Personal notes. June 24, 1939. Lynn Smith Papers, Correspondence, 1939–1940, Elbert A. and Clara Smith Collection, P 78–2, folder 95. Community of Christ Archives, Independence, Mo.

Smith, Wallace B., to Wilmer Andes. September 26, 1977. Red Brick Store: Nauvoo: First Presidency Papers "R" through "Z," 1977, RG 30-4, folder 10. Community of Christ Archives, Independence, Mo.

Sohm, Rex L., to Michael W. Reed. April 20, 1970. NRI historical files, Nauvoo, Ill.

Spencer, Daniel, and others to Emma Smith. August 22, 1844. Papers of Lewis C. Bidamon, Huntington Library, San Marino, Calif.

State, Church, and Civic Leaders Visit Famous Illinois Site." Journal History of the Church, May 4, 1938, 3. Church History Library, Salt Lake City.

Stobaugh, Kenneth L. "Getting a Foothold Again: The Development of the Joseph Smith Historic Center in Nauvoo." UP S6100.1. Community of Christ Archives, Independence, Mo.

———. "The Historic Site, A Living Document of the Past." Presidential address to the John Whitmer Historical Association, 1976, UP S6100. Community of Christ Archives, Independence, Mo.

Stobaugh, Kenneth, to Bishop DeLapp. Telephone conversations (transcription). February 28, 1962. Historic Properties: Nauvoo: LDS Property Exchange, 1962, RG 26, folder 191. Community of Christ Archives, Independence, Mo.

Stobaugh, Kenneth, to W. N. Johnson. October 23, 1963. Historic Properties: Nauvoo: Miscellaneous, 1963, RG 26, folder 196. Community of Christ Archives, Independence, Mo.

"The Restoration of the Joseph Smith Red Brick Store, Nauvoo, Illinois, 1843: A Special Project for the First Presidency for the Sesquicentennial of the Church." RG 26, folder 263, 3. Community of Christ Archives, Independence, Mo.

"To Rebuild Old Temple at Nauvoo." *Hancock County Journal,* in Journal History of the Church, March 9, 1939, 11. Church History Library, Salt Lake City.

"Two Basic Principles for Guide Service." NRI historical files, Nauvoo, Ill.

"Utah Mormons Visit Nauvoo." Journal History of the Church, October 4, 1905, 10. Church History Library, Salt Lake City.

"Visit City of Nauvoo." Journal History of the Church, July 24, 1905, 2. Church History Library, Salt Lake City.

Wood, Wilford C., to Arline Mulch. April 29, 1954. *Arline Mulch v. Wilford C. Wood,* complaint, Circuit Court of Hancock County, Illinois, in Nauvoo, Illinois, P 22, folder 69. Community of Christ Archives, Independence, Mo.

Wood, Wilford C., to G. L. DeLapp. July 8, 1952. Historic Properties file, Nauvoo: Correspondence and Miscellaneous, 194501954, RG 26, folder 186. Community of Christ Archives, Independence, Mo.

Wood, Wilford C., to Sister Mary Paul. August 23, 1952. Cited in "Nauvoo Temple Scripts," 1992. NRI historical files, Nauvoo, Ill.

## Books, Book Chapters, and Articles

"A Walk through Sts. Peter and Paul Catholic Church." Nauvoo, Ill.: n.p., n.d.

Alexander, Thomas G. *Mormonism in Transition: A History of the Latter-day Saints, 1890–1930.* Urbana: University of Illinois Press, 1986.

Allen, James B. "Nauvoo's Masonic Hall." *John Whitmer Historical Association Journal* 10 (1999): 39–49.

"An Epistle of the Twelve to the Church of Jesus Christ of Latter-day Saints in All the World." *Times and Seasons* 6 (January 15, 1845): 779–80.

Anderson, Vern. "Temple Building May Be LDS Prophet's Legacy." *Deseret News,* May 1, 1999.

Arrington, Leonard J., and Davis Bitton. *The Mormon Experience.* Urbana: University of Illinois Press, 1992.

Avant, Gerry. "Nauvoo's Impact." *Church News,* August 27, 1977.

———. "Play Beckons, 'Walk My Quiet Roads.'" *Church News,* August 21, 1982, 10.

Bennett, James O'Donnell. "Faded Mormon Glories Kept as Nauvoo Shrines." *Chicago Daily Tribune,* August 12, 1926, 15.

———. "'Weirdest Place in Chicagoland' Is Nauvoo, Ill." *Chicago Daily Tribune,* August 13, 1926, 9.

Bennett, Richard E. *Mormons at the Missouri, 1846–1852.* Norman: University of Oklahoma Press, 1987.

———. *We'll Find the Place: The Mormon Exodus, 1846–1848.* Salt Lake City: Deseret, 1997.

Bennion, Samuel O., to President Heber J. Grant and Counselors. January 21, 1928. George W. Thatcher Blair Collection 1837–1988, MS 15616, box 1, folder 23. Church History Library, Salt Lake City.

Bernauer, Barbara Hands. *Still "Side by Side."* Kansas City, Mo.: Bernauer, 2001.

Berry, Orville F. "The Mormon Settlement in Illinois." *Transactions of the Illinois State Historical Society* Springfield: Illinois State Journal Co., State Printers, 1906): 88–102.

Bingham, Justin Hall. "Packaging the 'Williamsburg of the Midwest': Nauvoo, Illinois, 1950–2000." Master's thesis, University of Illinois, 2002.

Black, Susan Easton. "How Large Was the Population of Nauvoo." *BYU Studies* 35, no. 2 (1995): 91–94.

Blum, Ida. *Nauvoo: An American Heritage*. Carthage, Ill.: Journal, 1969.

Blum, Mrs. C. J. "Mormons Plan to Re-Build Original Nauvoo Temple." *Nauvoo Independent*, December 21, 1961.

Blythe, Christopher James. "Emma's Willow: Historical Anxiety, Mormon Pilgrimage and Nauvoo's Mater Dolorosa. *Material Religion* 12, no. 4 (2016): 405–32.

Bodnar, John. *Remaking America: Public Memory, Commemoration, and Patriotism in the Twentieth Century*. Princeton, N.J.: Princeton University Press, 1992.

Brown, Lisle G. "Nauvoo's Temple Square." *BYU Studies* 41, no. 4 (2002): 4–45.

——. "'A Perfect Estopel': Selling the Nauvoo Temple." *Mormon Historical Studies* 3, no 2 (2002): 61–85.

Brown, Samuel Morris. *In Heaven as It Is on Earth: Joseph Smith and the Early Mormon Conquest of Death*. Oxford: Oxford University Press, 2012.

Buckingham, J. H. In *Illinois as Lincoln Knew It: A Boston Reporter's Record of a Trip in 1847*, edited by Harry E. Pratt. Springfield, Ill.: Abraham Lincoln Association, 1938.

Burton, E. B. "Historic Nauvoo." *Zion's Ensign*, 31, no 26 (June 24, 1920): 489.

Burton, Emma B. "Sister Emma Burton at Nauvoo." *Zion's Ensign* 31, no. 22 (May 27, 1920): 433.

Burton, P. R. "Old Nauvoo." *Zion's Ensign* 32, no. 45 (November 4, 1920): 795.

Burtons[, The]. "Another Sunday at Nauvoo." *Zion's Ensign* 30, no. 31 (July 31, 1919): 494.

Cannon, Brian Q. "'Long Shall His Blood . . . Stain Illinois': Carthage Jail in Mormon Memory." *Mormon Historical Studies* 10, no. 1 (Spring 2009): 1–19.

Cannon, D. James, ed. *Centennial Caravan: Story of the 1947 Centennial Reenactment of the Original Mormon Trek*. Salt Lake City: Sons of Utah Pioneers, 1948.

Cannon, Janath R. *Nauvoo Panorama*. Nauvoo, Ill.: Nauvoo Restoration, 1991.

Cawthon, Raad. "New Temple Is a Monument to History, Faith, and Hope." *Philadelphia Inquirer*, April 29, 2000.

*Charter and By-Laws of the Icarian Community*. Nauvoo, Ill.: Icarian, 1857.

Chidester, David, and Edward T. Linenthal, eds. *American Sacred Space*. Bloomington: Indiana University Press, 1995.

Colvin, Don F. *Nauvoo Temple: A Story of Faith*. Provo, Utah: Religious Studies Center, Brigham Young University, 2002.

Crellin, Henry G., Jr., "Archaeological Excavations at Nauvoo During the Summer of 1967." *Newsletter and Proceedings of the Society for Early Historic Archaeology* 107 (August 10, 1968): 2.

Dahl, Larry E., and Don Norton, eds. *Modern Perspectives on Nauvoo and the Mormons: Interviews with Long-Term Residents*. Provo, Utah: Religious Studies Center, Brigham Young University, 2003.

Dennis, Landt. "Old Nauvoo Anew: A Mormon Williamsburg Lives Again in Illinois." *Marathon World Magazine* 3 (1973).

Dermody, Tom. "Catholics, Mormons in Nauvoo Laying Foundation for Dialogue." *Catholic Post*, January 19, 2012. https://thecatholicpost.com/2012/01/19/catholics -mormons-in-nauvoo-laying-foundation-for-dialogue.

Doss, Erika. *Memorial Mania: Public Feeling in America*. Chicago: University of Chicago Press, 2010.

Dourg, P. "Destruction of the Temple of Nauvoo." *Deseret News*, August 24, 1850, 6.

Dutton, Natalie. "Zoning Should Help Nauvoo Grow in an Organized Way." *Hancock County Journal Pilot*, July 11, 2001.

Egan, Dan. "After 154 Years, Old Nauvoo, Mormon Faithful Still at Odds." *Salt Lake Tribune*, March 11, 2001.

———. "Tensions on the Rise Again in Nauvoo." *Salt Lake Tribune*, January 23, 2000.

Eliason, Eric A. "The Cultural Dynamics of Historical Self-Fashioning: Mormon Pioneer Nostalgia, American Culture, and the International Church." *Journal of Mormon History* 28, no. 2 (Fall 2002): 140–73.

Federal Writers' Project of Illinois, Works Progress Administration. *Nauvoo Guide*. Chicago: McClurg, 1939.

Fidel, Steve. "Nauvoo Expects Temple to Bring New Prosperity." *Deseret News*, April 9, 1999.

Flake, Kathleen. *The Politics of American Religious Identity: The Seating of Senator Reed Smoot, Mormon Apostle*. Chapel Hill: University of North Carolina Press, 2004.

———. "Re-placing Memory: Latter-day Saint Use of Historical Monuments and Narrative in the Early Twentieth Century." *Religion and American Culture* 13, no. 1 (2003): 69–109.

Fountain, John W. "Mormons Return to Place of Old Trouble and a New Temple." *New York Times*, June 29, 2002.

Frederick, James. "Historic Mormon Town Comes to Life Again," *Des Moines Sunday Register*, September 17, 1972, 12.

Givens, George W., and Sylvia Givens. *500 Little-Known Facts about Nauvoo*. Springville, Utah: Cedar Fort, 2010.

Godfrey, Kenneth W. "Volunteers Bringing New Temple to Life." *Logan Herald Journal*, April 5, 2001.

Green, Dee F. "Interior Partitions Found in Temple Basement." *Nauvoo Independent*, August 30, 1962.

Griffith, Will, and Katharine Griffith, eds. *Historic Nauvoo: A Descriptive Story of Nauvoo, Illinois . . . Its History, People, and Beauty*. Peoria, Ill.: Quest, 1941.

Haddock, Marc. "Celebrating in 1947 Pioneer Day." *Deseret News*, July 20, 2009, B2.

Hales, Brian C. *Modern Polygamy and Mormon Fundamentalism: The Generations after the Manifesto*. Salt Lake City: Kofford, 2006.

Harrington, Virginia S., and J. C. Harrington. *Rediscovery of the Nauvoo Temple: Report on the Archaeological Excavations*. Salt Lake City: Nauvoo Restoration, Inc., 1971.

Hart, John L. "Nauvoo Illinois Temple: Most Well-Built." *Church News*, May 4, 2002, 7.

———. "Yearning Is Fulfilled: Temple Is Back." *Church News*, May 4, 2002, 5.

Haws, J. B. "Wilford Wood's Twentieth-Century Treks: A Visionary's Mission to Preserve Historic Sites." In *Far Away in the West: Reflections on the Mormon Pioneer Trail*, edited by Scott C. Esplin, Richard E. Bennett, Susan Easton Black, and Craig K. Manscill, 251–76. Provo, Utah: Religious Studies Center, Brigham Young University, 2015.

Heaps, Julie Dockstader. "Nauvoo 'Beautiful' Once Again." *Church News*, June 29, 2002, 23.

Heinzmann, David. "When the Saints Go Marching In." *Chicago Tribune*, April 28, 2002.

Hinckley, Bryant S. "The Nauvoo Memorial." *Improvement Era* 41, no. 8 (August 1938): 461.

Hinckley, Gordon B. "Thanks to the Lord for His Blessings." *Ensign*, May 1999, 89.

"Historic Artifacts Include Tools." *Church News*, June 29, 2002, 7.

"Historic Nauvoo Buildings House Missionaries." *Church News*, November 7, 1953, 1, 12.

"History of the Community of Christ in Nauvoo, IL." http://www.nauvoochurch.org/about.php.

*History of the Reorganized Church of Jesus Christ of Latter Day Saints*. Independence, Mo.: Herald, 1973.

"History, 1838–1856, volume F-1 [May 1, 1844–August 8, 1844]," 259. Joseph Smith Papers, accessed December 7, 2017, http://www.josephsmithpapers.org/paper-summary/history-1838-1856-volume-f-1-1-may-1844-8-august-1844/266.

Howard, Richard P. "The Mormon-RLDS Boundary, 1852–1991: Walls to Windows." *Journal of Mormon History*, 18, no. 1 (Spring 1992): 1–18.

———. "The Nauvoo Heritage of the Reorganized Church." *Journal of Mormon History*, 16 (1990): 41–52.

Hughes, Jay. "Mormon Temple in Illinois Causes Unease." *Washington Post*, November 2, 1999.

Husar, Deborah Gertz. "Businesses Glad to See Temple Tourists Pouring In." *Quincy Herald-Whig*, June 8, 2002.

———. "LDS Church Outlines Project to Extend Visitor Experience in Nauvoo." *Quincy Herald-Whig*, March 14, 2018.

———. "Mormon President to Help Dedicate Temple." *Quincy Herald-Whig*, June 22, 2002.

———. "Nauvoo Businesses Bustling as they Brace for Tourists." *Quincy Herald-Whig*, May 1, 2002.

———. "Nauvoo Firm Gets Opportunity to Make Temple Windows." *Quincy Herald-Whig*, June 10, 2000.

———. "Ready or Not, Nauvoo Prepares for Crowds." *Quincy Herald-Whig*, May 1, 2002.

———. "Time Capsule Sealed Away during Temple Ceremonies." *Quincy Herald-Whig*, June 27, 2002.

Ihrig-Gilbert, Karen, and Eugene Shurts. "The Sisters of St. Benedict in Nauvoo 1874–2001." In "Nauvoo: The Way We Were" (walking tour brochure). Nauvoo, Ill.: n.p., 2010.

———. "1200 Mulholland." In "Nauvoo: The Way We Were" (walking tour brochure). Nauvoo, Ill.: n.p., 2010.

"Interview with Church President Gordon B. Hinckley about the Nauvoo Illinois Temple." *Meridian Magazine*, May 3, 2002.

Jackson, Roger P. "Designing and Constructing the 'New' Nauvoo Temple: A Personal Reflection." *Mormon Historical Studies* 3, no. 1 (2002): 204–28.

"Journalists Visit Reconstructed Nauvoo Temple." Press release, *Mormon Newsroom*, May 1, 2002. https://www.mormonnewsroom.org/article/journalists-visit -reconstructed-nauvoo-temple.

Kammen, Michael. *In the Past Lane: Historical Perspectives on American Culture.* New York: Oxford University Press, 1997.

———. *Mystic Chords of Memory: The Transformation of Tradition in American Culture.* New York: Knopf, 1991.

Kane, Thomas L. *The Mormons: A Discourse Delivered before the Historical Society of Pennsylvania.* Philadelphia: King and Baird 1850.

Kenney, Scott G., ed. *Wilford Woodruff's Journal.* 9 vols. Midvale, Utah: Signature, 1983–85.

Kimball, J. LeRoy. "The Era Asks about Nauvoo Restoration." *Improvement Era*, July 1967, 12–18.

Kimball, James L., Jr. "J. LeRoy Kimball, Nauvoo Restoration Pioneer: A Tribute." *BYU Studies Quarterly* 32, nos. 1 and 2 (1992): 5–12.

Kimball, Spencer W. "A Report of My Stewardship." *Ensign*, May 1981, 5.

Kimball, Stanley B., ed. *On the Potter's Wheel: The Diaries of Heber C. Kimball.* Salt Lake City: Signature, 1987.

King, Seth S. "Utah Mormons Restore Historic Village in Illinois." *New York Times*, September 9, 1970.

Kloehn, Steve. "Nauvoo's Prospects on Rise with Mormons' Temple." *Chicago Tribune*, May 25, 1999.

Kurki, Lisa. "Wood, Wilford C." In *Encyclopedia of Latter-day Saint History*, edited by Arnold K. Garr, Donald Q. Cannon, and Richard O. Cowan, 1359–60. Salt Lake City: Deseret, 2000.

Launius, Roger D. *Joseph Smith III: Pragmatic Prophet.* Urbana: University of Illinois Press, 1988.

Layton, Ida A. "A Sunday in Nauvoo." *Zion's Ensign* 30, no. 28 (July 10, 1919): 443.

Leonard, Glen M. *Nauvoo: A Place of Peace, A People of Promise.* Salt Lake City: Deseret, 2002.

Lloyd, R. Scott. "A Commanding Presence Returns to Nauvoo." *Church News*, November 11, 2000, 4.

———. "Historic Nauvoo Temple to Be Rebuilt." *Church News*, April 10, 1999.

———. "Rebuilding a Magnificent Temple." *Church News*, October 30, 1999, 7.

———. "Reminiscent of 1846, 331,849 'Throng' Temple." *Church News*, June 29, 2002, 10.

Lund, Julia A. F. "Relief Society Monument Unveiled in Nauvoo." *Relief Society Magazine* 20, no. 9 (September 1933): 507–11.

Lyon, T. Edgar, Jr. *T. Edgar Lyon: A Teacher in Zion.* Provo, Utah: Brigham Young University Press, 2002.

M. C. J. "Church Acquires Nauvoo Temple Site." *Improvement Era* 40, no. 4 (April 1937): 226–27.

Mabley, Jack. "Mormons of Nauvoo Did What They Had to Do." *Chicago Tribune*, April 5, 1977, 4.

Mackay, Lachlan. "A Brief History of the Smith Family Nauvoo Cemetery." *Mormon Historical Studies* 3, no. 2 (Fall 2002): 240–52.

Maffitt, Lloyd. "Nauvoo to Be Williamsburg of Midwest." The Hawk Eye, March 4, 1969, 3.

"Marked Route Guides Tourists to Historical Landmarks in Nauvoo." *Keokuk Daily Gate City*, September 7, 1939, 6.

Martin, Stephen A. "Church Leaders Make Rare Joint Appearance." *Burlington Hawk Eye*, June 28, 2002.

———. "First Temple Sunstone Placed." *Burlington Hawk Eye*, August 22, 2001.

———. "Former Monastery Will Be Torn Down." *Burlington Hawk Eye*, January 13, 2002, D1.

———. "Full Circle for Nauvoo Temple." *Burlington Hawk Eye*, October 25, 1999.

———. "Keokuk Hopes for a Good Impression." *Burlington Hawk Eye*, March 14, 2002.

———. "LDS Church Buys Nauvoo Catholic Monastery." *Deseret News*, September 11, 1999.

———. "LDS May Have to Wait to Get Nauvoo Temple Permit." *Deseret News*, October 18, 1999.

———. "More Tickets Made Available for Temple Opening." *Burlington Hawk Eye*, April 11, 2002.

———. "Nauvoo Clears Way for LDS Temple." *Deseret News*, October 20, 1999.

———. "Nauvoo Firehouse Gets a Vertical Lift." *Burlington Hawk Eye*, November 11, 2001.

———. "Nauvoo Gears for Tourist Flood." *Deseret News*, February 10, 2002.

———. "Nauvoo Temple Construction Building Hopes of Prosperity." *Deseret News*, February 14, 2000.

———. "Nauvoo Temple Now Official." *Burlington Hawk Eye*, June 28, 2002.

———. "Nauvoo Temple Tickets Are Going Fast." *Deseret News*, December 8, 2001.

———. "A New Beginning in Nauvoo." *Deseret News*, October 25, 1999.

———. "No Permit for Temple in Nauvoo." *Deseret News*, October 13, 1999.

———. "Once Feuding Saints Denominations Find Common Ground." *Burlington Hawk Eye*, June 24, 2002.

———. "Temple Fueling Nauvoo Economy." *Deseret News*, October 24, 2000.

———. "Temple News Rocked Nauvoo." *Burlington Hawk Eye*, January 1, 2000.

———. "The Spirit Here Is Amazing." *Burlington Hawk Eye*, April 28, 2002.

———. "Time Magazine Does Nauvoo." *Deseret News*, April 25, 2000.

Marty, Martin E. "Foreword." In *Mormonism and the American Experience*, by Klaus J. Hansen. Chicago: University of Chicago Press, 1981.

Marty, Martin E. "Muslims and Mormons in America." August 8, 2011. https://divinity.uchicago.edu/sightings/muslims-and-mormons-america-martin-e-marty.

"Masonic Temple Cornerstone Is Relaid in Nauvoo Sunday." *Keokuk Iowa Gate City and Constitution-Democrat*, July 19, 1954.

McBride, Matthew S. *A House for the Most High: The Story of the Original Nauvoo Temple*. Salt Lake City: Kofford, 2007.

Minert, Roger P., ed. *German Immigrants in American Church Records: Volume 10: Illinois North Protestant*. Rockland, Maine: Picton, 2011.

Misztal, Barbara A. *Theories of Social Remembering*. Philadelphia: Open University Press, 2003.

Mitchell, Katharyne. "Monuments, Memorials, and the Politics of Memory." *Urban Geography* 24, no. 5 (2003): 442–59.

Moore, Carrie A. "Good Will Is Gaining in Nauvoo." *Deseret News*, May 3, 2002.

——. "Nauvoo Temple Dedication Spurts Torrents of Tears, Joy." *Deseret News*, June 28, 2002.

——. "Nauvoo Temple Open House Begins on May 6." *Deseret News*, April 6, 2002.

——. "New Centerpiece Rises in the 'City Beautiful.'" *Deseret News*, May 2, 2002.

——. "Resurrecting a Temple." *Deseret News*, July 2, 2000.

——. "Yearning for Old Nauvoo." *Deseret News*, June 23, 2002.

Moore, Richard G. "LDS Misconceptions about the Community of Christ." *Mormon Historical Studies* 15, no. 1 (Spring 2014): 1–23.

"Nauvoo Greets 700 Mormons on Friendly Visit." *Nauvoo Independent*, June 29, 1939.

"Nauvoo Mission Unique; Tells Dramatic Story." *Church News*, September 11, 1971, 3.

"Nauvoo Restoration Buys Quarry." *Nauvoo Independent*, April 16, 1964.

"Nauvoo Restoration, Inc., Announces Construction of Visitors Center Here." *Nauvoo Independent*, March 13, 1969.

"Nauvoo Restoration, Inc., Organized at Meeting." *Nauvoo Independent*, August 2, 1962.

"Nauvoo Temple Construction is 'On Schedule.'" *Nauvoo New Independent*, February 9, 2000.

Nauvoo Tourism Office. "Nauvoo German—Icarian History." http://www.beautifulnauvoo .com/nauvoo-s-german—icarian-years.html.

"Nauvoo's Historic Business District." Denver, Colo.: GlennView, 2006.

"Nauvoo's Rich Past." *Des Moines Sunday Register*, October 7, 1979.

Newell, Linda King, and Valeen Tippetts Avery. *Mormon Enigma: Emma Hale Smith.* Garden City, N.Y.: Doubleday, 1984.

Nordhoff, Charles. *The Communistic Societies of the United States: From Personal Visit and Observation.* New York: Harper and Brothers, 1875.

"Old Mormon Temple Star Stone Is Discovered in Keokuk Attic." *Gate City*, September 27, 1962.

Olick, Jeffrey K. "Genre Memories and Memory Genres." *American Sociological Review* 64, no. 3 (June 1999): 381–402.

Olsen, Daniel H., and Dallen J. Timothy. "Tourism and Religious Journeys." In *Tourism, Religion, and Spiritual Journeys*, edited by Dallen J. Timothy and Daniel H. Olsen, 1–21. London: Routledge, 2006.

Oscarson, R. Don. "City of Joseph: The Original Nauvoo Pageant Remembered." *Mormon Historical Studies* 15, no. 1 (Spring 2014): 112–36.

"Over 1500 Watch Ground Breaking Sat." *Nauvoo Independent*, May 29, 1969.

Park, Loretta. "Rebuilding the Dream: Salt Lake City Architects Design New Nauvoo Temple." *Ogden Standard-Examiner*, May 1, 2002.

Petroski, William. "S.E. Iowa Set to Welcome Mormons." *Des Moines Register*, March 31, 2002.

Piercy, Frederick. *Route from Liverpool to Great Salt Lake Valley.* Edited by James Linforth. Liverpool: Richards; London: Latter-day Saints' Book Depot, 1855.

Piotrowski, Sylvester A. *Etienne Cabet and the Voyage En Icarie.* Washington, D.C.: Catholic University of America, 1935.

*Proceedings at the Dedication of the Joseph Smith Memorial Monument.* Salt Lake City: n.p., 1906.

Pykles, Benjamin C. *Excavating Nauvoo: The Mormons and the Rise of Historical Archaeology in America.* Lincoln: University of Nebraska Press, 2010.

"Rebuilding at Nauvoo." *St. Louis Post Dispatch,* December 13, 1970, 6.

Rich, J. C., to Edward Hunter. December 25, 1869. *Deseret Evening* News, January 7, 1870.

Richardson, Brian. "Hotel Business Booming with Temple." *Keokuk Daily Gate City,* June 19, 2002.

Roberts, B. H., ed. *History of The Church of Jesus Christ of Latter-day Saints, Period 2: Apostolic Interregnum.* Vol. 7. 2nd ed. rev. Salt Lake City: Deseret Book, 1932.

———. "Nauvoo in Winter." *Contributor* 8, no. 3 (January 1887): 3.

Romig, Ron, ed., *Emma's Nauvoo.* Independence, Mo.: Whitmer, 2007.

Rothman, Hal K. *Devil's Bargains: Tourism in the Twentieth-Century American West.* Lawrence: University of Kansas Press, 1998.

Rugh, Susan Sessions. *Are We There Yet? The Golden Age of American Family Vacations.* Lawrence: University Press of Kansas, 2008.

Russell, William D. "The LDS Church and Community of Christ: Clearer Differences, Closer Friends." *Dialogue: A Journal of Mormon Thought* 36, no. 4 (Winter 2003): 177–90.

Savage, Kirk. "History, Memory, and Monuments: An Overview of the Scholarly Literature on Commemoration." Online essay commissioned by the Organization of American Historians and the National Park Service, 2006.

Scherer, Mark A. "'Answering Questions No Longer Asked': Nauvoo, Its Meaning and Interpretation in the RLDS Church/Community of Christ Church." *John Whitmer Historical Association Journal,* 2002, 73–77.

Sessions, Perrigrine. *The Diaries of Perrigrine Sessions.* Bountiful, Utah: Carr, 1967.

Shackel, Paul A. "Introduction: The Making of the American Landscape." In *Myth, Memory, and the Making of the American Landscape,* edited by Paul A. Shackel, 1–16. Gainesville: University Press of Florida, 2001.

Sheridan, Carolyn. "Response to Temple Opening Overwhelming." *Fort Madison Daily Democrat,* January 9, 2002.

Simmens, Genny. "St. Mary's: End of an Era." *Nauvoo Historical Society Newsletter,* November 1998.

Smith, Charles J. "Things Moving in Nauvoo District." *Zion's Ensign* 35, no. 8 (February 22, 1923): 125.

———. "Work in Nauvoo District." *Zion's Ensign* 34, no. 7 (February 16, 1922): 109.

Smith, George Albert. "To the Relief Society." *Relief Society Magazine* 19, no. 12 (December 1932): 703.

Smith, George D., ed. *An Intimate Chronicle: The Journals of William Clayton*. Salt Lake City: Signature, 1995.

Smith, Joseph Fielding. *Doctrines of Salvation*. Vol. 1. Salt Lake City: Bookcraft, 1954.

Smith, Joseph, III. *The Memoirs of President Joseph Smith III (1832–1914)*. Edited by Richard P. Howard. Independence, Mo.: Herald, 1979.

Snow, Eliza R. *Biography and Family Record of Lorenzo Snow*. Salt Lake City: Deseret News, 1884.

Sowby, Laurie Williams. "Nauvoo, Nearby Towns Happily Anticipating Temple Open House." *Utah County Journal*, January 3, 2002.

"St. Mary Monstery [*sic*], Academy Sold; Sisters to Relocate." *Nauvoo New Independent*, October 14, 1998.

Stack, Peggy Fletcher. "Temple Put on Hold in Nauvoo." *Salt Lake Tribune*, October 14, 1999.

Stark, Rodney. "The Rise of a New World Faith." *Review of Religious Research* 26, no. 1 (September 1984): 18–27.

Stobaugh, Kenneth E. "The Development of the Joseph Smith Historic Center in Nauvoo." *BYU Studies Quarterly* 32, nos. 1, 2 (1992): 33–40.

Swearingen, Joy, and Doug Endres, "Items Too Numerous to Mention: Variety Drew Large Crowd to Joseph Smith Academy Sale." *Hancock County Journal-Pilot*, August 29, 2007.

Swensen, Jason. "Nauvoo History Comes Full Circle." *Church News*, June 29, 2002, 7.

———. "News Elicits Cheers and Tears in Nauvoo." *Deseret News*, April 5, 1999.

Taylor, John. In *Journal of Discourses*, 23:61–62. London: Latter-day Saints' Book Depot, 1883.

"Team Will Uncover Nauvoo Temple Foundations: Mormon Leaders Study Site." *Quincy Herald Whig*, May 5, 1962.

"Temple Broadcast a Pioneering Milestone." *Church News*, July 20, 2002.

"The Mormon Conference." *True Latter Day Saints' Herald* 1, no. 5 (May 1860): 102.

"This Magnificent Structure." *Church News*, June 29, 2002, 5.

Thomas, W. H. "Nauvoo Branch Organization." *Zion's Ensign* 33, no. 14 (1921): 221–22.

Todd, Jay M. "Nauvoo Temple Restoration." *Improvement Era*, October 1968, 10–16.

"Utah Architect Visits Nauvoo in Anticipation of Nauvoo Temple Reconstruction." *New Independent*, April 14, 1999.

Vallet, Emile. *An Icarian Communist in Nauvoo: Commentary by Emile Vallet; With an Introduction and Notes by H. Roger Grant*. Springfield: Illinois State Historical Society, 1971.

Van Biema, David. "The Invasion of the Saints." *Time*, July 2000.

Van Orden, Dell. "'Hallowed, Sacred Site Made Beautiful' out of Respect, Love." *Church News*, July 8, 1989, 3, 8.

VanSledright, Bruce. *In Search of America's Past: Learning to Read History in Elementary School*. New York: Teachers College Press, 2002.

Watson, Elden J. *Manuscript History of Brigham Young, 1846–1847*. Salt Lake City: Watson, 1971.

"What Is Nauvoo Restoration, Incorporated?" Nauvoo, Ill.: Nauvoo Restoration, Inc., n.d.

Young, Brigham. *Journal of Discourses*. London: Latter-day Saints' Book Depot, 1861.

Young, Richard W. "In the Wake of the Church." *Contributor* 4, no. 4 (January 1883): 148–51.

# Index

SCOTT C. ESPLIN is a professor of religious education at
Brigham Young University and a coeditor of *Far Away in the West:
Reflections on the Mormon Pioneer Trail.*

The University of Illinois Press
is a founding member of the
Association of American University Presses.

---

Composed in 10.75/13 Arno Pro
with ITC Avant Garde Gothic Std display
by Kirsten Dennison
at the University of Illinois Press
Cover designed by Jason Gabbert
Cover illustration: "Nauvoo, Sunglow on the
Mississippi," by Alan Fullmer

University of Illinois Press
1325 South Oak Street
Champaign, IL 61820-6903
www.press.uillinois.edu